Theorizing

Theorizing

Alan F. Blum

HEINEMANN
LONDON

Heinemann Educational Books Ltd

LONDON EDINBURGH MELBOURNE AUCKLAND TORONTO
HONG KONG SINGAPORE KUALA LUMPUR
IBADAN NAIROBI JOHANNESBURG
NEW DELHI

ISBN 0 435 82070 2
Paperback ISBN 0 435 82071 0

Published by
Heinemann Educational Books Ltd
48 Charles Street, London W1X 8AH
Printed in Great Britain by Morrison & Gibb Ltd
London and Edinburgh

Contents

ERRATA

Page

3   third line from bottom: for: 'we' read 'me'

48   first para, last line: should read 'where whatness is what is other than speech'

third para, first line: should read 'as internal to speech'

63   last para, second line: should read 'the otherness of what is is'

68   second para, eighth line: should read 'being; what'

99   penultimate line: for 'conditions' read 'connection'

140   fourth line from bottom: for 'preserve' read 'presence'

145   last line of quotation: should read 'perspicuously believe and with certainty do'

154   first para, twenty-second line: for 'casually' read 'causally'

158   first line of footnote: for 'thinks' read 'thanks'

236   first para, fifth line from bottom: should read 'that happen to be'

244   fourth line from bottom: for 'regional' read 'required'

261   third line from top: delete '?'

On the following pages, 'no-thing' should read 'nothing':
32 fourth para, second line. 69 first para, eleventh line.
71 first para twentieth line. 86 second line from bottom.
87 third para, fifth line from bottom. 126 third line from bottom. 133 fifth line. 135 second line from bottom.
168 fourth line. 172 fourteenth line.

On the following pages, 'Being' should read 'being':
49 last para, fourth line. 69 first para, tenth line.

The first six chapters make the essential argument. Chapters 7 and 8 exemplify this argument – showing various ramifications – for the discipline of sociology. Chapter 9 concretizes the argument of the first six chapters in a form that is possibly more graspable.

Since this is not a work on the history of thought, no claim is made for the exegetical fidelity of my remarks concerning the various views of historical authors. Ultimately, I am making reference to *my* view through various 'distorted' readings of those authors. The distortional character of all reading (and speaking) must be kept in mind not as a problem to be corrected, but as a method for affirming the commitment of the reader/speaker. It is through the distortions that the reader will discover – if he takes the time – the commitment for which this work speaks. This is not to say that I refuse responsibility for what I say about works, but that the reader must centre his attention on how I could say it as a method of preserving the intelligibility of the work.

That I could only show how I can speak by creating at ension in the speech of other works as the medium for such a display indicates not uncontrolled violence but only the fact that speech in the service of what is beyond words can only affirm itself through similar reconstructions of other authors.

Acknowledgements

Strictly speaking, this work is the product of a dialectical relationship begun at Columbia University with Peter McHugh and some of our students, a relationship accentuated and deepened through my participation with a lively group of students of New York University, and one which continues today. In this work I serve somewhat as an apostle for a collective commitment to a version of analysis which is a product – in the best sense – of the concerted interplay of interested minds and open souls, the interplay which Plato speaks of as friendship.

It lies in the nature of this relationship that these friends would not agree with what is said in this book, perhaps dissenting in major ways from both mode and substance of expression. This despite the fact that all of those friends have contributed to the book, indeed have written it.

Among those students I must single out Daniel G. Foss, Stanley Raffel, and Stephen Karatheodoris. Foss's imagination and critical distrust of easy formulation continually was conveyed to me over the course of our relationship at New York University, and he contributed to the intellectual re-organization of this work at crucial points, particularly through our conversations over the writing of his Ph.D. dissertation, *Method And Certainty* (New York University, Department of Sociology, 1971). Raffel continually listened, engaged and re-formulated, bringing an acute and constructive intelligence to bear on what was said, and saying himself in ways that always improved and deepened. His writings and conversations were a constant source of inspiration and reflection. Stephen Karatheodoris, a most remarkable student and friend, did everything a superior student could do and more besides – he began to teach – and thereby made it easier for me to fulfil the role of the teacher as a one who learns.

From the time of our association at Columbia, Peter McHugh and I constantly invented, exchanged, and criticized the ideas reflected in this book, working on them so concertedly and collaboratively that it is literally impossible to discriminate his ideas from mine. His criticalness was invariably the final censor, his inventiveness the incentive, and his friendship the context for our intellectual enterprise of which this work is only one particular expression. His influence is apparent on almost every page whether as a source of the speaking, or as the principal member of the hypothetical audience to which the speech is addressed.

Finally, I must acknowledge indebtedness to friends like Irwin W. Goffman, Alvin Gouldner, and Kathleen Zane who always engaged me critically and patiently, and to Ernest Lilienstein and Derek Phillips who have been enduring sources of support.

Introduction

The following work contains a variety of analyses which appear eccentric and is organized through a language that appears unorthodox. The analyses were not designed to be eccentric nor is the usage designed to be unorthodox. I found it the most truthful way of speaking, a mode of speaking which my commitment requires.

I could attempt to teach you to read the following work but such an effort would deny my argument. Therefore I will not characterize the book or present you with a position from which to read it for that would create a beginning for you which you ought recover for yourself in your own reading. I will not then anticipate objections which you might raise (and which I have inventoried myself in assembling this work over the resistances generated by innumerable concrete exchanges) by attempting to convincingly disarm these objections, and instead I shall trust you to achieve the reading which I require (which is less of a concrete 'position' than a level of involvement). My writing is intended then, to invite you to re-constitute yourself through the very inter-action of the reading as one engaged in the 'problem' of the possibility of reading itself as exemplified in the relationship between speech and its grounds.

I

Aristotle's Problem

I

It is indeed strange that Aristotle felt compelled to consult his predecessors on some questions but not on others. For example, in speaking of 'wisdom' he can say in conclusion . . . 'these then are the beliefs in kind and in number which we have concerning wisdom and wise men'[1] where the 'beliefs' in question refer only to statements such as 'we believe first, that the wise man knows.' In such cases the 'we' might refer to the silent collective of anyman and everyman who has ever thought intelligently; this collective does not have to be delineated. What is strange then, is that for other questions Aristotle held himself to the requirement of having to make this anonymous 'we' public and reportable. For example, while lecturing us on the meaning of 'cause,' he undertakes a painstaking, methodic survey of the differentiations within the 'we.' What then drives Aristotle to treat the 'we' in one case as an anonymous ground or resource that is only to be affirmed, and on the other hand, as a determinant collective with distinctive parameters and persons?

Aristotle says that 'it is because of wonder that men began philosophizing and do so now' but he does not consult Anaxagoras, Empedocles, Parmenides, or Plato in support of this, for he says only that 'it is clear' that this is so.[2] Why then, does he consult such predecessors when he speaks of 'cause'? Or again: when he speaks of the arts as being of a higher sort than experience and experience as higher than memory and memory as higher than sensation, and when he says that the arts are lower than the sciences but that among the sciences, the theoretic are higher than the practical and the productive,[3] why does he not

---

[1] *Metaphysics*, translated by Hippocrates G. Apostle, Bloomington: Indiana University Press, 1966, 092a.

[2] An example of making wonder a topic can be found in M. Heidegger, *What Is Philosophy?* translated by J. T. Wilde and W. Kluback, New Haven, College and University Press, n.d.

[3] These hierarchies are frequently mentioned for example in the *Metaphysics*, *op. cit.*, books A, a, B, and E, or in the *Nicomachean Ethics*, Book I, A and B. Also see R. McKeon's 'General Introduction' to the modern library edition, *Introduction to Aristotle*, New York: Random House, 1947, XV–XXV.

consult his predecessors with the same methodic vigilance that he employs to track down 'cause'? Why for these matters, does he assert 'we believe' and 'we know the fact' and 'we consider' and 'we agree that' instead of conducting a sweeping survey of what his specific predecessors actually said? What distinguishes the questions which Aristotle refrains from asking from those which he poses and explores? Why does he seem to turn to his predecessors for certain questions while remaining content with the answers which *he* puts forth for others? Does perhaps the turn to one's predecessors become such an integral feature of serious questioning that the absence of such a turn comes to announce a failure of nerve? To put it squarely, can Aristotle's assertions about 'wisdom,' 'philosophy' and the like, be seen as instances of a failure to turn, or is such an apparent failure in itself a turn of sorts?

Aristotle opened every one of his works by consulting his predecessors, and yet he does not consult them on every matter of usage.[1] However, even when Aristotle ostensibly fails to engage in such consultation – as when he says 'all men agree' – he is still consulting, for the anonymous collective depicted in 'all men agree' constitutes a lively and determinant point of reference for the inquiry. The original question was then posed prematurely for the problem is not why does Aristotle consult on some questions rather than others? But, given the omnipresence of consultation, *how* does Aristotle make reference to his predecessors?

For the truly important questions, Aristotle consults by invoking the anonymous first person plural; in subsuming 'he' (or 'they') and 'me' under the 'we' Aristotle invites the 'you' to participate in a tradition. The grounds of membership in such a tradition is a decision for silence, a decision not to challenge the understanding which the 'we' conceals. It is this kind of consultation in which he engages while discussing philosophy, wisdom, truth, the sciences and arts, and the Good. In these cases Aristotle does not pose questions of his predecessors, but evokes them by making reference to their status as collectivity compeers. What he leaves unsaid actually makes such reference.[2]

What we might want to say is that these truly important questions pose and accept as an environment of knowledge the parameters of the form of life of the classical Greek version of theorizing. Such a form of life is secured and treated as a sub-position or resource for prosecuting other inquests. Thus, when Aristotle queries the meaning of 'cause,' his tradition functions as a resource; yet, we must recognize the possi-

---

[1] Besides the *Metaphysics*, the reader might consult as examples the *Physica*, *Rhetorica* and *De Anima*. It is only in the works on logic that such consultation is absent.

[2] Are we not making transparent here from another angle the problems which sociologists speak of under rubrics like 'consensus' and 'common culture'?

bility that this unity is more apparent than Real, for it masks the difference between Aristotle and the other relevant tradition of his day.

Since the 'we' is an omnipresent feature of intelligible speech – of language (this is what is intended by the idea of a 'public language') - it seems gratuitous to re-assert it. Yet, what is re-asserted is not this 'we-ness,' but *my* decision to relate to this 'we-ness' in a particular way. Differentiation is as omnipresent a feature of speaking as 'we-ness' because the necessary difference between speech which *says* and that which merely chatters is that saying (in asserting that it has some-thing to say, some-thing worth hearing) makes the claim that it is not speaking about what merely appears because what merely appears (to anyman) need not be said. Since to speak that which need not be said is merely to chatter, on its every occasion speaking generates for itself the requirement of fulfilling its responsibility to its claim to 'see beyond' what appears. It is in this sense that speaking is differentiating through an authorial claim to know.

On some occasions Aristotle fragments this 'we-ness' by speaking about a 'they.' To do such discrimination is to explicitly re-centre 'me' as a differentiated member of the 'we.' The news in Aristotle's writing is conveyed in that which follows this explicit differentiation, for it is only in lieu of this device that he recognizes the grounds of his claim to write, i.e., that *he* knows and *they* (and you) do not. In contrast to 'we agree' Aristotle treats the use of 'they' as a mode of differentiating himself from his past as knowledge from opinion.

Yet 'we agree' enunciates the same claim to knowledge and unless he recognizes this Aristotle would have to treat his speaking it as redundant. In uttering 'we agree' and in refusing to address the responsibility which the speaking requires by its very character as speech, Aristotle masks the claim he makes in speaking by hearing 'we agree' concretely as a description of our doing agreement (hence, he announces that he speaks trivially). Aristotle does not hear 'we agree' as a disclosure of the committed character of his speaking because he uses 'we agree' as an occasion to relax rather than to reaffirm his responsibility.

'We agree' terminates discussion by bringing together 'we' (Aristotle) and 'they' (predecessors) in a provisional unity: its use points to a togetherness which the author intends to construct for his resourceful use; it seeks to deflect us from addressing that togetherness as a topic. In contrast, his use of 'they' as a mode of differentiating him from them alerts us (you, the reader) to this requirement: that the problem of reconciling 'they' and 'me' is your task, and that subsequent writing will be devoted to furnishing the materials for enabling *you* to decide this reconciliation. When he differentiates 'them' from 'we' he says: this is a question that requires talk (a topic) and *you* ought to decide between 'them' and 'me.' This usage conceals the fact that *he* establishes the conditions for the reader's decision; the questions to which 'we agree' (could) make(s) reference are precisely those which could challenge the conditions for such decisions. The question of how Aristotle's differentiation between 'them' and 'me' is designed to convince '*you*' is then related to his decision to take responsibility for the concrete topic but not for that which authorizes his claim to speak. Or, he hears that authorization to reside in a *matter* that can be decided by a neutral party. This is the grounded claim of research: that it distinguishes itself from chatter not by seeking to understand itself as a responsible saying, but by inducing a 'you' to vote on whether its chatter is (true, accurate, newsworthy) witty or artful.

II

In the first book of the *Metaphysics*, Aristotle begins with his notion of the four causes in hand and proceeds to read his predecessors as concrete developmental points in the career of the idea. When commentators speak of Aristotle's *dialectical* treatment of his predecessors, they can only mean it in this sense, for there is nothing *dialectical* about Aristotle's treatment of the classical form of life.[1] This is to say, that he is not 'dialectical' in his examination of science as the search for first causes and principles, nor in his conception of knowledge as a scale from sensation to comprehension, nor finally in his conception of the distinction between theory and practice. However, some might see his dialectic as evidenced in his treatment of cause, essence, substance, and motion.

Aristotle's dialectic consists in his tactic of arranging previous opinions about an idea as a linear development of partial perspectives which he then synthesizes and codifies in an action that differentiates them from him. Thus, his notion of cause is a synthesis inherited from them and to which he holds them responsible by demonstrating how they fail to theorize under the constraint of the synthesis.

There is a formal parallel between the 'mistakes' of Aristotle's predecessors and the 'mistakes' of Socrates' interlocutors: both predecessors and interlocutors constantly seem to take a 'part' of the idea for the 'whole' but in the dialogues of Plato the movement in thought between part and whole is shown as the movement that is inquiry. That is, the 'dialectic' is shown as a critical and violent contest within the mind that is re-presented in interaction. In Aristotle, the relation between part and whole (between thought which thinks partially and thought which thinks totally) is re-presented as a linear development

[1] Everyone *calls* Aristotle dialectic: e.g., McKeon, Mure, Jaeger, *et al.*

4

which builds upon itself mathematically rather than dialectically. Whereas Socrates relates to his interlocutors (as re-presentations of falseness) in an ironic mode, Aristotle relates to his predecessors mathematically. One relation to the past is ironical and subversive, the other is linear and 'progressive.'

Aristotle takes as his starting point the totality of ordinary discussion of a question as framing the limits of intelligible speech about the question, and *within such limits* he then proceeds to recover the subject of the speech. The predecessors re-present the various predicates that have been (and can be) attached to this basic subject. His work codifies such predicates through an explication of the subject to which they are addressed. Inquiry functions as the task of recovering the subject which was lost through speech (and yet which is omnipresent) by re-asserting the primacy of the subject-as-subject. Consequently, previous formulations are reduced to various speeches about an underlying matter whose status is pre-supposed as an unexplored point of departure in all speech. Though rooted in the security of the communal subject, each predecessor fails to address this rootedness itself. What is missed is the 'whole' or first to which their myriad speeches make reference, and their 'mistakes' result from taking speech for the whole. But this 'whole' is the communal conception of 'cause' as revealed by an intelligence operating retrospectively and archaeologically upon common culture.

A similar movement occurs in Plato with this important exception: the history of the discussion does not provide its own limits and consequently, the subject of the historical discussion is only a facsimile of the Real subject. Each predecessor is exemplified as a typification of the conflict between the aspiration of the Real subject to express itself in speech which can only speak predicatively. Thus, the subject of the historical discussion is only a hint that the Real subject has been covered over and this Real subject is not (as in Aristotle) the pre-supposed notion of 'cause' which underlies causal talk, but the very grounds of speech itself which provide for the character of causal speech as speech worth speaking. The Real subject is how cause ought to be spoken to exemplify true speaking and consequently, the Real subject is truth and not cause.

The 'mistakes' of the interlocutors are then the mistakes of those who take the subject of speech to be the Real subject and since the Real subject is the *Physis* through which speech emerges to speak about what is worth speaking, even Aristotle's self-consciousness about ordinary usage exemplifies such a mistake. Aristotle does not truly hear causal speech as anything more than speech *about* the idea of cause and consequently, he is prevented from theorizing about the idea of cause. To theorize about cause would be to address the way in which cause comes to be, it would be to ask 'what is cause?' not as a subject already secured in discussion to which predicates are applied, but as itself a predicate covering over the real subject – the isness of 'is' – of which causal speech is just a partial expression.[1] It would ask not for the essence of cause, but for how cause essences.

From Plato's perspective, all of Aristotle's speech on cause fails to address the fundamental question of how men can speak. The interlocutors then re-appear in a different guise as men who are divided against themselves, as men whose speech is not at one with its true subject: the interlocuters become many examples of the segregation of thought from 'that for the sake of which it thinks' personified by men whose soul (and thought) are divided, are many. Each dialogue then exemplifies the tension between the unity of true thought and the divisiveness of concrete thought, and each dialogue displays this tension through the concrete example of an idea-as-topic.

Whereas Aristotle's predecessors are out of touch with their pre-suppositions or assumptions, this means only that they are not properly 'reflexive' where reflexivity is understood as having a communal grasp of the possibilities of conceptualization which will make their perspectiviality transparent. Thus, Aristotle's predecessors are not yet fully formed members of the scientific community, and how could they be since Aristotle invented science? Thus, his predecessors fail simply because they precede him: his predecessors fail because he has established their radical differences vis-à-vis himself and it is a concrete difference in time.[2]

In contrast, Socrates' interlocutors may not make their perspectives transparent, but this is not their Real problem; they are not incomplete members but rather, too complete, for they mistake the subject which organizes their speech for the subject for which they speak. They mistake that which they subject for that to which they are subject. They do not 'mistake' the part for whole, but in treating speech as Real, they confuse one set of limits – the concrete parameters of intelligible discussion – with another – the Desire to speak truly – which grounds and provides for any discussion.[3]

[1] This issue is well discussed in W. Marx, *Heidegger and the Tradition*, Evanston: Northwestern University Press, 1971, where Aristotle is depicted as asking for the whatness of a thing rather than for the whatness of whatness.

[2] For Aristotle, previous speech about cause becomes wrong only in relation to a difference which Aristotle him-self creates, where any consideration of the conditions for such a creation is silenced through invocation of the 'we agree.' Such speech becomes wrong when it does not co-respond to Aristotle's standard (which is a synthesis of these same false speeches). Speech becomes wrong for Aristotle because it is pre-historical – before Aristotle – since Aristotle himself is the first (the beginning of history).

[3] Speech about cause becomes wrong for Plato when it takes its own possibility (its cause) for granted, when it takes the possibility of speaking for granted. For Plato, what is 'false' is to exist as an uncritical speaker – a speaker who shows no

III

Socrates' interlocutors – particularly in the dramatic Sophist dialogues – continually mistake a random or concrete feature for the essence of the thing under discussion, and such mistakes seem to result from their taking what is correct from their own experience for what is true.[1] At first glance, this seems to be what Aristotle's predecessors are accused of – of mistaking a part of the thing for the whole – but the difference is deeper.

Socrates often tells his interlocutors that he is anxious to teach them to choose what is clear in preference to what is high sounding and impressive. What is 'high sounding' is not necessarily a 'part' of the idea under discussion for it may depict the whole range of empirical uses of the idea. The question is rather, to what does the 'high sounding' contrast? What is 'high sounding' as what sounds good ought to be contrasted to what is good (as being is contrasted to Being). Men should not lose their heads to what appears good for what matters is that which *is* good.

The high sounding is spoken because it rings true and impressively to men and thus to choose the high sounding is to choose what rings impressively in the ears of men. It is to choose that which engages the senses which means: that which is easily noted because it is securely in sight. In contrast, Socrates recommends that instead of gratifying fellow slaves (men, those to whom the 'high sounding' appeals) we direct our speech to pleasing the gods.[2] Socrates recognizes the possibility of organizing intelligible speeches around alternate standards and the question to consider pertains to the character of the standard. The mistake of his interlocuters results from their failure to raise their thought to face the highest standard – the standard of the Logos – and not the standard of what men want to hear.

Those who are controlled by the impressive and high sounding are

---

faithful immersion in the critical problem (the eternal crisis) of speech and language. What is wrong is to rest secure in the conventions of speaking by showing no Desire to surpass these conventions; to show faithlessness to this Desire. The falseness of such a speaker is the alienation of one who does not experience what he speaks, who does not dwell in his resonances.

[1] Cf. P. Friedlander, *Plato*, Vol. 2, Pantheon Books, 1965, 1964, for his commentary on *Meno*.

[2] See the *Phaedo* for this reference: In my usage, it corresponds to Hegel's distinction between truth and correctness; see *The Logic of Hegel*, translated by W. Wallace, Oxford University Press, 1873, 305, 352, 354. This corresponds to the distinction between the existential and predicative senses of 'to be' discussed in C. Kahn, 'The Greek Verb "To Be" and The Concept of Being,' Foundations of Language, Vol. 2, No. 3, 1966. Also see Socrates' comments to Polus in *Gorgias*, 472, 482.

those who cannot think beyond diversity, for the high sounding is connected to the dispersiveness of the mouthings of men. The high sounding impresses itself upon the senses of men, it is a matter of the eyes and ears and mouth; the ordered character of the high sounding is provided by the orderly character of the body, for it is the body which impresses a unity upon speech. The high sounding is a metaphor for the artfulness of rationality and the inability to discriminate beauty (order) from the Good, or Art from dialectic.

Thus, in the *Republic*[1] where Socrates presents the divided line analogy to Glaucon, mere thinking is differentiated from knowledge not on the principal ground that it mistakes part for whole (that it lacks a communal perspective) but for two more striking reasons: first, thinking depends upon foundations which it fails to question, it moves downward in the wrong direction and never seeks to make its own foundations transparent;[2] and secondly, thinking dwells upon copies, images, and reflections rather than on originals and consequently, the 'wholes' with which thinking is pre-occupied – e.g. ideas – are reflections of originals which ground them.[3] Thinking does not treat its images *as* images, but as trustworthy objects. The metaphor is used to suggest (in keeping with the spirit of the Sophistic dialogues), that faulty thinking is not partial thinking but thought which moves in the wrong direction and which is attracted by the wrong music. Genuine thought as thought that listens to itself is thought that seeks to 'hear' its foundation and its origins resonate in what it speaks. Genuine thought turns back upon itself and in so doing repudiates the simple, secure, and pleasurable.

To close the eyes and ears to the high sounding is then to resist the influences of the common by standing within the common-speaking community ironically, to treat its conventions as icons of an unexplored and decisive foundation. To resist the high sounding – what appears good – is to engage a language critically, to weed out that which is critical and decisive to speech from what is peripheral and extraneous. To engage the critical by seeking to hear it even while the eyes and ears are flooded by the noise and prattle of the extraneous; to hear the music despite the chatter. To lose one's head to the high sounding is to fall under the spell of images (sounds) of the Good, rather than to the

[1] The *Republic*, translated by F. M. Cornford, Oxford University Press, 1945, 509d–511e. Good discussions of the divided line are contained in the following: J. Klein, *A Commentary on Plato's Meno*, Chapel Hill: University of North Carolina Press, 1965, Part 5; S. Rosen, *Nihilism*, New Haven: Yale University Press, 1969, pp. 156–185; and (for exposition), J. E. Raven, *Plato's Thought in the Making*, Cambridge University Press, 1965, Chapter 10.

[2] It fails to *hear* its foundation.

[3] It fails to *hear* its origins.

Good itself, it is to succumb to words rather than to listen to language.[1]

For Socrates, to speak is to speak 'in tune' with what is heard, where what is heard is what speech says.[2] This is the sense in which speaking is listening to the resonances which the speech says rather than to what it speaks. What speech says is its togetherness with Reason and true speech is that which shows how it hears this togetherness. The mistakes of the interlocutors are then mistakes of men who do not listen to what they say because they do not speak in a listening way.

Opinions are high sounding and impressive insofar as they ring true to the eyes and ears.[3] To engage in authentic thought is to close the eyes and ears to that which impresses and is high sounding. It is to resist the politicization of speech, the concretizing of speech. This means to close the eyes and ears to the pressure to treat speech as first rather than as achieved. Our togetherness under the control of the impressive and high sounding is 'taken up' in discussion as a moment in a movement to re-create this togetherness around something which not only *seems* but *is*.

Plato's predecessors are limited by the senses because the senses produce such high sounding music that they succeed in impressing a unity upon the thoughts of men. Men do not recognize that the ideas they discuss are hollow sounding unities which are actually achievements of a higher unity that pre-figures and grounds. Men take what is merely correct for what is true and when they are trained to listen to the impressive and high sounding against the backdrop of the truly musical, the high sounding begins to sound hollow. Yet the high sounding can only sound hollow against the backdrop of the truly musical and the truly musical can only be heard by beginning with the

---

[1] To resist the high sounding is to refuse to limit one-self to what *appears* as independent of that which it is an appearance of because such a limitation denies the very claim embodied in significant speech – the claim to see beyond what appears, to have some-thing to *say*. To resist the high sounding is to understand the apparent as a disclosure of what is and it is to know that one begins by facing the underlying even as it appears to be other than it is. To fall under the influence of the high sounding is to treat the apparent as first, as Real, rather than as an appearing of the Real.

[2] For this conception of what speech *says*, see M. Heidegger, *On The Way to Language*, New York: Harper and Row, 1971.

[3] See for example Klein's statement *op. cit.*, 'Recollection is now identified with the "binding" of right opinions to which we subscribe "from heresay." To "bind" then means to find reasons for them in one's own thinking . . . the finding of Reasons for something in one's own thinking is precisely what we mean by understanding and learning. The goal is knowledge (epistêmê). Should this goal be attained, that which was formally opined (doxaston) and merely remembered will stand firmly and stably on its ground: it will be something "known" (epistêton). The known itself by itself is removed from the vicissitudes of time. The term "recollection" refers now directly to the effort (meletê) of understanding and learning." Pp. 248–249.

high sounding and hollow. Therefore, Plato's predecessors fail only because they have not mobilized the capacities which both he and they share as human and not because they precede him in time, or only show 'perspective' where he shows knowledge.

The limitations which Aristotle ascribes to predecessors are also a result of their unmusicality, for these predecessors fail to recognize that the high sounding has a music of its own. They lack methods for hearing the high sounding as correct or incorrect and their task is to decide from among that which sounds impressive and rings in their ears, that which is worth perpetuating. Aristotle is concerned with the hollowness of the high sounding only in the sense that what is impressive diverts us from inspecting its foundation in fact. To authenticate the high sounding as true rather than as hollow is to determine if what it speaks is correct. To determine if the high sounding is true is to see whether it sounds alike to all men, for it is only under these conditions that we can control for its 'impress' upon the senses and arrive at judgements about it which are true. True judgements about the high sounding are arrived at by deciding whether all men hear the same music on the grounds that if they do, the acceptability of the speech cannot be a product of its high sounding character since the high sounding appeals differently to men.

Aristotle's predecessors were limited by their inability to distinguish that which appeals to them from that which is correct (appealing to all men), and they lack the method for discriminating between the authentic and the inauthentic. Aristotle's world was inhabited by men whose attention was exhausted by what they spoke and understood in concrete speech and not by the silent togetherness of speech and language. Aristotle and his predecessors begin and end with the 'high sounding' – and within that context seek to decide upon the authenticity of the spoken without reference to what it covers over. Aristotle and his predecessors never leave the level of words for language.

The common enterprise in which Aristotle and his predecessors were engaged was the project of recording and preserving the true opinions of men as inherited in intelligible speech; to accomplish this, they required principles for converting the many speeches into one standardized speech to which men could uniformly orient, and they needed methods for conducting inspections of such speeches in order to decide whether they were worth perpetuating and preserving.[1]

---

[1] To Aristotle, the high sounding as what sounds (appears) good is connected to a body at a time and place; what sounds good contrasts to what *is* good as perspective differs from knowledge. For Plato, the high sounding is not equated with perspectiviality because all men tend to hear it. What sounds good (and is not) for Plato is that which gives pleasure – the security and trustworthiness of common-speaking. Though the apparent is not the Real for Aristotle, this is only

IV

The dialectical character of Plato's work then becomes clearer: predecessors and interlocutors cannot re-present inadequate 'positions' which are later surpassed, but rather, display moments in the career of mind which are omnipresent and omnirelevant at all times and places and in the most lofty of thoughts. These 'moments' constitute that through and against which thought thinks, that from which it seeks to free itself even in its act of assimilation, that which is at once external to its unity and the medium through which this unity is achieved. Charmides, Meno, Thrasymachus, Protagoras, Zeno are moorings which thought inherits and creates for itself and then seeks to assimilate to itself in its re-constitutive movement. Meno might be vain, ambitious, and slow witted but as such he impersonates the mind's *essential* conflict with vanity, ambition, and pleasure, a conflict that is not external to thought but is one through which thought assembles itself as thought that is worth thinking. To provide for the experience of thought as Plato does is not to cite the inferior opinions of others, but is to show this otherness as a moment in the segregation of thought from itself and as a stage in its re-articulation in a unity that assimilates this otherness.[1]

Whereas Aristotle's Anaxagoras becomes a contributor to the historic symposium on 'cause' whose pre-history Aristotle terminated by appointing himself moderator of the symposium, Plato's Anaxagoras typifies the steering of thought away from itself. Thus, Anaxagoras' otherness is discernible in different ways.

Aristotle organizes the surfaces of pre-existing discussion and opinion by synthesizing in terms of dimensions which he sees as under-lying such a discussion when viewed in retrospect. Thus, his conception of 'cause' appears as the achievement of an archaeological excavation which he performs upon a corpus, while the very possibility of such an excavation is controlled at the start by what he speaks of as his achievement.[2]

---

because of the perspectivial character of what appears as it presents it-self to *one* who sees and hears it; since what appears can only be *present* for a one it represents the fragmentation of the unity which Aristotle ascribes to the idea of rational 'knowledge.'

[1] Since both Plato and Aristotle *use* their predecessors, neither should be treated as providing descriptions of the pre-history of social thought (as we should not be seen as describing Plato and Aristotle). Thus, Cherniss's attempt to take Aristotle to task for bad historiography is just foolish as McKeon and others have pointed out: for that enterprise rests upon a correspondence version of reading and history. C. H. Cherniss, *Aristotle's Criticism of Pre-Socratic Philosophy*, Baltimore: Johns Hopkins Press, 1935.

[2] The difference between the author – whose very writing in asserting *his* knowledgeability serves to differentiate 'them' from 'you' and himself ('me') –

To relate to one's speech Rationally is to seek to re-produce one's commitment as an achievement in the very speech itself. This is not to *describe* one's achievement causally for that masks the essential relatedness of the commitment to the speech which it grounds by concretizing the achievement as matter. Neither is it to celebrate the achievement aesthetically as pure creative *praxis*, for what would make the achievement itself – as method – the *telos* and good of speaking (which is egocentric and romantic). To show the speech as an achievement is to *show* one's speaking as the achievement of a bringing to appearance of that which is beyond speech itself; that the author of the speech – that which authorizes the speech – is beyond speech (the speaker) itself and that the speaker orients to this difference between man and God (between speech and language) as the difference that is Real (as the origin-al difference) by showing his faithfulness to this difference as that which is good.[1]

The opinions to which Aristotle orients are only intelligible as speeches and Aristotelian theorizing attempts to synthesize speeches. Thus, the assertion in which something (true or false) is asserted about something becomes the unit to which the manyness of speeches are reduced and the reduction generates the subject paradigm as the minimal intelligible unit.

This paradigm which is limited by the boundaries of ordinary discussion and by a concrete standard of intelligibility lays down a ground plan for thought by authorizing its true direction; it stipulates both the boundaries of intelligible speech and the correct route for the mind to follow in its achievement of such speech. These stipulations are secured by ideas of significant speech, of correct form, of synthesis, and of inquestive responsibility. Such a paradigm then conceals the question of its own possibility: of what a thing must be to be a some-thing rather

---

and those from whom he claims to differ is a difference which he ought to re-create in his writing as an achievement. This would show how the commitment which his differentiation re-presents is wrenched from the common speaking as an achievement.

In contrast, Aristotle hides the achievement of the difference with which he begins and from his position he externally 'relates' to others by characterizing, judging, evaluating, and describing.

[1] Thus, Aristotle criticizes his predecessors as partial, incomplete moments in the history of the idea of 'cause' as it emerged from its sensuous grasp in pre-history towards its culmination in his synthesis. Each thinker is judged in reference to the standard constructed through the several contributions of all thinkers. Aristotle's contribution is then to codify and organize the ordinary discussion of cause and the product of such an enterprise is a standard for locating the perspectiviality of each predecessor. Aristotle's reading is then designed to affirm the adequacy of organized, methodic thought which is at one with its nature when it explicates conventional opinions in terms of the paradigm of the mathematical speech.

than nothing, of what it is to speak 'about,' of what the connection is between the something that is spoken about and that for the sake of which speech is about.

Thus, the subject-predicate format to which Aristotle reduces speech is itself the achievement of a monumental act of thought, an act of thought which wrenched its conclusion from concealment in the mysteries of the anonymous 'we.' The achievement *qua* achievement is only discernible in the relationship between Aristotle and his predecessors when the relationship is depicted as a moment in this achievement.

In this sense, the relationship between Aristotle and his predecessors could re-present the relation between the origin and end of inquiry by displaying how his authoritative speech about cause was itself pre-figured by an authoritative conception of significant speech where such a conception was itself re-constituted out of his encounter with the myriad speeches of his predecessors (such as their very speeches about cause). Consequently, when the opinions of his predecessors are depicted as the materials upon which his inquesting reflects – as the beginning matter – this conceals the unity which both he and they share, as a unity which is covered over by their differences and of which these differences are icons.[1]

Aristotle's authoritative version of cause stands to the usage of his predecessors as the correct version stands to perspective, interest, and opinion. Thus, the dialectical development of his idea of cause from out of the contest between predecessors and himself is not glimpsed; he substitutes the recitation of concrete opinions (as history) for dialectic, where such a history is itself made possible by the standard in terms of which it is at once read and of which it is a production. This is to say that Aristotle's very encounter with his predecessors is itself a moment in the unity of that which moves and concerns us, of that which comes to be, and as such, the encounter belongs to the unity from which it has to be wrested. Yet, Aristotle's speech transforms the meaning of this unity – the Oneness of 'to be' – into the unity of a relationship of similarity between different men or opinions.

What 'cause' *is* is a compendium of his predecessors' speeches and the test of Aristotle's speech lies in its success in restoring the unity between his predecessors and himself, i.e. in showing his one speech about cause to be at One with their many speeches. The unity about which he

---

[1] Aristotle's formulation of 'cause' neither existed all along as the *apriori* in terms of which he searched their work, nor appeared as the mechanical re-production of such work. Either of these options masks the struggle of thought with its origins: by presenting his formulation of cause as the synthetic *description* of those who preceded him, Aristotle glosses the very experience of theorizing out of which his formulation emerged. The experience in question is what permitted Aristotle to even begin to read their works as concealing the formulation recommended by his.

remained silent is resurrected as the goal of inquiry, but now in the form of a unity that re-presents the concrete synthesis between externally related opinions. Thus the 'we' invoked silently glosses not the inheritance of Being, but the 'we' of common belief, opinion, usage, and custom: the anonymous collective is made transparent as common culture, and the task of theorizing is identified in the stages of differentiating and re-constructing such a culture in order to typify its Oneness as the Rationality of common sense.

In this way, Aristotle's theorizing ends where Plato's begins, for it is the communal rationality which Plato accepts as his point of departure. Aristotle successfully segregates communal rationality from Reason[1] and creates for theorizing the task of explicating common sense by re-forming it as a Rational speech. Common sense and the essential tension between Reason and communal rationality presented by Plato then re-appear in Aristotle as the conventional tension (later to be institutionalized as 'epistemology') between the plurality of perceptual possibilities and the standard of agreement generated by a unitary conception of knowledge. In Aristotle, Dialectic comes to be paradigmatically personified as the conflict between the individual and society (between the individual as 'perspectivial experience' and society as the standard of warranting speech which is independent of such contingencies); whereas Dialectic for Plato is exemplified in a conflict within the soul between the goal to which thought aspires and the restrictions under which it labours.

As the custodian of conventional wisdom, Aristotle consults his predecessors as developing instances in the capacity of thought to report upon its methodic character.[2] Ordinary usage frames the possibility of such an explication and the deficiencies of predecessors are instances only of ordinary thought's inability to comprehend its myriad concrete possibilities. The difference between Aristotle and his predecessors is a difference in 'perspective,' for the totality of ordinary usage escaped them in the severalness of their individual enterprises. He arrives to pick up the pieces and to supply the perspective (the order and sanity) lacking in a pre-history which can only be seen as ideological; Aristotle will cure ideology through objectivity and method and he will begin by identifying the whole of which each predecessor only glimpsed a part.

Aristotle's standard for reading his predecessors is the result of a

---

[1] For the difference between rationality (reason) and Reason, see M. Heidegger, *The Essence of Reasons*, translated by T. Malik, Evanston: Northwestern University Press, 1969.
[2] We are not recommending the newsworthy character of the charge that Aristotle is commonsensical, for this has been debated by philosophers and critics alike. Rather we seek to provide for this characterization by making it intelligible in terms of another conception of inquiry.

contact with these selfsame predecessors. The contact was itself grounded in a destiny which Aristotle and predecessors shared and out of which he wrested the standard. While Aristotle acknowledges the dependence of his synthesis upon those who contributed to its production,[1] the mechanistic image of such a dependency in Aristotle (the synthesis of countervailing usages) conceals the effort and violence through which his very conception of the synthesis was uprooted from the security of its past. Aristotle reads his predecessors in such a way as to suppress the dialectical contact between his conception of theorizing and the past from which it had to be wrenched. Consequently, the conflict between the past as a sub-position and as a position to be surpassed is hidden under his re-presentation of the conflict as an orderly and cumulative process of growth. Aristotle reads his predecessors so as to hide the experience that is theorizing; he hides the experience by speaking about it rather than by displaying it through his very work.

V

In the *Phaedo*,[2] Plato examines the idea of cause, and his examination is nothing like the methodic and exhaustive survey undertaken by Aristotle. Plato uses that discussion as an occasion to address those matters upon which 'we' tend to agree – the classical version of knowledge – where Aristotle uses the latter as a resource for examining the question of cause. Thus, Socrates does not cite Anaxagoras' conception of cause as a partial or underdeveloped contribution to the history of the discussion, but as a way of symbolizing thought that is uprooted from its Reason. In Plato, one's predecessors take on life as moments in the growth of knowledge and the interaction is displayed as an aspiration to know over the resistances of the impressive and high sounding. Plato's predecessors are re-presented to exemplify the otherness of Unity dispersed in speech, and they are situated in

[1] For example, note the inventory of 'Problems and Difficulties' and the comments upon these which open the third book of the *Metaphysics*. The impression is of a thoroughly fair and responsible historical consciousness and of an indebtedness to predecessors and this impression is only shattered when we recognize the monstrous act of disrespect displayed in this concretization and externalization of others. The predecessors are not situated within the evolution of the inventory as moments in its reconstruction, but are confronted by it as a massive external imposition. The problems and difficulties are not re-experienced in *his* writings but are presented as the gift of a great mind which had so surpassed predecessors as to radically destroy the unity between he and them.

[2] The *Phaedo*, translated by H. Tredennick in the *Collected Dialogues of Plato*, edited by E. Hamilton and H. Carns, Bollingen Series, LXXI, 1961.

dialectical juxtapositions to this unity on every occasion. Indeed, the very action of displaying these predecessors is an act of juxtaposition since the display is created by an authorial rationality which the predecessor re-presents through speeches which negate this vision.

Therefore, Anaxagoras is not pre-theoretic and unresponsive to the totality of possible usage; it is not that Anaxagoras exemplifies perspectiviality and partiality. Rather, the perspective which Anaxagoras shows – the kind of speech he makes – is one that is not worth making. Only superficially does Anaxagoras mistake the parts for the whole; deeply, he makes reference to the way in which thought becomes segregated from its Reason, to one way in which speech can be segregated from language.

Plato discusses theorizing through the metaphors of body and soul, and Anaxagoras exemplifies thinking typified by the soul's increasing subordination to the body. The kind of explanation which Anaxagoras offers re-presents this subordination because it treats cause concretely rather than Rationally. It is not that his conception of cause is only part of the story or is only one way to use cause, but its very use makes reference to the fact that Anaxagoras does not understand what it is to be, and a philosopher who does not understand this cannot speak responsibly about anything. The unity which Anaxagoras cannot see is not the unity of common culture in its commonest sense – the unity typified by the ordinary discussion of cause – but the relationship between his speech about cause and that which causes cause (and everything else) to be.[1]

Plato then treats his predecessors as actors; they are constructed to impersonate the experience of theorizing by exemplifying the otherness which theorizing has to overcome; they re-present not the otherness of the false opinions of 'other' men, but of thinking which disperses under the influence of the eyes and ears and which in such a dispersion must attempt to collect itself under the impetus of theoretic Desire.

The 'we' of Plato – of author, reader, and predecessor – is brought securely to hand through the speech of a predecessor who serves to encapsulate the undifferentiated solidity of the collective, of the beginning. The beginning is then addressed through the author's differentiation of self from reader as one determined to speak the unsaid as that which is concealed beneath the solidarity shared by reader and predecessor. Through the metaphor of history – of concrete

[1] Thus Plato wants to re-experience this unsaid unity in speech and this is the very unity upon which Aristotle secures his speech. Plato will not examine cause *dialectically* if that means with fairness, objectivity, and responsibility towards the totality of usage. Rather, Plato will address the questions of wisdom, philosophizing, truth, and knowledge by using the discussion of cause to make such reference. Plato's discussion will begin where Aristotle ends (with 'cause') and will terminate where Aristotle begins (with 'philosophizing').

'pastness' – the predecessor impersonates the solidarity of the secured and unthought beginning which the origination of the conversation typifies and which the authorial speech moves to assimilate in its struggle to collect itself.

The predecessor as the icon of the historicity of thought serves to make explicit the tension between the impulse of theorizing and the conventionality or security of its beginnings. Plato's dialogues are inhabited by predecessors wrapped in the bodies of interlocutors, whose contests display the essential tension between the aspirations of thought to understand how it thinks and the opinion of society that it knows of what it speaks.[1]

The difference between Aristotle and Plato can be seen in the ways in which they use the notion of inter-action. Plato shows thinking – which is the conversation within the soul – through the *icon* of the external social encounter as that encounter dramatically gathers the togetherness of speech and logos. In contrast, Aristotle treats thinking not as an internal conversation, but as a medium or vehicle for translating thought already achieved and acceptable as a 'position' into a commodity. Whereas Plato uses interaction as an icon of the conversation that is thinking, Aristotle uses interaction as an instrumentality (a method) for bringing one man's thought into contact with an other.

Thus, the writing that displays thinking does not show thought as the action that is the soul's ascent towards Being, but as inter-action. The writing of one man – Aristotle – stands to the writing of the other as two external courses of action and the problem of thinking is essentially a *social* problem of convincing through inter-action, rather than of displaying – through an icon – the movement of inwardness that is thinking. Whereas Aristotle treats theorizing as *essentially* communication, the communicative context for Plato is an *occasion* (or condition) for showing the movement of theorizing.

VI

Let us consider the 'we agree.' What does it do? Does its use alert us to Aristotle's wish to remain silent about those matters for which it is

---

[1] Plato then evokes the forgotten history of social life by using that selfsame life as a point of departure for theorizing. The very history which Aristotle silences under the 'we' becomes 'that for the sake of which' Plato's actors act. Plato's actors impersonate the 'society' which has fallen out of touch with the true subject concealed in the 'we.' In this way, the achievement which the 'we' masks is re-experienced within the encounter as the conflict between the impersonations of actors who enact the conventions of 'society' and the authorial rationality which these impersonations at once stimulate and negate.

invoked? When Aristotle uses 'we agree' instead of explicating previous opinion to show how the agreement was produced, can this be read as his method of saying that these questions are settled for him, or that such questions can be treated as settled because they will go nowhere? That is, to say 'we agree' rather than to engage in consultation with predecessors is to insinuate that the questions are not worth speaking about?

On the other hand, for a Greek like Aristotle these are the very questions – wisdom, truth, philosophy, the Good – which have to be treated with the greatest respect. In this case 'we agree' cannot announce the triviality of the question nor yet its self-evidence. So what does 'we agree' do? Furthermore, the importance of these questions is noted in the fact that on most inquestive occasions Aristotle begins by remarking upon them, i.e. although he does not 'take them up for discussion' as he takes up cause or motion, the fact that he starts from them suggests their relevance.

For example, Aristotle says that dialectic does not start from any opinion but only those that 'stand in need of being talked about,[1] and he claims that no sensible man will take up for discussion some opinion which is evident and which creates no problem,[2] nor will he discuss opinions held by no one.[3] Since Aristotle simultaneously *starts* from such opinions and takes them up for discussion, they must be issues that stand in need of being talked about, issues that are neither self-evident nor obvious. Yet, the fact that he does not direct the same questioning to these opinions as he does to others shows that despite the problems which these opinions present, they will be treated *as if* they are self-evident and create no problem. Here then we find a class of opinions that are genuine problems, that are worthy of being discussed, that are neither self-evident or obvious; on the other hand these opinions will not be taken up for discussion in the same way in which other opinions are addressed. They will be remarked upon, defended, justified, without consulting predecessors to determine how they opined. Thus, if these opinions create problems they cannot be the same sorts of problems which other opinions raise.

Why then, does the man who always consults his predecessors decide not to consult for this class of important problems? The problems are worthy of being discussed and they are worth being assessed through an inventory of intelligent opinion and yet he does not engage in such an inventory. Perhaps the problems are so important that such consultation would be profane? The meanings of philosophy, wisdom, truth, theory, practice, and the Good – the meanings which resonate

---

[1] *Topics*, 101b, 3–4.
[2] *Rhetorica*, 1356b, 37.
[3] *Topics*, 104a, 5–8.

through such notions – raise questions of Logos, of the order which pervades and grounds all things with intelligibility. These questions are important and yet cannot be taken up for discussion. Why is it then, that this class of most important questions – given that answers to them are not self evident – cannot be converted into topics of discourse?

That about which they ask is unspeakable: it is not for man to give solutions or answers (in the conventional sense) to that which they question. Only a God can give a 'solution' to these questions whereas man can only dream or point.

That to which these questions point is beyond the pale of questioning and answering. If discursive topics enunciate the limits of speech by pointing to the inarticulateness of any answer – its inability to 'complete' the mystery and wonderment out of which the question grows – the importance of these questions reside in their status as reminders of speech's impotence to formulate its achievement in some ultimate complete speech which is itself unachieved (unconditioned).

Consequently, 'we agree' typifies the community of wide-awake men who decide to limit their questioning to that which can be topicalized, i.e. brought before the eyes and ears of men in the form of complete and intelligible speeches (like external things). 'We agree' reflects the decision to question only that which can be made to respect the authority of the question as self-evident rather than as masking a deeper authorization. 'We agree' shows the impulse to question only that which can be constituted to preserve the possibility and security of the question.

This use of 'we agree' shows a version of questioning in which answers are 'responses' to questions that are in some sense external to them as 'stimuli': where questions are ways of transferring responsibility, of animating the inanimate by topicalizing. The question is seen as reflecting a desire to complete itself through an answer anticipated to fill it in; questions and answers progressively complete what is empty or lacking; questions symbolize deprivations and needs which answers gratify and complete; questions are erotic, sensual, passive (women) waiting to receive and to consume while answers are instrumental and active (men) moving to give and to produce.

In contrast to this is a version of the question itself as a way of showing an answer. In asking a responsible question shows it-self as an answering-to – a responding-to – a suppressed history of questioning and answering of which it is a residual trace. The question answers – which is to say that in its speaking it responds to a history which its speech marks but cannot name. The question answers by preparing itself in its very posing as a response (as a speech that is responsible to that which animates it). This type of question is not satisfied by a response because its very speech is intended to display that to which *it* is responsible, and thus, it is more of a reminder than a cry of pain. It is this sense of questioning that the use of 'we agree' elects to disregard.

'We agree' then settles the issue in the only way Aristotle knows, for in speaking it, he transforms the ideal of Logos into the consensus of common belief and opinion: 'we agree' divests the Logos of its mystery by converting it into a 'shared assumption.' Thus Aristotle invokes 'we agree' on those occasions when the truly important question of Logos presses to the surface and demands to be spoken: 'we agree' performs the service of permitting him to abstain from either profane consultation or vain self-celebration. The very utterance of 'we agree' serves to hide the differentiation of author from reader beneath the unity of a common assumption by transforming Logos into the assumptions and understandings of a common culture, into the shared and 'given' starting point of an inquiry.

To attempt to address the Logos goes nowhere since any attempt is grounded in that which it addresses; yet, to consult opinions about the Logos is barbaric for it suggests that the Logos has not been grasped by one who so questions. The option is to transform the unspeakable into common belief and in so doing, to exempt it from authentic questioning. Thus, the wise man knows his limits and the limits of his subject matter.[1] Whereas for Plato, the good is divined as the only source and topic of speech despite the re-cognition that it cannot be spoken (re-produced through words) but can only be shown (its 'thatness' can be made reference to as the reason for speaking), for Aristotle this unspeakability constitutes a 'problem' – that the good must be assimilated to words (and thus becomes 'common culture').

Aristotle's use of 'we agree' marks his ambivalence and prudence, for what the 'we agree' conceals cannot be addressed by his programme. This is the appeal of the suspension of doubt. What is doubted will be re-experienced, so we withhold doubt as the grounds of this promise. But the re-experience is not forthcoming. Instead, this withdrawal is used as a positive resource or 'assumption' never to be faced again. He decides to let the Logos lie by excluding it from the purview of rational interest, or by transforming it from the unsaid and powerful to the self-

---

[1] For example note the following in the *Nicomachean Ethics*, 1094B, 19: 'The man of logical training will only seek such a degree of certainty in each branch of study as the character of the objects studied permits. To demand demonstration from a statesman is an error of the same kind as to be content with probable reasoning in a mathematician.' In other words, the wise man will recognize the limits and this is reiterated throughout his corpus. We address this matter in greater detail in the following chapters, however, for a different conception of limit, the reader might consult M. Heidegger, *What Is Metaphysics?* translated by R. Mannheim, New York: Anchor Books, 1961, pp. 49–50.

evident and common. 'We agree' then comes to signify our agreement not to address what the 'we agree' leaves unsaid, and it appears not as a limitation or failure of the programme but as a positive and constructive feature.[1]

The tension shown by the 'we agree' is a result of the fact that its use masks the difference between author and reader under a coerced unity. 'We agree' is at once a creation which in its very unification enunciates a difference; it points to the dialectic between unity and difference.

'We agree' should read: since we ought agree, let us. Why ought we agree? We ought agree because productive speaking requires terminating discussion. How though do we achieve 'we agree' aside from through stipulation and force? How do we come to 'we agree' and what is its weight?

'We agree' points to a level of solidarity or one-ness that is created by an other (a one who departs from the one-ness through his authorial existence). 'We agree' is an authorial conception of what needs to be trusted, as 'fact.' How does 'we agree' come to be? By what is its expression ruled?

Whereas 'we agree' ought be seen as the achievement of the author and not as a description of fact, Aristotle employs it as a device to mask belief as knowledge (difference as unity). The question is not, what is the essence of 'we agree?' – but, how does 'we agree' essence? What is the essence of 'we agree?' asks how 'we agree' rules (by terminating discussion, by pointing to what 'we share,' etc.), but how does 'we agree' essence? asks for that by which 'we agree' is ruled, it asks how we ought hear 'we agree' in the strongest sense.

Authorship raises the problem of unity (that 'we agree' enough to speak together) and difference (that despite this togetherness, it is *I* who speak to *you*). If 'we agree' why do *I* speak to *you*? If we differ, how can 'we agree?'

The force of the 'we agree' is that it is a characterization of what we have in common that does not touch what we (Really) have in common. In Aristotle, the relation between 'we agree' and 'they' is the relation depicted in the movement of inquiry. We disagree in order to create 'we agree' (in order to unify difference), but we can only disagree within limits prescribed by 'we agree.' The referents for our agreeing and disagreeing are then matters of opinion (we agree on this . . . disagree on

---

[1] On this point one might consult Ortega Y. Gassett, *What Is Philosophy?* New York: W. W. Norton and Company, 1960, p. 54:
'Hence the sciences . . . advance by making out of their own limitations the creative principles of their concepts. In order to improve they do not try to take a Utopian leap over and beyond their own shadow or to surpass their own fateful limit; on the contrary, they accept this latter with pleasure, and holding it close, installing themselves inside it with no regret, they succeed in reaching plenitude.'

that . . .). 'We agree' points to the collective who decide to limit their speech, the community of co-speakers who *happen* to share a language; 'we agree' is an organizational device. Yet 'we agree' can also point to the fact that we could agree, to the possibility of agreement that both lies beyond those limits and grounds them. 'We agree' points to the possibility of language itself and to the eternal and Rational community depicted in man's critical relationship to language. This Aristotle knows too, but does not want to take up. This is to say that 'we agree' points in the most concrete sense to our sharing of a common language; analytically, it makes reference to the solidarity depicted in metaphors like Being, the Good, limit, and horizonality.[1]

For Plato, 'we agree' enunciated the need of speakers to rest secure in their conventions and he treated such usage as an occasioned manifestation of the practical need to communicate. Plato sought to show in his writing the faithfulness of suspending such a constraint even though its suspension created risk and 'objective uncertainty' for the author; he demonstrated the thoughtfulness of authorial existence within the tension of such a creation. The authorial existence he displayed served to re-present in microcosm the faithful mode of existence as a way of life both Rational and Good.

In contrast to Aristotle Plato attempts to make the 'we agree' transparent, which is not to claim that Plato is pre-suppositionless and never uses the resources of common belief to develop his inquiry. Indeed, Socrates frequently indicates to his interlocuters that they must assume in advance a stance of knowing that which the very discussion is to bring about.[2] Yet the concern of Plato's dialogues is always to address the question concealed by the 'we agree,' to address the question of collectedness and unity which the invocation of 'we agree' covers over. That is, Plato does not seek to hide the differences between men beneath the unity of a common culture, but attempts to use the resources of common culture in order to evoke the deep unity which these differences cover over.

For Plato, the true subject is the 'we' to which Aristotle makes frequent reference and passes over. But the 'we' of Aristotle as the 'we' of custom and belief still covers over the resonances of the 'we' as the power that forces itself to the surface in any and every inquiry and

[1] The crucial (critical) relation masked by 'we agree' is not the relationship between its use in speech and the communities which it makes possible, but refers to the difference between that to which it makes reference (whether its 'functions,' or a concrete level of solidarity) and that which makes *it* possible. For Plato, 'we agree' enunciated the difference between being and Being, between common speech and the possibility of language, between speaking 'we agree' and the possibility of saying any-thing (rather than nothing).

[2] Socrates makes such remarks about virtue in *Meno* (80b–81a), about knowledge in *Theaetetus*, 196D, and about language in *Gorgias*, 481.

which undergoes a transmutation at the lips of Aristotle in becoming the secure 'we' of custom and belief. Plato himself uses such utterances as signs which mark the reluctance of men to speak about truly important matters, the tendency of men to withdraw from that which they ought to face.

In the *Phaedo*, Plato uses the metaphor of the soul's immortality to make reference to the resonances covered over by the 'we agree.' That is, that our use of the notions of 'equal things' and 'equality' is only intelligible under the assumption that we have knowledge of perfect equality in advance. The notion of the soul's existence before birth is then to be read not as a concrete description of Socrates' religious ideology, but as a myth designed to address the very Logos about which Aristotle's 'we agree' silences questioning.

In the exchange with Simmias, Socrates directly confronts the grounds of intelligibility by re-explicating the character of theorizing as *anamnesis*, as a re-membering of the resonances concealed by the 'we agree.' Socrates then *uses* the agreement which he, Simmias, and Cebes acknowledge – their agreement that they are speaking intelligibly – to address that which the agreement leaves unsaid, the question of its very possibility. Socrates does not leave the 'we agree' behind as a secure 'assumption' from which to investigate life, death, body and soul, for he uses these very ideas to address what the 'we agree' itself leaves behind.

Aristotle's contact with his predecessors is treated by him as something to characterize without his re-cognizing that this contact is shown in his very writing. To characterize in this way is to mask the latent contact as a moment in his achievement of a resourceful position. By characterizing for the reader he prevents the reader from experiencing his (Aristotle's) differentiated position as an achievement and thus he prevents him from experiencing the movement of the soul that is thinking.[1]

Aristotle wants to transform the difference between 'them' and 'me' (as a social situation) into a unity (re-presented in the 'we agree'). 'We agree' reflects the commonality of knowledge and *you* (the reader) are to judge. Aristotle lays the ground for the democratic process of science as knowing by starting with the mathematical conception of difference

---

[1] In both Plato and Aristotle the reader learns the 'position' of the author by seeing it contrasted with others. The reader and writer interact in this way. Yet, whereas this contrast is depicted in Plato as real movement – as the achievement that is thinking – as thoughtfulness struggles with the un-thought in an origin-al and foundational way, Aristotle's presentation masks the achieved character of his thought.

Aristotle disregards what he deeply has in common with predecessors and starts with their difference as secure. Plato begins with what he shares as one sense of the 'we agree' and creates the difference through his writings in the *aporia*.

and the image of knowledge as a concrete social relationship. Aristotle wants to produce many 'we agrees' from difference, many social relationships.

Plato's interest is not in the creation of 'we agree' but in its interrogation. He wants men to begin to experience the 'we agree' in which they live by hearing it for what it says instead of masking it under positive speech or employing it as a resource.

VII

Where commentators speak of Aristotle's dialectic they intend the following: that he regarded as preliminary to any serious work the need to examine previous opinion about the problem at hand by re-arranging such opinions with reference to his inquestive interests.[1] Dialectic as the inventory of opinions re-presents Aristotle's obligation to community, for he acknowledges how his statement of the problem inherits the tensions of previous formulations.[2]

Dialectic is then conceived as the playful discharge of inquestive responsibility prior to the serious business of inquiry, and consequently dialectic is severed from inquiry as that which stands before relates to that which comes after. Dialectic as a corrective to the one-sidedness of inquestive belief ensures that such belief is grounded in a communal start, for only from such a standard beginning can accurate and intelligent work result. Yet, the inventory is already part of the serious work because it organizes the parameters of serious discussion. The inventory organizes the parameters of serious discussion not because of *what* it turns up, but because it is itself a result of applying the conception of serious work which it is designed to prepare.

Aristotelian dialectic is then a social experience in the most concrete sense, for it depicts the consultation of Aristotle with other opinions that are external to him; dialectic is a metaphor for social contact between ego and everything that is alien (non-ego) to him. Yet, the Platonic notion of dialectic as a conversation within the soul suggests that this contact is not paradigmatically expressed in the exchange between externally related opinions, but is a relation internal to the theorist between belief and knowledge. Dialectic as a metaphor for thinking is not an ordinary contact (like a review of the literature), but exemplifies the relationship of thought to Logos. Aristotle's inventory

[1] When commentators then speak of Aristotle's dialectic they intend it in the Aristotelian sense, i.e., they accept Aristotle's version of his work by formulating the work in terms that are coherent with his recommendation.

[2] But this obligation has to be understood analytically as the succeeding chapters attempt to make clear.

can never characterize Platonic dialectic because it presents the achievement of knowledge as an externally related succession of opinions which masks the experience of dialectic as a conversation within the soul. It is only within the limits of *this* use of dialectic that the idea of dialectic as preliminary to the serious work of inquiry is intelligible. Aristotle's re-definition of dialectic serves to sever thinking from inquiry by presenting inquiries mechanistically, and by depicting history not as a movement within the mind, but as an exchange between differentiated individual selves.

Furthermore the conception which Aristotle uses to differentiate *preliminary* dialectic from subsequent inquiry not only concretizes dialectic, but deceptively depicts inquiry as if it was independent of his inventory of opinions. This is not merely to say as McKeon and others have, that Aristotle uses history for philosophical purposes, but rather that his theorizing displays in its course a commitment to one decisive version of history – a decision to collect authoritative usage and to suppress the question of possibility. Thus, Aristotle's subsequent 'research' is not independent of his inventory of opinions (the inventory he calls 'dialectic'), for it continues that inventory in the guise of a language of assertions and of the relationships between assertions. The problem is then two-fold: Aristotle transforms the meaning of dialectic into the concrete inventory, and he conducts inquiries that exemplify such inventories. For example, if Aristotle's speech about motion looks different than his review of previous opinions about motion, such a concrete and external distinction obscures the deep condition of his study that it be responsible to the analytic requirements of an inventory.[1] These segments of his work relate as intersecting moments in the investigative impulse to rationalize and formalize ordinary belief and opinion. Because Aristotle's inquiries are all inventories, they are no different from his review of predecessors.

Thus, Plato's dialectic could never depict the playful examination *prior* to serious work, because all serious work is essentially an instance of dialectic. Furthermore, Plato's dialectic does not make reference to the requirement of solidifying a common and responsible beginning because it is designed to dissolve the security of the beginning in the *aporia*.

Consequently, when Aristotle invokes 'we agree,' he is recommending that we have nothing further to learn from contacting other opinions and that we ought to begin by consulting ourselves. This is only intelligible given his very concrete notion of other opinions, a notion which equates other opinions with other men and which further equates dialectic with an inventory of other opinions (and of other men). In

---

[1] This can be seen clearly in his opening discussion in *Physica* to which we attend in Chapter 3.

this context, to begin with our selves means to begin with a notion of our limit in hand, with the recognition that our work (our serious work) can never start unless we limit our concern to what is at hand. It is *this* notion of dialectic which grounds the repudiation of questioning as necessary by differentiating between the playful and prior and the serious and subsequent.

To invoke 'we agree' is to repudiate at that point, the attempt to consult other men on the grounds that such consultation would disperse one's attention and inquestive focus at exactly the moment when concentration and organization is required.[1] In contrast, a view of dialectic as a conversation within the soul acknowledges that the use of other opinions is only a method for dramatizing this conversation; such a view further acknowledges that inquiry by its very nature is a public marker of this conversation regardless of whether or not it respects this fact.

To Aristotle, Plato's kind of dialectic then becomes a rubric for the impractical questioning that fails to recognize its limits, which is not just questioning the obvious and self-evident, but is a questioning of that which cannot yield answers. In this sense dialectic is a questioning which delays the start of the work. Dialectic is only relevant as the kind of questioning that ensures a common start and the inquirer must distinguish between those questions which can be dialectically engaged (with profit) from those which cannot.

'We agree' as 'we have nothing more to learn from others' means that we might as well start with our selves, i.e. that we might as well begin with the position that we know. What we know is not that to which the 'we agree' refers, but is rather the limits of questioning in which we recognize our unity. 'We agree' means that we recognize our limits. Hardheaded, Aristotelian dialectic as the preliminary inventory of opinions is then an attempt to secure an authoritative foundation for knowledge by forcing each man to begin with the authority of the intelligible speech so as to guarantee his common start with all men. It is an attempt to induce men to re-experience in a communicable way – to learn – by limiting their attention to what is learnable. What is learnable is that which men can discover for themselves; yet such discoveries consist of assertions that can be recorded and preserved and the creation of an authentic record requires that men accept their common limit.

To experience knowing is to establish an identity between what men see for themselves and what is there to be seen, and it is to learn to see for oneself what is there to be seen. Yet, what is there to be seen can only be decided communally, for without such a standard it would only

[1] 'We agree' then serves as an organizational device, i.e., as a theorist's version of the social organization of method.

dissolve into what is seen for oneself. The myriad possibilities of seeing for oneself has to be reduced to the one thought of that which is there to be seen.

Unless dialectic is directed to equalizing the differences among men in a common origin, it can only create an undisciplined and idiosyncratic interest, an interest which undermines the requiredness of a common start. Dialectic must then serve as a preliminary operation for equipping different men with common information so that their conclusion will be assessable.

If the speeches of many men are to be compared the speeches must be amenable to judgements of similarity; similarity is only applicable to a population of men who are already decided to be similar in some intelligible and relevant way. Science is a method of forcing such similarity upon men by organizing them around their most intelligible resource – their ability to speak to one another through a language of assertions and to evaluate the claims which the assertions recommend. Aristotelian dialectic guarantees through the violence of this limitation, the solidarity of such a community.

To create such a community is to instruct each man to renounce the Desire (shared with all men) to question matters which cannot be spoken standardly. It is to instruct man to renounce the desire to remember, or to hear the beginning as an end. Thus, one is to repudiate one kind of unity the unity of Desire) to accept another unity (his co-presence in a community of intelligible speakers). To accept the authority of the latter is to decide to sever one's speech from history and is to begin with speech as limit. 'We agree' then instructs one to begin with self in the concrete sense: with concrete, intelligible speech, with the authority of the senses and of the spoken, with the experience which one confronts for one-self. The Aristotelian 'we agree' destroys the Desire released by the *aporia*.

Aristotelian dialectic is then intended to serve as a corrective for the differentiating tendencies of science. Science authorizes the individual to experience for himself (to attend to *his* experiences) and yet, such authorization can create a dispersed collection of mouthings without any common standard; consequently, science guarantees the standard by controlling the original differentiation which it recommends as a difference within the limits of a unity. Aristotelian dialectic guarantees that the differentiation required for the adequate re-experience of knowledge is rooted in a unity – the unity of the many who accept this limit as the point beyond which questioning will not proceed. The failures which Aristotle ascribes to predecessors are then failures of not preparing the solid beginning, their tendency to speak under the auspices of interests which undermine the common beginning. Yet, this very failure makes Aristotelian dialectic possible, for if men always spoke under such auspices Aristotle would have no problem.

Aristotle's problem is to supply a method for reconciling differentiated beliefs by authenticating that which is true and excluding it from that which is false. The triumph of the method is that it supplies the procedure for reconciliation and its success depends upon whether it can reconstruct differentiated belief (the many speeches) as knowledge (the one speech). The failure of Aristotle's predecessors is guaranteed by his dialectic which can only be utilized where there are differences. Without such differentiation, all of Aristotle's works would either be paraphrases of 'we agree' or descriptive inventories of opinion. Without such differentiation, Aristotle would either be silent or redundant.

Aristotle's procedure is grounded in the threat of contentiousness introduced by divisive and dispersed opinion and it is designed to unify by orienting men to the common which their dispersed mouthings cover over. The common is not something deep, but a concrete relevance to which their differences can be referred; the common refers to the fact that despite the idiosyncracies of their speech, they speak. What men have in common is that they speak. The failure of his predecessors is then a failure to understand their commonality as co-speakers and is a failure to adapt their speech to the requirements of this commonality. The disorder of knowledge and the disorderliness of the beginning are both rooted in the same condition, that thinkers have not been responsible citizens. Aristotle's solution is to appoint himself the law giver.

Whereas Aristotelian theorizing regards the differences between men as a menace which must be controlled because it promises to disrupt the unity of the start, Platonic dialectic treats such differentiation as that which must be faced because it *is* (an expression of) in itself a unity. Plato uses these differences to recover the unity-in-diversity, whereas Aristotle's intention is to minimize such differences in order to discover a unity whose creation will permit us to differentiate correct from incorrect opinion. The achievement of unity which is treated by Plato as an analytic re-construction – a re-membering or *anamnesis* – is regarded by Aristotelian dialectic as an empirical discovery.[1] Aristo-

---

[1] This is reminiscent of Wittgenstein's instructions to look for possibilities and not for facts, or for that which is before our eyes rather than for 'discoveries.' See his *Philosophical Investigations*, New York: McMillan, 1953. For example, note Cavell's characterization of Wittgenstein:

'Instead of accumulating new facts of capturing the essence of the world's definition, or perfecting and completing our language, we need to arrange the facts we already know or can come to realize merely by *calling to mind* something we know,' in *Existentialism and Analytic Philosophy*, Daedelus, summer, 1964, p. 964.

Of course this 'calling to mind' drives for – its impulse – has been re-formulated by ordinary language philosophy to stand for the intelligible range of communal usage, whereas *anamnesis* was used in a radically different sense by Plato. In this

telian differences derive from a conception of the external relations between selves which can only be overcome externally through the imposition of force and method (i.e. through the imposition of an alien law which is external to men just as they are external to one another).

The problem which Aristotle then sets for himself is the task of eliminating differentiation among men in order to create an empirical unity, by accentuating these very differences. This is accomplished by instructing men to trust the authority of their senses and of 'right sounding' speech: that they can only start from (trust) the clear and speakable, from what they can see for themselves with their eyes and ears.

For Plato, the task is otherwise: differences are eliminated not by being avoided or 'controlled' but by being addressed in order to confront the unity which they are (which they cover over). The differences are neither crucial nor interesting, for they are concrete expressions of their originating ground. To follow Aristotle's programme is to make the reconciliation of such concrete differences the goal of inquiry by trivializing the idea of unity through its transformation from that which grounds the different looks of A and B into that which A and B have in common. Whereas differences are icons of unity for Plato, Aristotle starts with the reality of original differences.

Differences for Plato as different concrete moments in the conversation within the soul called thinking, are transformed in the Aristotelian programme into the concrete contacts between one course of thinking (one man) and another; Plato's unity as the dialectically evolving identity between thought and its foundation – a unity which is expressed in the ideal of speech which speaks thinkingly – is altered to refer to the common understanding which two thinkers share.[1] The relationship of thinking to itself (the relation of thought to unity) is converted into the *social* relationship of contact and of 'mutual orientation' between two selves whose thoughts are treated as secure.

Whereas both Plato and Aristotle understand thinking as the movement from convention to nature,[2] the experience of such an

---

sense, Wittgenstein's counsel to 'return concepts to their original home' has been modernized by conceiving of 'origin' as making reference to everyday rather than to *arché* (to the 'firstness' of concrete usage rather than to the 'firstness' of the primordial resonances of Logos). The problem of this transformation is that it affirms the authoritative character of empirical usage while failing to accredit the very action of such an affirmation as licensed by a conception which transcends ordinary usage itself.

[1] M. Heidegger, *Identity and Difference*, translated by J. Stambaugh, New York: Harper and Row, 1969, for a contrast of these two relationships.

[2] See Leo Strauss, *Natural Right and History*, Chicago: University of Chicago Press, 1953, Chapter 1 and *What Is Political Philosophy?* Glencoe Free Press, 1959, Chapters 1 and 3, for lucid discussions of the unitary character of this conception among the Greeks.

achievement is differentially displayed in their writings. Just as Plato transforms the very reading of his predecessors into a moment within this experience – into an icon of the conversation within the soul – Aristotle externalizes this experience by treating it as the cumulative result of an exchange of opinions between literate men.

Aristotle's hierarchy of knowledge[3] – from things known better to us to things known better in nature and from sensation to knowledge – is nowhere personified in his reading of his predecessors, for such reading begins with his knowledge already secure, which it then employs as a standard of evaluation. The possibility of the standard itself is not re-experienced in his work and the authority of the standard is only defended and justified through the inventory of opinions which it itself produced.

The inventory of opinions as the reading of predecessors – Aristotle's particular dialectic – appears heuristic rather than demonstrative because both discovery and demonstration are wrenched from thinking and are themselves differentiated from one another so as to preserve their isolation from thinking.[4] The difference between heuristic and

[3] G. R. Mure has a useful discussion of the analytic character of Aristotle's hierarchy and of the idea of hierarchy in general in his book, *Aristotle*, Galaxy Books, 1933, especially pages 57, 182, 183, 186; also see his *Introduction to Hegel*, Oxford, at the Clarendon Press, 1940, Chapters I through VI and his 'Foreword' to F. G. Weiss, *Hegel's Critique of Aristotle's Philosophy of Mind*, The Hague: Martinus Nijhoff, 1969.

[4] For examples of this distinction, A. Stigen, *The Structure of Aristotle's Thought*, Oslo: The Norwegian Council for Science and the Humanities, 1966, particularly Chapter 3. Since this book was written under the influence of McKeon, the latter's interesting article 'Truth and the History of Ideas' in his *Thought Action and Passion*, Chicago: The University of Chicago Press, 1954, should be consulted. In this respect McKeon's work deserves special comment.

One value of his article is that McKeon's treatment of Plato's and Aristotle's uses of history in itself exemplifies the Aristotelian approach to predecessors. For example 'For Aristotle, dialectic is not the method of science, and Aristotle's dialectic treatment of other philosophers, whatever its utility to scientific inquiry, could never be confused with the actual collection of data or demonstration of conclusions which are essential to the constitution of a science.' (p. 60). This preserves first, the authority of Aristotle's characterization of dialectic, and his assumption that no matter how his treatment is characterized, that such treatment differs from his method (of demonstration). We regard this as too concrete: our whole point is that one can see his method *in* his critique if critique is understood analytically rather than as a concrete recitation of previous opinion or as Aristotle's report on his intention in doing critique. This is to say, that what Aristotle reports to be preliminary is still an end and what *he* takes to be serious (and subsequent) has the analytic character of the preliminary. Again, this is not to pronounce upon what Aristotle meant in a descriptive sense, but is to display through a reading of what he meant, what we mean.

Analytically Aristotle's critique and method like Plato's are one, and the failure to appreciate this results from reading Aristotle literally and by seeing his critique as dialectic and his method as demonstrative. What McKeon wants to

demonstration conceals their unity in the experience of thinking because thinking has long since been wrested from its primordial status as a conversation within the soul and shaped into its mould as a contact between selves.

We see Aristotle's attitude toward theorizing in the way he reads his predecessors not because of their mutual influences (the influences

---

say is that 'from Aristotle's point of view . . . they are different,' but since McKeon's own thesis recommends that the question of Aristotle's 'point of view' just like the question of Anaxagoras' point of view to Aristotle, serves to affirm the authorial conception of inquiry which brings the point of view to life, what Aristotle 'had in mind' can only be a demonstration of McKeon's conception of philosophizing. Thus we would argue the following: McKeon writes as if he is exempt from his thesis, for his thesis recommends that his attempt to ground his distinction between the authors (which is what a point of view characterization is) only disguises his authoritative version of inquiry and consequently, the differences he locates as analytically crucial only take on life as Aristotelian designations. This is to say that while we are not disguising *our* Platonic reading of Aristotle (for a speaker has to stand somewhere) McKeon masks his authority under the guise of a descriptive interest in the so-called history of ideas.

For example on page 61 he says that the treatment of previous philosophers 'is for Aristotle a (dialectical) conversation . . . preliminary to the serious work of philosophy . . .,' and his understanding of the relation between critique and method in Aristotle is controlled by this perspective. Yet, even though Aristotle might understand himself this way, we see the critique *as* the method and thus McKeon's understanding of Aristotle and Plato re-capitulates Aristotle's authority while speaking as if it does not. This is not to label McKeon Aristotelian or some such thing but is rather to accuse him of not grasping the fu implications of his thesis – or better, of not showing the courage of his position.

The major problem is that McKeon's characterization of Aristotle as segregating critique from method and of Plato as unifying them is based upon a concrete conception of both critique and method as externally related and is supported by his reading of the distinction between heuristic and demonstration. Thus he says 'to judge between the histories of thought envisaged in the philosophies of Plato and Aristotle is to judge between their philosophies' . . . while ignoring that to judge in the present case is to *use* one of their philosophies to do the judging. Consequently 'to judge' between masks under an objective rubric the fact that the issue has already been judged. In other words to speak of the judgement – as an instance of philosophy – as a judgement is to mask the very authority which McKeon employs. His paper exhibits a peculiar kind of nihilism, then, for it conceals its authority behind a classificatory method authorized by the Aristotelian tradition itself and thus suppresses his very real commitment behind the scholarly apparatus of the historiography of ideas. Again the point is not that McKeon is incorrect; but rather, in describing the practices of his predecessors as he does, he brings to the surface an authoritative method of reading. This appears particularly striking in quotes such as 'Plato discerns the "spirit and intention" of predecessor while Aristotle (when accurate) recovers what a predecessor *said*.' (p. 82). This is terribly misleading for the notion of what a philosopher *says* (not speaks) is here segregated from 'spirit' and 'intention' in the most concrete sort of distinction. What has to be addressed is the method of reading and it is in this sense that McKeon's method of pluralistic characterization refuses to face itself.

between his method of reading and his method of theorizing) but in his various segregations of history from knowing – of heuristic and discovery from demonstration and proof – for his preservation of such distinctions testifies to the unity of the experience of knowing which his very writing seeks to suppress. Aristotle's reading of his predecessors exemplifies his theorizing (it *is* his theorizing) and this is seen in his every effort to keep these moments apart.

VIII

Whereas Aristotle's writing *relates* in the sense that it characterizes (it relates to what it characterizes), it leaves the possibility of the author (as an achievement) unexplored. Plato's writing is intended to display the possibility of Plato him-self as a Rational achievement.

Plato is always writing only and exclusively about the theoretical life and his very writing exemplifies the movement and courage essential to such a life; his writing exemplifies the action that is such a life. Socrates is not a description of this life, but an icon; Plato's predecessor Socrates is used to exemplify the co-existence of Desire and irony which typifies the theoretical life.

Though both Plato and Aristotle write about predecessors, Plato relates to his predecessor as an apostle, while Aristotle relates to his predecessors as a genius. Plato shows him-self an apostle for the Desire re-presented in Socrates not by describing Socrates accurately, but by using Socrates to show the requiredness of faithfulness to that which ought move men. Socrates is used to exemplify the ideality of a theoretic life and the struggle of life to co-exist faithfully and loyally under the auspices of such an ideal.

Aristotle treats his predecessors as moments leading up to him. As the genius, Aristotle begins history and owes to no-thing. The source of Aristotle's differentiation from the common lot of men is his genius. Just as Socrates is that for which Plato writes – the source and Reason of his apostasy – Aristotle writes for unity and communality: whereas Plato's commitment is to an exemplification of the theoretical life as a form of heroism, excellence, and virtue, Aristotle's commitment is to his own differentiated talent and genius as the source and ground of his achievement. Whereas Aristotle wants to transform faith into knowledge substituting agreement for faithfulness, Plato wants to show the truth of faithfulness itself. Paradoxically (to modern ears) Plato wants to show the truth of faith, the Rationality and Reason of faith; Plato wants to show that truth is faithfulness.

The Reason of faith is the Good which inspires it and faith is exemplified in speaking which exposes its committed character in the very act of speech. Speech exposes its stand-point (the point on which it stands) by re-creating this 'point' in any matter it speaks about. Faith is 'tested' rationally not by giving reasons for it (for that submits to a conversational standard of rationality), not through mere celebration of the *fact* of faithfulness (for that is narcissistic), but by analyzing any matter in a committed way as a showing of that to which faith is faithful the failure of the limits to comprehend the unlimited.

'We agree' then rules by terminating discussion (differentiation) and we have shown how Aristotle uses it in this way. Yet 'we agree' ought serve as an occasion for collecting thought – as an incentive for addressing the very foundation of 'we-ness' in the relationship between Being and nothing. This is the sense in which 'we agree' is ruled, for it comes to *be* as an appearance of what is and of the difference between Being and nothing as a difference. Whereas 'we agree' ought point to and remind us of what is first (that by which it is ruled) by making us stop and think, Aristotle uses it as a secure base for action, assuming of course that he is first. Aristotle the genius treats his past as concrete and different in kind from him-self whereas Plato the apostle treats his past as a feature of his present that needs continual re-affirmation in order to convince one self rationally that such a faith is good.

IX

Theorizing is the attempt to bring the experience of thinking to speech. If thinking is a conversation within the soul, what one speaks *about* ought be exemplified as a moment in this conversation. One's predecessors re-present the unthought origins of one's own thought which this very thought seeks to surpass. Theorizing begins with what men have in common and since author, reader, and predecessor are men, inquiry begins with what they have in common as men. What they have in common is that they are all moved, caused, and summoned by that which moves, causes and summons all things. Beneath the superficial commonality of their 'mutual orientations' to one another is a deeper unity – the Oneness of Being in which all men participate. To treat one's predecessors as external and different is to treat the reader and all men in the same way; to ignore the Oneness of author-predecessor-reader is to ignore the author's Oneness with the very beliefs he seeks to surpass. To treat predecessors as externally connected moments, is to mask the achievement of one's authority through the self-centred invocation of the immunity of genius. In all inquestive work the action of writing raises the question of how the unity between men is to be addressed.

The difference between the author, predecessor, and reader is that he has listened to what they share. The author knows that what they share needs re-thinking, and their deep unity consists not in the *what* of what they share, but in the fact that what they share can be re-thought. The most important matter to re-think is that what they share has not been thought. This is how Heidegger can say that the most thought-provoking thing is that we are not thinking.[1]

The problem of the author is to induce the reader to join with him to hear what they share by constructing a relationship with the predecessor as the icon of a thinking experience, as itself an instance of the re-thinking to which author and reader are directed. Author and reader share their humanness – their capacity to re-think that which needs thought. The author's problem is to re-create an exemplary thinking experience for a reader whose horizons are controlled by the security of the unthought, the pleasurable, and the common; to have the reader re-experience their human solidarity which the dispersive forces of the high sounding and impressive cover over.

To cite the falsity of predecessors, and their omissions, gaps and stupidities as failures is to compare their performances (performances which the author has himself created) with the standard of true speaking in terms of which they fall short. To use the standard resourcefully for such citation while not exposing its committed and Rational character as a standard that is achieved masks the possibility of re-experiencing the standard itself as that which emerges out of the Desire to surpass this selfsame arena of falsity and otherness. Because such usage concretizes the standard as a neutral object – present and apparent to the on-looker – it divests the standard of any moral weight as a Good on the grounds that what is merely present is not worth saying. In differentiating predecessors from oneself in this way, the author recommends that the relation of what he knows to belief is an external succession of opinions, a matter of his concrete superiority to them, a matter of his genius. Yet, since authorial knowledge is itself wrenched from the same milieu of convention, opinion, and falseness, and only exists as knowledge in its essential contrast to such opinion, to make the predecessor radically other is to cover over the essential conflict which thinking experiences in its effort to re-think what needs thought. All characterizations of predecessors have to evoke within their very occurrence a sense of the achieved character of the characterization.

Aristotelian criticism does not re-present the relation of thought to its possibility and grounds because it assumes it-self as secure, and in so doing it hides the relationship out of which *it* emerges. Logos gives

[1] M. Heidegger, *What Is Called Thinking?* New York: Harper and Row, 1968

all men the power to engage in the thinking experience, and what men need to know is how they can aspire for knowledge on the basis of what they share. Thus, in differentiating self from predecessor, the author treats himself as if his speech has no history aside from its character as the product of a series of external, cumulative contacts with previous opinions. In differentiating self from predecessor, what is shared is trivialized and the differences between men become analytically crucial. Such self-centredness points to the authority of individual concrete talent and genius as the source of authorial knowledge rather than to the Good for which the author is an apostle. As these differences get accentuated, the ground for re-experiencing oneness as the highest unity rather than as the common become forgotten.

To speak thinkingly is to show the organic relation of the unthought and the thought as re-presentations of different developmental points in the career of truth, knowledge, and mind. The relation of author to predecessor is only a metaphor for this relationship. Consequently, the presentation of predecessors as different in kind from author is to re-present the relationship of thought to itself as a relationship between things which are different in kind (as mechanical relationships) and disregards the essential unity of thought and that which it thinks (the essential togetherness of language and Being).[1]

The difference with which Plato begins is the difference between the unity of the common and the unity of the possible and resonant which the common-speaking covers over. In contrast, by beginning with the unity of the common Aristotle transforms the idea of Oneness. Similarly he re-interprets difference which no longer depicts the otherness of the common that negates the Logos in its very act of speaking (the difference between the common and the Logos), but as the differences between the many possible ways of speaking about the common (as a difference within and grounded by the limits of the common).

Aristotle's 'we agree' then masks the relationship of thought to itself – it masks the experience of this relationship – by announcing a new and authoritative conception of the relationship that is thought. 'We agree' provides for the unthought unity of Aristotle, predecessor and reader and his inventory of opinions is meant to contrast against this, the thoughtful. Though 'we agree' is a result of this kind of inventory, it is written about as if it was an inheritance rather than an achievement. The relationship between 'we agree' and the inventory is

[1] In one sense, Aristotle's use of 'we agree' seems to demonstrate his unity with predecessors and reader, for such usage appears to mark the resourceful employ of common custom and opinion. Yet, there is a difference between using the unity of the common as a resource, and re-experiencing this unity as something other than the commonness which *it* shows (i.e., as a unity which *it* covers over).

35

not re-experienced dialectically, it is not discussed in a manner that preserves the experience, and instead comes to stand through the imagery of the external relations of assumptions, premises, and heuristic to demonstration and proof. Aristotle does not then show how the work of inquiry makes essential reference to the achievement of the 'we agree' or how inquiry *is* essentially a re-membering of what the 'we agree' leaves unsaid.

Aristotle ignores the character of his beginning as an achievement by forgetting the question of how he could begin as he does. That he does not take this as his task means that he does not show how the beginning arises out of wonder, philosophizing, the search for wisdom, truth, *et al.* These are the resonances which underlie the 'we agree' and to which it points as the experience of achieving the beginning. Because Aristotle treats his beginning as a Real beginning, he treats it as secure. The experience of securing it is re-produced in the inventory of opinions.[1]

The reader is then induced to accept a position external to the experience of the 'we agree,' i.e. to accept the assumption on the basis of belief and authority. The reader is treated externally.[2] In the same

---

[1] Thus, the familiar notion well expressed by G. S. Kirk and J. E. Raven, *The Pre-Socratic Philosophers*, Cambridge University Press, 1957, 'Aristotle gave more *serious* attention to his philosophical predecessors than Plato had done . . . however his judgements are often distorted by his view of earlier philosophy. . . .' (p. 3). This is a very strange characterization. We have been trying to show in part that this notion of seriousness is one which underpins received authoritative versions of inquiry and is Aristotelian in origin. If we can succeed in making this conception of seriousness strange, we will succeed in opening up the question of theory to other lines of development. The trick, however, is to make Aristotle's conception of seriousness problematic not (as Kirk and Raven suggest) because of its possible inaccuracy (for example in the way Cherniss does), but on the grounds that it is not Really serious.

[2] Some might suggest that the treatment of Aristotle in this chapter is sufficiently unsympathetic to justify the accusation that we are externalizing him just as we show him to externalize his predecessors. In one sense, we have been trying to show how essential Aristotle is for our speaking about the very problems which he covered over, and further, that this concealment is rooted in the deep unity of thought with respect to Being. Thus, though Plato and Aristotle are concretely differentiated, we have been using these differences *to point to* the deepest level of their Oneness. Our respect for Aristotle is displayed in our attempt to assimilate him to Plato as moments in the career of true thought.

For example, note in McKeon's article how one sympathetic to Aristotle actually succeeds in concretizing him by taking him at his word; such 'sympathy' serves to concretize the predecessor at first, situating him in a field of differentiated selves, and then by distributing characterizations. We are seeking to reconstruct Plato *and* Aristotle as One by seeing them not as differences in kind (as different thinkers) but as different moments in the evolution of truth (as different moments in the concept of thought). Aristotle is essential to us because in seeking to rationalize him we use his writing as an occasion to make reference to the ideal of Rationality. He belongs together with us because it is through him that this ideal surfaces. The point to keep securely in mind is that we are not interested in

way, the reader is exposed to Aristotle's presentation of his relation to predecessor as an external relation, for the Oneness in which *they* are rooted is sacrificed by his differentiation of him-self from them – a differentiation seen in the inventory of opinions which covers over the unity from which it was wrenched. Where Oneness is forgotten, differentiation emerges as analytically central; Oneness is divested of its analytic character and true and false thought are equated with correct and incorrect opinion where correctness itself is grounded in the ability to achieve a consensus of belief and opinion.[1]

X

We might ask, how does Socrates relate to the 'we agree?' Concretely he negates, distrusts, undermines; he does everything that Aristotle fails to do. Yet Socrates is Plato's figure and so it is Plato who relates to the 'we agree' through Socrates. Plato uses Socrates to address the problem of 'we agree' in this sense: that the problem of Socrates is used to excite the Desire to understand and to enact the theoretical life. Plato invented the problem of Socrates as an exemplification of the theoretical life, as the eternal focus for our imperative question – how ought we live thinkingly amidst the un-thought without losing our souls to self-interest as it is variously manifested in the icon of genius and in its appearances as artfulness, courage, and authenticity: to be artful, courageous and true without losing one's head to aesthetics, pride, and experience. Socrates is used to centre the tension between the common and the extra-ordinary, between pleasure and Desire, between security and character, between productive speaking and critical speaking, between the faithfulness of irony and the faithlessness of positivity.

---

describing Aristotle or Plato even though our speech might sound as if we are: we are making points off them to make reference to an ideal of Rational thought. Thus, the objection that we are distorting Aristotle just as we claim he distorted his predecessors misses the point that we use Aristotle to make reference to the rational grounds of our Desire to distort (just as we must read him as doing the same). We are all involved in proposing and affirming and not in describing. The problem is not distortion, but to expose the Reason for the distortion as the Reason that is good. Whereas our reading of Aristotle seeks to create the tension of an *aporic* by not understanding him concretely, his readings of predecessors create the most concrete differences between he and they: this is because we want to show through our reading how our reading is possible (its grounds) and such a creation of tension is necessary, where he assumes his possibility as secure and thus creates not tension but concrete disagreement.

[1] These issues are pursued in the following chapters.

Plato uses Socrates to centre the eternal question of how the theo-retical life ought be exemplified in the existence which is theorizing, the question of what kind of hero we want to exemplify, what kind of courage we want to affirm. The problem of Socrates forces us to re-examine that which the 'we agree' masks (though not necessarily in the way Socrates did) because the figure of Socrates is an icon for that eternal concern which 'we' must face – the concern of how to affirm loyalty to this 'we-ness' in the existence that is 'me,' my existence as a man.

The great tradition in theorizing is the tradition that re-members the problem of Socrates, and 'we agree' in the strongest sense means that 'we agree' that the problem of Socrates is the problem to re-member. To re-member the problem of Socrates is to re-member the moral grounds of speaking as a saying and the imperativeness of constantly re-asserting these grounds even while employing them. To show the Good while orienting to showing itself as a faithful responsi-bility. To submit speech to this demand – to attempt to say what ought be shown – is to show that towards which the saying aspires as that which is Good, it is to take the risk of faithful speaking.

In this chapter, we have opened a line of thought by taking up for discussion some matter that needs thinking. Our pursuit of the resonances of 'we agree' raises a tissue of concerns which we can now begin to anticipate; what we see is not so much a solution but a path. We are engaged in re-arranging what we already know, but the re-arrangement begins to lead us into strange territory. We keep trying to find our feet.

2

Science

Although 'being' is used in so many senses, it is evident that of these the primary sense is whatness.[1]

But all the sciences, marking off some being or genus, conduct their investigations into this part of being, although not into unqualified being nor into their part of being *qua* being, and they say nothing concerning whatness; but starting from the whatness of their subject, which in some sciences is made clear by sensation but in others is laid down by hypothesis, they thus proceed to demonstrate more or less rigorously the essential attributes of their genus.[2]

None of these sciences examines universally being *qua* being, but cutting off some part of it, each of them investigates the attributes of that part.[3]

Aristotle, *Metaphysics*

I

In speaking about being, Aristotle makes reference to what the sciences do; if the primary sense of being is whatness,[4] the sciences *mark off*

[1] *Metaphysics*, Z 1028a.
[2] *Metaphysics*, E 1025b.
[3] *Metaphysics*, 1003a.
[4] In that Aristotle conceives of whatness as the whatness of a being rather than of whatness itself. See W. Marx, *op. cit.*, for this distinction. Such usage as Heidegger's has been criticized as a species of 'linguistic bewitchment' by philosophers as diverse as Carnap and MacIntyre. They uniformly read Heidegger's conception of Being in the most concrete way – as a category or genus – and his intent as descriptive. Passmore's very fair précis of Heidegger in his *A Hundred Years of Philosophy*, New York: Basic Books, Second Edition 1966, pages 487–498, seeks to correct many of these concretizations. Also, Rorty's 'Introduction' to *The Linguistic Turn*, Chicago: University of Chicago Press, 1967, places Heidegger well vis-à-vis his contemporaries. Yet MacIntyre re-iterates these same charges – 'his basic mistake . . . is to suppose that because an expression is used in some one context with a particular grammatical form, it can be transferred without change or loss of sense to any context in the same grammatical form.' p. 44. He says further – after anticipating a Heideggerian objection to this descriptivist imputation – that Heidegger uses 'alleged etymological roots (as) prime evidence of what the word really means.' p. 46 (as if Heidegger is interested in *what* words

some part of whatness *saying nothing of whatness itself*, and conduct their investigations into this part, into its attributes. Furthermore the sciences say nothing of their part of whatness *qua* whatness but instead begin with the part of whatness which they have secured and from such a beginning, proceed to demonstrate and investigate.

The sciences are then characterized by what they fail to say or by what they say nothing about, i.e., by what they leave unsaid. But if the sciences say nothing about whatness itself, their silence simultaneously says something – it says that they are saying nothing about whatness. In speaking about the particular whatness that they 'mark off' the sciences simultaneously make reference to 'whatness itself' from which their delineation emerges. In a peculiar way then, the sciences are characterized by what they fail to speak, because what they speak makes reference to what they truly say and what the sciences truly say is that they will have nothing to do with whatness in general.

It is with this truth that science begins: by limiting itself and establishing this limit as its beginning. Science begins by marking off a

---

'really mean' in that sense). 'Unfortunately he first mistranslates his authors and makes philological mistakes in his etymologies. But worse still, he never explained how etymologies could be clues to concepts. What Heidegger fails to grasp here is of the first importance.' p. 46. But this is an uninspired reading: Heidegger's 'mistranslations' and 'mistakes' are instances of his analysis and only appear as 'misses' to one with a correspondence notion of reading; the idea that Heidegger 'never explains' exposes the critic as one who has a concrete notion of explanation, and as one who fails to *see* the so-called explanation in the speech as an integral feature and not as some separable 'self-characterization.' The critic is holding the author responsible to requirements that he (the critic) has imported, such as 'being accurate in translation' and 'giving evidence for concepts,' but these are the critic's criteria, for the corpus of Heidegger's work is explicitly directed to making transparent the kind of mind that the critic shows, the kind of mind that would make such demands, and consequently Heidegger's work is directed to exposing such demands. So how can MacIntyre repeat these questions? He evidently does not listen, he does not understand Heidegger's work (or he wouldn't repeat such charges). MacIntyre's critique only displays *his* authoritative conception of reading which he masks as a description of Heidegger under the epithets of attributed 'mistakes' and 'failures.' Thus MacIntyre congratulates himself for scoring off Heidegger with points such as: he mistranslates, he distorts authors, he assumes uniformity of usage, he treats Being and non-Being as names, etc., while the understanding that produces such charges is taken as a topic of Heidegger's very writing. MacIntyre plays the role of the dummy resurrected from Heidegger's writings to contest them, but since he can only mouth what has been surpassed in these writings, he can only remain an unconvinced protagonist, rather than an interlocuter, for he is external to the dialogue and in his turn, externalizes the other whom he reads. If MacIntyre had an analytic notion of reading and critique he would address Heidegger's commitment – the election which grounds his work – instead of citing concrete 'failures' to which Heidegger is unresponsive as a matter of principle. If MacIntyre was anything but a drone he would confront that principle.

part of whatness either through sensation or hypotheses: science posits a part of whatness as its beginning and upon this secure foundation, proceeds to investigate and demonstrate the attributes of this whatness.

To so limit whatness, to mark off and collect a part which it segregates from whatness in general – this is how science begins. Science attempts to create access to whatness by limiting it to a part; science can only speak about a part of whatness and therefore limits its attention and its interests to what it can speak.

But, does science even speak about a part of *whatness*? Aristotle says that science does not speak about *its* whatness *qua* whatness, so how can science speak about whatness at all? If science restricts its interest to its part of whatness without respect to the whatness from which the part is differentiated, then *what* is the part? In speaking about its part science skips over whatness itself, for to speak about its part is to speak about a re-presentation of whatness without reference to the *what* which the part re-presents. To secure its part of whatness, science requires of itself that it transform this part into something else, something other than whatness. Science then begins by cutting off a part of whatness but in the very action of the cut, it transforms its part into something other than whatness.

II

Aristotle's characterization of science covers over an origin that is even deeper than what he speaks, for in beginning with its part of whatness, science concretizes whatness. To conceive of whatness as a some-thing with dismembered parts is to conceive of whatness as a genus and the part as a species. This is to say that Aristotle conceives of whatness as a genus which the sciences secure in dismembered parts or species and thus lays the possibility for an oraganon of science which is a hierarchically organized series of species of the genus whatness. In making each of these species a genus in itself, science does more than mark off a part of whatness, for it creates an altogether new notion of whatness.[1] This is to say, that science re-conceptualizes 'what is' in that it re-thinks Being. Or to put it otherwise: Aristotle *uses* science to make reference to his re-thinking of Being, a re-thinking that eventually comes to ground science as we know it.[2] (Just as we in this reading use

[1] Which is to say that even though Aristotle speaks of *what* science marks off as whatness, this is a new notion of whatness as some-thing with parts (some-thing identifiable, speakable).

[2] Thus, though Aristotle does not do (e.g., in the *Physica*) what we have come to regard as physics (and see the following two articles for this – J. Owens, 'Matter

Aristotle's conception of science to make reference to our re-thinking.)[1]

Science then begins with a part which only acquires life as part of a whole and yet, in segregating its part from the whole, science treats the part with which it begins as the whole. To begin in the way it begins, science must forget its history and in such an action must limit its attention to a part which has survived. Through the action of marking off, science re-produces that history in a part which it secures as a starting point for that which it intends to finish. The part survives because science 'marks it off' and limits itself to the part. Science begins in the positive action that is speech, but this positive action itself is a negation of that for which the speech speaks. In marking off a part of whatness, science silences whatness itself.

The sciences 'start from' the whatness of the subject, which in some sciences is made clear . . . but in others, is laid down. . . . Science secures its whatness as its beginning by making it (this whatness) clear or by laying it down. Making clear and laying down is the action that initiates science and the action completes the experience of wresting from oblivion the 'what' that is made clear and laid down. Science discerns its whatness and makes it clear, lays it down, as that from which the science starts. Science starts from what it itself makes clear and lays down. Thus, science makes clear and lays down its achievement as a beginning from which to start.

No matter whether this whatness is apprehended or posited (i.e., is laid down), it is secured, and in this securing is established as that from which science will proceed. The source of this whatness as a power which bids men to make it clear or lay it down is external to whatness as it comes to be laid down; in laying down the whatness of a part of

and Predication in Aristotle' in E. McMullin, ed., *The Concept of Matter in Greek and Medieval Philosophy*, Notre Dame University Press, 1965; and G. L. Owens 'Tithenai ta phainonena,' in J. M. E. Moravcsik, ed., *Aristotle: A Collection of Critical Essays*, New York: Anchor Books, 1967), he nevertheless lays the ground for all respectable thinking. Thus the objection that for example Aristotle's physics has been superseded by Newtonian physics should not be construed as an objection to our point (for this change see R. Harre, *Matter and Method*, New York: Saint Martin's Press, 1964 and M. Heidegger, *What Is A Thing? op. cit.*). Our concern is with the possibilities which Aristotle's re-thinking of Being provoked, possibilities which were internal to his conception and that are still with us. Strictly speaking then, what we are calling Aristotle's conception is *his* only in the metaphorical sense that we can see it through him and his writing. Thus, our concern is really not with Aristotle's re-thinking *per se* (as something which belongs to Aristotle) but with a conception of Being which we recognize today and which is as much the product of Aristotle's successors as Aristotle. We use Aristotle to make reference to this conception and not to situate him vis-à-vis those who followed in a history of thought.

[1] Therefore, for science to achieve its part and to establish its action of limiting and securing whatness, science must conceive of whatness as a genus whose parts stand to it as species, but then must mark off each part as a genus in itself.

whatness, that which gives the part its character as a part of *whatness* is forgotten.

The sciences then start from the whatness of their subject and in their turn subject themselves to the authority of their start: the sciences lay down the whatness of their subject as the authority to which they will be sub-ject.

Subject has different resonances. As that of which something is asserted it is the thing of which something is said and ultimately it is the underlying matter to which predicates are tied.[1] Science starts by laying down a thing of which it will speak and then proceeds to speak in conformity with the authority of the subject. Science starts from its subject and speaks under the auspices of this selfsame subject: science lays down an authoritative path and confirms itself as instance of this selfsame path. Science seeks to speak about its subject but in speaking serves to exemplify the very authority of the subject of which it speaks. Because science starts from a part of whatness it can only speak from within the limits of the start; consequently, all of its speech-making will confirm the authority of the subject from which science starts.

Science secures its part by concretizing whatness and by thinking of whatness as a concrete genus. Science thinks of whatness as the highest genus of all and secures a species or part to serve as its beginning. The whatness that science concretizes appears in the form of the subject (in the same way that the whatness concealed by the 'we agree' appears through the utterance as common opinion and belief). Science secures a part of whatness by forcefully deciding to speak about a subject. Though the subject is part of a larger unity, science limits itself to speaking from the security and whatness of the subject and does not speak of the unity. Science speaks about its subject and not about how its subject is possible and thus, science speaks about its subject as if it was some-thing. This is to say that science speaks about the subject which it subjects and not about the subject to which it is subject.

Thus, science begins with two things – with whatness and its part – where there is only One. That is, by treating its part as it-self Real, science makes of the relationship internal to the Oneness of whatness an empirical relation between whatness as the One and its part as an Other. In the language of Parmenides and *The Sophist*, science treats Non-Being as if it was Being by seeing nothing as some-thing.[2]

---

[1] See Heidegger, *What Is A Thing? op. cit.*, for the possibilities internal to the subject-predicate conception.

[2] Parmenides' conception is presented in Heidegger, *Introduction to Metaphysics;* and L. Taràn, *Parmenides, A Text With Translation, Commentary, and Critical Essays*, Princeton: Princeton University Press, 1965; also see *The Sophist*, translated by F. Cornford, Indianapolis Library of Liberal Arts, 1957. I have also had a number of discussions with Daniel Foss over these issues in the course of his preparation of his dissertation.

Whereas science should see the relationship between whatness and its part as a relationship internal to whatness itself (which would prevent it from seeing its part as a 'part' at all, but more like an appearing and coming-to-manifestation of whatness), science instead sees the relationship as external – as a relationship between two things. Science starts with a difference as Real: science starts with a concrete notion of the apparent as a Real object rather than as (an appearing of) a disclosure of that which lies beneath.

Science then begins with both kinds of false thinking discussed in *The Sophist*: in treating whatness as a whole with parts, it sees that which is similar (a One) as different, and in treating whatness as a genus, it sees things which are different (in the way that Being differs from the highest genus) as similar.[1] To say that science begins in error is to say that it begins by conceiving of Being concretely: First, by taking what is as a complete whole it takes what is not a thing (no-thing) and concretizes it as the thing that is a determinant totalization; secondly, by breaking what is into parts it makes of what is essentially one (what can *be* outside of what is?) two, and thus treats nothing (for *that* is what is outside of what is) as some thing. The two mistakes are to treat no-thing as some thing, and to treat nothing as some-thing and both mistakes are animated by the identity of no-thing and nothing.

The beginning of science is then an end, for in cutting off a part of whatness and in laying down its subject, science makes its beginning secure. In securing its beginning science acts, and in so doing completes, ends, and terminates the wonderment out of which its beginning emerges. In beginning, science proceeds to cut itself off from the origin which its beginning limits. If science begins in an act of limitation, then its beginning is an end. The wonder which led to experiencing the idea of whatness as itself a genus is hidden.

Science then begins in negativity, with what is other than whatness; in limiting whatness to the whatness of that which it subjects it segregates whatness from that to which it is subject and makes its subject something other than whatness. Science thus segregates its subject from the whatness to which *it* is subject. From this beginning – from the otherness of the subject external to whatness – science proceeds and can only proceed as an instance of what is other than whatness. Science speaks about what is other than whatness because science limits itself to a subject which is only produced through an act that violates whatness. Science is only possible through its violation of whatness.

---

[1] The two kinds of errors can be found in *The Sophist, op. cit.*, 263 B. D. For treatment of Being as a genus, see R. G. Collingwood, *An Essay on Metaphysics*, Oxford: Clarendon Press, 1940, Chapters 1 to 5. Most important is Heidegger's *An Introduction to . . . op cit.*, especially Chapters 1 and 2.

Science

Aristotle says, science starts from the whatness of its subject only in the sense that this whatness is accepted. Science submits to the authority of the whatness of what it can subject because this whatness is either clear or reasonable, and yet science refuses to allow itself to become troubled by the question of the whatness of its subject – of the possibility of its subject. Science then submits not to whatness at all, but to cannons of clarity and reasonableness.

Subject as the topic or theme of discussion is the topic which science accepts as clear and/or reasonable. Science accepts what its topic-as-topic is, its clarity and rationality, and excludes the question of topicality itself. Science begins from the understanding of its topic – it secures this understanding – and ignores the question of what a topic must be to be a topic. Science accepts the topicality of its topic but does not ask of topicality in general or of its topic *qua* topic. In starting from its topic science simultaneously accepts the topicality of its topic and in this action excludes the question of topicality as itself a topic for its consideration. The idea of subject as topic masks the distinction between time and eternity by transforming that which is critical or central into a 'discursive theme.'

III

Think of topic as a part of speech which organizes discourse. On this view, topic as a part of speech is the part which organizes the selfsame speech. Topic is that theme which organizes the speech and the idea of topic makes organizing capacity equivalent to centrality. Although 'topic' evokes a sense of the critical or central character of discourse and suggests the critical element which authorizes speech, it transforms this subject into a theme – a common theme – as that which is concertedly noticed and acted upon.[1]

Science transforms the idea of subject (as that which is central) into topic because science conceives of thinking as a communicative exchange like a conversation. Let us understand a topic as that which excites notice or attention because of its currency or 'relevance.' A topic organizes the attention of the many precisely because it appeals to the 'eyes and ears.' The parameter of notice-ability of the idea of topic contrasts in a critical way with the covered-upness of a subject that is central. Topics emerge for science as *problems*, as themes for

[1] If science appropriates to itself a topic, this means that science decides to submit to the authority of a discursive theme and to subject itself to a notion of concerted notice-ability which it lets lie; in laying down this theme, science lets it lie.

45

discussion which excite notice because of their currency. Yet a subject which is central cannot be a mere problem because it is an eternal ruler: the relationship of speech to Being through language is not a 'problem' to be 'noticed' but it is an omnipresent covered-up feature of being human.

Topic organizes the notion of what appears historically through the ideas of presence and time: that what appears (is notice-able) is what is present, is what is seen. What is seen is present at a time and a place. To identify our subject with topic(s) is to give ourselves to the present, it is to fail to distinguish time from eternity.

The idea of topic grounds the identification of concrete subjects whether as 'problems,' 'objects,' or as agencies for subjecting matter. The idea of topic licences the creation of some intelligible matter as the theme to be discussed and so, the imagery of topic appears as that which is important to say. Yet the importance of topic bears no relation to centrality or foundation but to that which can be most comprehensively communicated and exchanged: the idea of topic (as surrogate for subject) lives off exchange value and organizational capacity – it lives off the most concrete understanding of speech – instead of drawing its power from its proximity to what is. The idea of topic not only masks the notion of topicality, but topicality itself only expresses a degenerate understanding of that which is worth saying.

In this view what is critical to speech is that speaking speaks about some-thing; that which speaking speaks *about* is what underlies speaking as its matter. The underlying matter of speaking as its subject is what speech (in its many possible appearances) speaks *about* and science emerges when men recognize the matter which underlies their speeches, when they orient their speaking to that matter, and when they subject their speaking to the authority of that subject. Science emerges when men orient to the critical character of the matter about which speaking speaks; this object is subjected, it becomes subjected matter.

To speak with authority is to speak 'with' (alongside of, together with) that which authorizes speech. Speech disperses when it has no-thing to say (when it is not in tune with its author), and organized speech is speech that is addressed to its author and to the unity between its speaking and its author. Similarly, insofar as the many men seem to speak with authority – to speak with their author – the some-thing about which they speak and which author-izes them, serves to make of them a unity. Thus, to subject one-self to the authority of some-thing (some matter) is to create the condition for the exercise of authority in that men are simultaneously ruled by the subject of which they speak, and rule by grace of having a subject *about* which to speak.

The subject as a unity is the author of speech because it authorizes speech, it creates speech. The subject and author is both the creator and the authority to which the speech returns. As speech speaks under the auspices of its unity with that which authorizes it and creates it, it speaks under the rule of that which it rules, of that which it speaks *about*. The subject as author – both in the sense of authority and creator – is personified in the notion of subject matter.

To have some-thing to say is then to speak from authority and the authority is grounded in having some-thing to say. Men who have no-thing to say produce dispersed mouthings just as if they were many men: men who have no-thing to say are not together in their togetherness; by speaking this way and that, from here to there, they show themselves to be men who are divided among themselves; whereas men who have some-thing to say are at One with themselves because in saying some-thing they show their Oneness.

The subject is a One and a many. As a One, it serves as a standard to which speaking is addressed and in this unity establishes itself as the authoritative and rational One from which men speak and to which they orient their speaking. As a One it is that to which men subject their speaking. As a many, the subject contains within itself all of the many speeches which can be made of it, and thus serves to ground the differentiations men achieve through speech. As a many, it allows men to subject the dispersiveness of speech to intelligible controls. As both a One and a many the subject serves as that to which all speaking must return: in its Oneness it authorizes the limits of intelligible speech and in its manyness it provides for the limits of intelligible speaking from which the One (true) speech is to be re-collected.

To secure its subject as a beginning is then to secure a collectedness under the control of an authoritative limit. Science, in marking off a part of whatness and in starting from such a part succeeds in establishing limits for rational speech and in such an action, succeeds in suppressing the question of the Rationality of the achievement. Science begins with the givenness of its subject (topic, authority) by ignoring the question of what the Givenness gives.

Yet, Aristotle says that science does not appropriate for itself the problem of appropriation – of subject matter, of subjecthood, of what a subject must be to be a subject – but instead, marks off a subject from subjecthood in general and then proceeds to investigate. Science does not take the hint that its subject matter is subjecthood and instead, silences this concern by treating its subject as secure and by starting from the security of its subject. Science submits itself to its subjected matter and not to that by which it (science) is subjected.

Science subjects itself to the subject of its speech and starting from the authority of this subject proceeds to speak; science proceeds by making this subject transparent, by qualifying, explicating, and exploring the relationships which are internal to this subject, but always

47

in a manner that preserves the authority of the subject-*qua*-subject. Science never really questions its subject because it never raises the question of how it subjected its subject and of how it wrenched its subject from unconcealment.

To address the question of subject is to ask after the relation between speech and whatness where what is other than speech.

IV

Aristotle's remarks about science – about the whatness of science – show that the whatness assigned is displayed in science's standpoint with respect to whatness itself. More deeply, these remarks make reference to a conception of language.

If whatness is conceived as internal speech, science marks off a part of speech and then proceeds within the limit of this mark – not to question speech itself – to make matters increasingly intelligible within such a limit. The question of the whatness of science, of the what that science is, turns into the question of the whatness of speech, of the what that is speech as itself a totalized complete speech. Language as the subject whose whatness is to be determined is conceived as the whole (the genus, the over-arching categorization, Being) from which the sciences mark off a part.

The whatness of science as the whatness of its speech is that matter of which it speaks (which it subjects), and thus science-as-speech appears as the subject whose whatness is to be determined by identifying the matter to which its speech is subject. Science is the subject for which whatness is secured and whatness can only be identified as that which pervades and underlies the speech that is science. The question of the whatness of science is the question of the whatness of the speech that science happens to speak. Yet, if whatness belongs to science as the thing spoken about belongs to the speech, then science also belongs to whatness.[1] Science as speech belongs together with whatness because whatness lets speech speak, it gives speech its subject. Science belongs to whatness and is its subject in the sense that whatness is the subject that possesses science (that possesses speech). Thus, whatness does not merely mean what something is, but is that which persists in its presence and endurance, that which concerns and moves us.

Science belongs to whatness as speech belongs to whatness because science (speech) belongs to what moves all things and brings them to be. Science belongs to whatness as a possession of whatness and thus whatness as the subject which possesses is the subject of science. Could

[1] See Heidegger, *On The Way to Language*, *op. cit.*

we then say that science's subject is truly that which possesses it and not that which it possesses? Is science authorized by the matter which it subjects or by Being to which it is a subject?

Whereas Aristotle describes science as the relation of a part of whatness to whatness, as the concrete relation of speeches, he opens the possibility for a relationship obscured: that science belongs to whatness not as a part relates to a whole or as speeches relate but by thinking whatness where whatness is other than speech.

Aristotle says that sciences ignore all senses of subject other than as subjected matter (even though their very being shows their involvement in an other sense of subjecthood) and that this is no limitation because it is what the sciences do. Thus, Aristotle's subject is what the sciences do – how the sciences appear as forceful methods of subjecting matter – instead of what they ought do. In this sense, Aristotle is speaking about science as his subject in the same way that the sciences themselves speak (according to Aristotle).

Whereas the whatness of science asks what belongs to science, the science of whatness asks how science belongs to whatness? Yet Aristotle's very description of science shows that science does not belong to whatness and that the very whatness of science is seen in its refusal to belong to whatness. The whatness of science consists in its refusal to belong to whatness and so, science distinguishes itself by not belonging to whatness. Aristotle's characterization is then empirical, for he tells us how science *exists* through its disdain for what owns it; he says that science ought not to think whatness because that is not what science is.

What the sciences ignore is how they could do as they do. They ignore precisely those matters which led Aristotle to differentiate himself from his predecessors; the sciences which Aristotle describes are like the Aristotle whom we have formulated. They do not grasp the 'we' in 'we agree' in any but a professional sense. They see the 'we' as masking a common limit rather than as pointing to a communal fate.

For science to belong to whatness is to think whatness and this is what science refuses: the whatness of the speech of science is seen in its refusal to think whatness itself. Science marks off a part of whatness and in so doing displays its stance towards whatness; science is silent about whatness, but it is a silence that says much.

Science belongs to Being but does not speak about this relationship; this is a fact. Science does not speak about how it (its speech) belongs to Being. About what relationship does science speak? It speaks about the relationship of Being to science, about what belongs to science. Science speaks about the relationship of its speech to its subject (its authority), but it never speaks about how this authority is itself authorized. Science speaks about what it has in its grip, rather than that which grips it. All of science's speech is directed towards exemplifying its authority instead of addressing that subject from which it receives its grant and by which *it* is authorized.

Science speaks about what it appropriates and owns, about what belongs to itself, and in all of this speech science never touches it self, it never addresses what it really is. Science speaks about what it owns (what it subjects) but not about that which owns it (to which *it* is subject). What then is the true subject of science, that which science owns or that which owns science? Is the true subject of science that which causes science to be or that which science causes to be?

This constitutes no problem for Aristotle because (empirically) science can be seen as a refusal to speak about what owns it and thus, Aristotle classifies the sciences by their silence towards this question. The sciences appear when thinking appropriates authority for itself, and science is distinguished to everything inferior by its will; science wills of itself that it speak only of itself and of what it owns and not of what owns it. The strength of science rests upon this resolve, for in so limiting its attention science guarantees its authority. In limiting itself, science author-izes a subject about which only science can speak and thus, the very limitation of science results in its creative achievement. To create is to make a One from the many, and science accomplishes this by forgetting that it is itself one of the many things that belong to what moves all things.

Science attempts to complete the many by concretizing them as a one and this can only be accomplished by starting from a beginning provisionally totalized as complete. Yet if this beginning is complete, *that it is complete* is accomplished as a showing of its essential incompleteness. When science predicates what is it hides from itself the fact that what is *is* Other than its what is since its whatness is prefigured by that which it is not.

In marking themselves off, the special sciences will create the opportunity for a science of whatness, but it will not be *their* concern. There should be a special science of whatness, a special concern with how science(s) and speech belong to whatness, but this will not be a concern of the special sciences because they are not interested in whatness in that sense.

V

Aristotle's special sciences are like the special men whom Plato described so well – those who mark off some being and conduct their investigations into this part, saying nothing concerning Being nor of their part of Being *qua* Being. These special men were called Sophists but they re-appear in all of the dialogues disguised as typical interlocutors. These interlocutors personify the special sciences which Aristotle describes and they are always made to submit to the scrutiny of the science of sciences which Plato's authorial rationality depicts.

Socrates says: 'In itself, an art is sound and flawless so long as it is entirely true to its own nature as an art in the strictest sense – and it is the strict sense that I want you to keep in view.'[1] This 'strict sense' which he instructs Glaucon to 'keep in view' is the relationship of the art to whatness or Being. When Socrates says, that in the strictest sense an art is perfect in itself he means that it should be understood as a way of making reference to whatness and to how it belongs to whatness for only in the unity of an art with whatness do we catch a glimpse of the perfect art. Cornford elaborates this idea as follows:

> The ruler in his capacity as ruler, or the craftsman *qua* craftsman, can also be spoken of as the craft personified, since a craft only exists in the man who embodies it and we are considering the man only as the embodiment of this special capacity, neglecting all personal characteristics and other capacities he may chance to have. When Socrates talks of the art or craft in this abstract way as having an interest of its own, he means the same thing as if he spoke of the craftsman *qua* craftsman.[2]

The art is then personified through the character of an actor whose only interest is to address this relationship and to act under its auspices. The interlocutor is always shown as one who forgets or repudiates this standard in his conversation through his contrast to the authorial re-presentation of the standard in the character of Socrates. Thus, whether in speaking about the art or the person, we are speaking about the movement within the soul idealized as true thinking. In neither case do we speak about the art or person as it is (as it exists), but about what it ought to be.[3] What the art ought to be is a moment in its evolving understanding of itself as a One with Reason. What the person ought to be is the evolving consciousness of the unity of his speech and Reason. To think of the strict sense of the practice is to think essentially about the practice and all other senses are discarded: the strict sense is that which makes the practice intelligible – which makes it something rather than nothing – and though other senses are speakable they are strictly speaking nothing. Speaking about other senses does not touch what the practice *is* even though such speech is the easiest speech in the world. To think about the strict

---

[1] *The Republic, op. cit.*, 1. 342 (p. 23).
[2] *The Republic, op. cit.*, pp. 21–22.
[3] Aristotle's empirical conception of science parallels Thrasymachus' conception of 'ruler' in the *Republic* in the exchange with Socrates, 336B–347E.

sense is to think of what is critical to the practice – crucial, central, that without which the practice would be nothing.[1]

Among the Greeks, Reason was not used as a faculty or mental process, but as 'basis,' 'origin,' 'foundation,' or 'ground.' In asking for the Reason of a being a Greek asks for its ground or condition for being what it is and not something else. In Socrates, Plato exemplified essential thinking as speech which listens to what its very speaking covers over and which addresses such music rather than what is before the eyes and ears. Today we operate with a conception of rationality that formulates the idea as a standard or maxim for intelligible conduct. The versions of rationality that we find today are either idealizations of mathematicity or descriptions of ordinary procedures; 'rational' then comes to stand for an exhibition of the planful and intelligible character of a practice. It is in this sense that Aristotle displays the rationality of the sciences, for the sciences always operate intelligibly within the limits of the part of whatness which they secure. The two kinds of rationality which inquiry makes intelligible might be differentiated through the use of the 'R': rationality as planful and accountable practice which understands its conduct as a demonstration of its rule could be referred to as (practical) rationality; in contrast, Rationality refers to the practice which addresses the question of how it belongs together with Reason. Thus Rationality is exemplified as speech which speaks under the auspices of what it is, whereas rationality is personified in all formulation or description of conduct which seriously preserves the authority of the limit from which such formulation and description proceeds.

We might consider the plight of the practice which is not responsible to the question of how it belongs together with Being. Such a practice is not responsible to the question of its Reason; the Reason for its doing as it does is either self-evident or conventional, and consequently *the question* of its Reason is not worth thinking. Such a practice is typified in Aristotle's description of science. In this respect, recall the exchange between Socrates and Gorgias which opens *Gorgias* where Socrates seeks to induce the Sophist to formulate the meaning of his art, the art of rhetoric.[2] Gorgias responds successively: it is the art that deals with words, it is the art that secures certain effects upon an audience such as persuasion. Now, though Socrates does not claim to know what rhetoric is, he knows the difference between an analytic and a concrete conception; he knows that a number of activities 'use' words, and he

[1] To keep one's eye upon the strict sense is to keep in view the Reason of the practice where such Reason depicts the way the practice belongs to Being. The Rational inquirer is the one who shows in his speech that he addresses this relationship of belonging together.

[2] *Gorgias*, for Gorgias' response to Socrates' questioning, 449–456.

knows that speaking about the *effects* of an activity does not address the question of what it is. The gist of the exchange is that Gorgias conceives of the art of rhetoric as a practical activity – a technique – and thus exemplifies the thinking that is divided from itself. He does not hear the question as asking for what rhetoric *is* in the deepest sense, as an attempt to evoke from him his stand in relation to whatness. It is not that such a conception – formulable in a tidy, little formula or calculus or definition – is available as a solution to the problem of the meaning of rhetoric; it is rather, that Gorgias *does not even address the problem*, he does not even know that he does not know, he is rooted so unreflexively in the eyes and ears. Finally Socrates commits himself,

> It aims at pleasure without consideration from what is best; and I say that it is not an art, but a knack, because it is unable to render any account of the nature of the methods it applies and so cannot tell the cause of each of them. I am unable to give the name of art to anything irrational. . . .[1]

Whereas Gorgias assumes the security of the whatness of rhetoric, it is just this security that Socrates wants to dissolve. Socrates does not want to replace one formulation of the essence of rhetoric with another superior statement; rather, he wants the interlocutor to recognize that this security is something *given* and consequently, he wants to induce him to ask the question – what gives the Given?

Note that the irrationality of rhetoric consists in its inability to provide an account of the *nature* of its methods, which in the Socratic idiom means the Reason for the project: rhetoric cannot give an account of how its method shows the unity of the project with its nature because rhetoric does not even address its nature. That is, to say that rhetoric cannot give an account of its methods and 'cannot tell the cause of each of them' suggests that rhetoric does not address what it is, rhetoric can speak but in so speaking it does not address what 'causes' its speech, what makes its speech be. Rhetoric does not address its unity with Being, how it is in the grip of Being, or how it belongs together with Being.

The knack then, in contrast to the art, treats its nature as secure and well-founded, as that which is in hand. To say that the nature of the practice is in hand suggests that the question of this nature raises no problem, for it is secure. *What is secure is the understanding of the security of this nature.* To treat the nature of the practice as secure is to cut off possibilities for exploration because that which would be explored is beyond security and to explore the insecure is folly or madness. To treat the nature of the practice as secure is to accept the practice in its authoritative, conventional form. This is how Nietzsche

[1] *Gorgias, op. cit.,* 465.

can suggest that the practical understanding of a practice is decadent.[1] By *practical*, we intend: the understanding that tries to comprehend the practice while using the selfsame practice as the standard and limit of authoritative understanding.

Yet, the requirement to understand the practice without using it as a resource seems to create irreconcilable demands. The apparent tension between these demands can lead one to abandon the interests of the practice, or to forego the interests of Rationality. In the latter case, the practice abandons the attempt to provide for itself in any way for which its practice itself cannot provide. The practice then rules that the rational treatment of itself is the treatment which conforms to the essential rule of the practice. The practice authorizes itself as the limit of rational self-exploration; it decides authoritatively to explore itself only under the auspices of its practical interest in itself. In this way, the rational practice appears as the practice which elects to provide for itself as an occasion of the selfsame practice; it is the practice that analyzes itself as an instance of itself.

Science epitomizes this practical mode of understanding. If scientific self-understanding is unreal knowledge this means that it everywhere represents conduct not as an icon of Reason, but according to science (rationally rather than Rationally). To paraphrase Heidegger: whenever real knowledge places the Reason of conduct into the limelight, natural knowledge (science) looks the other way because its truth is thereby disputed. Science keeps to its own. Everything that comes before it is subsumed under the statement: it is and remains mine, and *is*, as such, as being mine.[2] Thus, science as the paradigmatic practice becomes absorbed in the conduct *it* represents (the conduct it represents scientifically), and comes to regard these representations alone as true, as real knowledge. The rational practice then starts from the pre-supposition of its own authority (its truth) as a standard and resource for its inquiry; conduct in conformity with this truth *is* rational insofar as it only becomes intelligible in relation to this truth. Yet, such practice is not truly Rational, because it does not understand its truth as the mere concept of truth, it does not know what it truly is.

It is usually assumed that Socrates' interest in ideas such as virtue,

[1] 'My objection to the whole of Sociology . . . is that it knows from experience only the decaying forms of society and takes its own decaying instincts with perfect innocence as the norm of sociological value judgement. Declining light, the diminution of all organizing power, that is to say, the power of separating, of opening up chasms, of ranking above and below, formulates itself in the sociology of today as the ideal. . . . The unconscious influence of decadence has gained ascendancy even over the ideals of certain of the sciences, in Frederich Nietzsche, *Twilight of the Idols*, 1858.

[2] M. Heidegger, *Hegel's Concept of Experience*, New York: Harper and Row, 1970, p. 60.

justice, piety, or courage was to create an exemplary model or procedure for adequate definition, and consequently these examples are inspected in order to recover his latent theory. Yet, this is a superficial reading of the Socratic task, for it fails to capture the character of his interest in X as an occasion for initiating inquiry into that which the X covers over; the fact that the X was not a calculus to be distilled in rule or formula but was a secured occasion to provide incentive for rational analysis by exemplifying the course of action of an ideal of inquiry. Socrates served as Plato's impersonation of the true art in contrast to the 'knack' of science and of true thought in contrast to the untrue.

In Socrates' exchange with Polus in *Gorgias* they speak about practices like rhetoric and power, and Socrates attempts to elicit definitions. When Socrates rejects the various definitions offered by Polus what we get is less a theory of definition than a notion of how one ought to think so as to be seen as thinking Rationally. To think Rationally is to display through speech one's unity with Reason. It is in these dialogues that the idea of inquiry as a movement of the soul appears. Adequate definition is a surface feature of a Rational, well-ordered soul in the sense that defining as a movement in the conversation within the soul serves to make visible the dialectical conception of that movement. The problem of the dialogues is not the problem of how to produce a good definition, but how to recognize a good man, and one way of recognizing such a man and of distinguishing him from the false and shrunken souls who abound is through his speech (his inquiry). The problem of the dialogues is not the problem of definition, but of how speech makes reference to the soul. Thus, the dialogues present science through the metaphor of sophistry and in so doing depict the respective ideals of a well-ordered art and a well-ordered soul.

Aristotle's sciences are self-sufficient islands just as Socrates' interlocutors are men sufficient unto themselves. Aristotle's sciences and Socrates' interlocutors refuse to address anything beyond the authority which they exercise and consequently, their attention is concentrated in the matter which they subject rather than by the (higher) subject to which their very speech belongs. These arts and men are exercised by what they own – their property – and consequently, they are limited by their selves (whether as the subject matter of a science or as the technique of a skill). These arts and men limit themselves to self and saying nothing of that to which self essentially belongs, they prosecute their inquiries and speak of many things.

VI

Whereas Plato's conception of science – as it ought to be and as it exists – is formally displayed in the *Republic* in the separation of the different 'objects' of Mathematics and Dialectic, the contrast between these sciences is presented in the exchanges of each of the dialogues. In this sense, the *Charmides* is particularly instructive.[1]

In that exchange, Critias attempts to respond to Socrates' question concerning *sophrosyne* or the meaning of temperance, i.e., the kind of knowledge of one self that accepts the bounds which excellence lays down for human nature.[2] Eventually, Critias defines *sophrosyne* as self-knowledge in a way that appears quite consistent with the temper of Socrates' various conversations and inquiry; yet Socrates rejects the formulation.

If temperance is roughly equivalent to self-knowledge and if all knowledges are sciences, then temperance is a kind of science, i.e., the science of self. Further, if all sciences have objects of their own (subjects which they subject), what is the object of knowledge of the self? When Critias replies that this 'object' is knowledge-of-knowledge or knowledge that one knows, etc., Socrates argues the circularity of this conception, for the object of a science must be external to its practice or else how can science decide when it has this knowledge or of what it consists? Socrates then attempts to show that to have knowledge of knowledge is not to have wisdom of what kind of knowledge one has.

The issue is strikingly revealed here in Critias' formulation which identifies knowledge with what is known and unknown to us and which consequently limits us from venturing beyond ourselves. When Socrates says that the object of a science must be external to its practice he intends: that the subject of a science must not be that which is owned by the science for then the very issue of appropriation will never be put into question; rather, the subject must be that which owns science, i.e., that which is external to its practice and through which its practice comes to be. If we understand the *practice* of a science as its concrete speech about its object, to say that its subject must be external to the speech is to say that its true subject must be other than the object *about* which it speaks. *External* does not mean (in this sense) 'something different from,' but rather, that which is unsaid (or, as we put it earlier: that which speech *says*). Thus, 'internal' and 'external' to a practice are used by Socrates in this dialogue to stand in the relationship of speaking (internal) and saying (external). To Socrates the important question is: what is the Good of the science? The Good is not an object

---

[1] *Charmides*, edited by B. Jowett in *Plato: Collected Dialogues, op. cit.*
[2] See Friedlander's discussion, *op. cit.*, pp. 67–81.

internal to the science; as the subject which causes all things to be, it is that which owns science and which is external to its practice. Although the Good appears 'internal' in the concrete sense that it grounds and founds the organization of any practice, it is precisely this grounding character which provides for its 'externality.' The Good is not a unique result of the practice and is not 'internal' to any one practice; as the source which authorizes all practice, it is 'external' to any one particular practice.

Critias' formulation of temperance as self-knowledge draws the limits of knowledge at the limits of self: though this catches the ordinary sense of temperance as 'doing one's own business' and 'keeping to one's own,' it hides the question of what kind of knowledge one has when one knows.

In other words to say that *sophrosyne* is knowledge of one's knowledge is to forget that any formulation of what one knows – as a formulation – is achieved and hence stands as a result of the contest through which speech comes to life, a contest which the formulation itself marks but fails to encompass. It is to mask the essential incompleteness of all formulative work (the fact that the formulation cannot provide for itself) under the assumption that to speak about one self speaking is to complete the inquest into the grounds of self. Yet, to speak positively about one self as other is to forget that such speech is only possible as an appearing of what is genuinely Other to it, to that which makes this very relationship between self as speaker and as topic for it self possible and intelligible. To say that self-description is self-knowledge is to hide the question of the Good of self-knowledge and of the suppressed unity from which it is wrenched. Since one implication is that this unity knows no boundaries of art, the notions of 'minding one's business' or 'doing one's work' is parochial and authoritarian.

Socrates raises the question of whether a collective organized along such lines would have a Good, and he suggests that it might be efficient but not 'well and happy.' The import of this comment is that Critias' conception would make the organization of the sciences look like an anomic division of labour and by creating the authority of specialization and limited objects of study, would serve to destroy the dialectical impulse. It would prevent men from seeing the togetherness of language and Being and by creating islands of autonomous and self-sufficient speakers would identify moral authorization with rules of grammar and would withdraw Being as a Rational concern.

As early as the *Charmides*, we see in Plato the distinction between the special sciences of which Aristotle spoke and the science of sciences and they are not conceptualized as a hierarchy of genus-species relationships. Critias' formulation would situate the particular sciences within their proper places and would create nothing superior to them: in contrast, Socrates wants to consider a knowledge that is not a technical science but is concerned with the Good of the particular sciences; yet, this will be a science that is more than the empty re-duplication of the factual sciences, for it must address the meaning and purpose of the special sciences and see them in relation to the unity of *Logos*.[1, 2]

At frequent points in the dialogues, Socrates indicates that *sophrosyne* cannot stand as 'doing one's business' or as specialized knowledge, but rather as knowing what belongs to the self in an essential way. Since what self owns and appropriates to itself does not belong to it essentially but is an accomplishment of action, what belongs to the self in an essential way is that to which self belongs and which owns it. If *sophrosyne* is to know how one belongs to Logos, it is to know this relationship of 'belonging together' between it-self and Logos. Thus, in the *Lysis* while discussing friendship, Socrates says that we are friendly to 'that which by nature belongs to us' and it is that which we must love: we love and seek to preserve, cultivate, and develop that which by nature belongs to us rather than that which is merely like us.[3]

This distinction re-produces the contrast between how speech belongs to whatness (to the subject which owns it) and how whatness belongs to speech (to that which is subject to it), for to know what belongs essentially to self is to know how self is owned by whatness and how they belong together essentially. Self knows what belongs to it when it knows that to which it belongs, and to love is to Desire this unity. To love knowledge can only be to love and desire the unity which lies covered over by the dispersiveness of speech.

Aristotle's characterization of science then re-produces the concrete notion of *sophrosyne* as knowledge and with it, the various limitations of self-formulations. His characterization provides for the authoritative and rational rule of self as mind which takes its Oneness for granted and which accepts as secure what it owns and what it is given. Through the *Charmides*, we can make this characterization of science more transparent, for it promises to lead to a conception of knowing which begins and ends in itself rather than in the experience of thinking, and which re-defines knowledge of self as *self-consciousness*. The way is prepared for Descartes and the epistemological project.

---

[1] Friedlander, *op. cit.*, p. 26.

[2] It is only when scientists address the relation of their sciences to this unity that we can speak of *sophrosyne*. For it is only when one knows the meaning and purpose of the science and how he comes to do as he does that he speaks responsibly under the influence of the unity of Logos.

[3] *Lysis*, translated by J. Wright in *Plato: Collected Dialogues, op. cit.*

VII

Aristotle's characterization of the sciences, just as Critias' characterization of *sophrosyne* has to lead to external and concrete relations
among the sciences. What is shared by the sciences is the most superficial, common unity when contrasted to what differentiates them;
though they share 'an interest in knowledge as cause and principle' and
the use of the common resources of method, they are differentiated with
respect to their subject (matter). What the sciences share is that they
can speak and they differ in terms of the matter which they subject
– the objects they speak about. In the deepest sense then, their similarity consists in their concerted and required use of 'we agree' to speak
about these different objects. In their manyness, the special sciences
cannot concert, for what truly unifies them is excluded as a concern
from their special projects. Yet, though they cannot come together, the
science of metaphysics will re-present their coming together by taking
together as its subject (matter) their common resources – the principles
and methods which they use in their respective projects. Yet, metaphysics will study its subject (matter) – their common resources – in the
same way that *they* study *their* subjects; that is, the subject of metaphysics will not be different in kind than the subjects of physics and
mathematics – a different kind of subject – but will be different in
degree – higher, loftier, etc. Thus, metaphysics will be another special
science though it will subject a different subject to scrutiny through
discourse. It is here that Aristotle elects to investigate the 'we agree'
and to establish this investigation as itself a special science. Metaphysics
will seek to unravel the structure of the 'we agree' as it is employed in
common by the different sciences: yet metaphysics will treat this
'structure' as matter to subject.[1]

In the first book of the *Metaphysics*, this subject is cause; it is that
which their speech is *about*. Aristotle listens to what his predecessors
speak (rather than what they say) by hearing their speech as directed
to the subject of which it is *about*. The subject of their many speeches
as that subject (object) to which their speeches are subject is the whatness of their speech. Their speeches appear as the many possibilities for
speaking about the object to which it is subject. Thus, the speeches can
only be seen as speaking about cause. Although the many speeches
might touch many things, what brings the speeches to life as a One

[1] Recall the way in which Aristotle reads his predecessors. He externalizes them
because he reads them under the auspices of the interest of the special sciences;
he secures a part of whatness and asking nothing of whatness in general, he
proceeds to characterize, relate, and assert. He finds the some-thing about which
their speech speaks and establishes this as the subject; it will serve to rule and
authorize limits for his reading of them.

speech for Aristotle is his capacity to see them as speaking of the same-thing. The predecessors are treated as a unity because in their severalness they speak under the same subject, they subject the same matter.[1]

Aristotle differs from his predecessors not as science differs from 'common sense,' but in the way metaphysics or the first science differs from the special sciences. The predecessors start from limiting a particular part of cause and after securing it, proceed to investigate; in this sense, the predecessors are icons of the special sciences.

How then can the predecessors fail? For if the special sciences must do as they do, so must the predecessors: on what grounds can they be held responsible if they are just doing what any scientist does? Because they differ from Aristotle as the special sciences differ from metaphysics, Aristotle can only mean that the special sciences are inferior to the science of metaphysics. Yet if this is so, why does he constantly assert that the sciences ought to do as they do, that they ought to avoid the questions of metaphysics? Who is Aristotle fooling? If the special sciences are thoughtless why does he recommend that they persist and endure in their thoughtlessness? What kind of teaching is this?

Obviously it is because the special sciences are thoughtless that metaphysics becomes possible, for metaphysics comes to be when it takes up for discussion the problems which the special sciences refuse to face (and which Aristotle counsels them to continue to avoid). metaphysics stands to the special sciences as Aristotle relates to predecessors, by seeking to restore in speech the subject to which the many possible speeches are directed.

Aristotle reads his predecessors not as one of them, but as a metaphysician. This means that Aristotle's reading exemplifies metaphysics. Yet, if Aristotle's reading exemplifies metaphysics, we have already seen how the invocation of the 'we agree' conceals all of the concerns of thoughtful metaphysics depicted in Plato's work. Consequently, Aristotle must re-define metaphysics which he does by re-defining Being as an object for a special science. What a curious situation: metaphysics as the science of Being has to preserve its authority by sacrificing Being for science. Metaphysics differs from the special sciences because it takes up whatness as its topic, and Aristotle differs from his predecessors as metaphysician to special scientist (as one

[1] If Aristotle and his predecessors are together in their subjectitude to the subject of cause of which they speak, then their many speeches stand in the relation of predicates to this underlying matter which rules them. Because Aristotle does not want to make yet another speech – to do more predication – he conceives of the inventory as a way of closing off interminable predication so as to arrest the subject from its dispersion through speech and to secure it as a subject worth starting from.

concerned with whatness in general stands to one who limits oneness, etc.). Thus, Aristotle's reading of his predecessors has to show his metaphysics; and yet, he reads his predecessors by suppressing just that question of whatness which he claims to be taken up in inquiries called metaphysical.

Because Aristotle still speaks as if he takes up whatness in general, what he intends is this: that he takes up whatness in general from the perspective and interest of science and consequently that he (like them) does not take up whatness at all. Aristotle is a special scientist parading as one dedicated to Being and it is extremely important to comprehend his claim: it is based upon his transformation of Being into a common subject of speech. If metaphysics does not differ from the special sciences in kind and differs only through the selection of a special subject (object), then the contrast between them is supplied through the formulation of their subject. The subject of metaphysics is the 'highest' subject of all in the sense that it is the commonest.

Aristotle's metaphysics instead of differentiating itself from the special sciences is intended as a demonstration of the authority of the special sciences themselves. Metaphysics seeks to show how a special science can address whatness while still preserving its character as one of the sciences.[1]

Since the subject of Aristotle's science is not Being, the question of how speech (cause) belongs to Being cannot be addressed, for Aristotle has already decided that being is that which belongs to speech and that to uncover the subject of speech is simultaneously to recover the Being of speech. Thus, Aristotle hears the speech of his predecessors as saying what cause is, and what is unsaid in their speech is the whatness of cause and not the cause of whatness.

Aristotle's question – what is the whatness of cause – assumes the security of cause as a resource for addressing what it is. That is, he poses the question of how cause belongs to itself, by conceiving of cause as the subject and of any intelligible answer to 'what is cause?' as generated from the range of predicates which have been attached to cause through the history of rational discourse.

'We agree' then serves to silence the Platonic voice, for Plato's interest is not in the whatness of cause – in how whatness belongs to cause, or in how Being belongs to speech – but, in how cause (speech)

---

[1] For example, by focusing upon the ways in which cause has been *used* by his predecessors, Aristotle does not investigate 'whatness-in-general' but limits himself to the range of ordinary usage which he has elected to 'mark off' and from which *he* decides to start. The subject or whatness of causal speech is the object (subject) to which he formulates their speech as attaching. The subject of the speech about cause which both he and they share is the underlying topic of cause which their many speeches partially touched in the same way that predicates qualify a subject.

belongs to whatness. What is unsaid (and hence, the true subject) is not the whatness of cause, but whatness itself. Plato's concern is with how cause *says* Being (how cause belongs together with Being) and not in the being of cause, or in how cause appropriates being to itself as an essence appropriates parameters.

Aristotle then appears as one of his special scientists: he limits himself to a part of whatness and proceeds to investigate. 'We agree' silences Plato's voice in the sense that it strives to quiet the desire to surpass the limit of the special science; it accomplishes this by stipulating that we ought to agree on what we have inherited by limiting our attentions to the givenness of the inheritance rather than to its achievement. Just as Aristotle silences Plato's voice by invoking the 'we agree' as the rule which authorizes the limits of ordinary and common speech and belief, science secularizes the question concealed by the 'we agree' by transforming it into the assumption of the common. 'We agree' marks the agreement not to re-open the question of whatness and authorizes this refusal as the very paradigm of rational inquiry.

Aristotle treats his predecessors in the same way that the special sciences treat their speech and thus, Aristotle's science of metaphysics relates to the special sciences as one of them. Furthermore if the science of Being is (analytically) no different from the special science, it then earns its extraordinary status on the basis of the extraordinary character of the subject of which it speaks (its object). Yet, since the subject is just another topic no different in kind from the topic of the special sciences, from what peculiar property of topicality can it borrow its special character? This property is commonality: that which is common to the special topics.

The similarity of Aristotle's metaphysics to the special sciences must not obscure this crucial difference: despite the fact that they all concert in their use of 'we agree' to limit discussion and to subject some matter, the special sciences differ from metaphysics as predecessors differ from Aristotle in the sense that it is metaphysics which analyzes the sciences and Aristotle who analyzes his predecessors. The capacity of metaphysics and Aristotle to do analysis is grounded in their interest in the structure of the 'we agree' which they *all* utter. What is interesting to metaphysics and to Aristotle is of course that to which the 'we agree' points – to the objects it subjects, the topics it appropriates – and Aristotle's image of the organization of such objects as world creates his ontology, while his image of the organization of such topics as knowledge creates his oraganon of the sciences. Yet the primary (critical) interest of metaphysics – of Aristotle as metaphysician – is in the *common* method through which 'we agree' comes to appropriate these different objects. Metaphysics studies 'we agree' as a method of appropriation in the sense that it attempts to formulate the range of grammatical possibilities for speaking convincingly; Aristotle's categories and logic provide one solution to such a problem.

Thus, Aristotle's metaphysics actually adds a new subject to the appropriated matter subjected by the different sciences and to the whatness from which these appropriations emerge: this new subject is the standard tacitly formulated as an order which governs the possibilities for rational and economic discourse about things as objects. Metaphysics subjects as its matter grammaticality; the possibility and grounds of the methods of appropriated speaking which intervene between Being and matter. Grammaticality is the Aristotelian version of the organizing potential of 'common culture' as the authoritative resource for intelligible speech. We can now begin to anticipate the outlines of those two modern offshoots of the Aristotelian science of Being – epistemology and sociology.

It is Aristotle who converts Being into a topic (a speech) which is only different in degree from other topics. The otherness of what is obliterated and Being is concretized as the source of speech which itself can be spoken. Being comes to stand for the most concrete ground of speech rather than as a metaphor for the intangible source of speech which is essentially that which is other than speech. Being is identified with the concrete conditions of causes that ignite the occurrence of speech as a performance and as such conditions come to be situated in the firstness of perspective (historicism) which is symbolized either as interiority (the 'person') in epistimology, or as commonality (the 'society') in sociology.

3

Showing, Hiding: Belonging-Together

I

According to Aristotle the principle sense of 'nature' is whatness[1] and the question 'what is the nature (whatness) of science?' has often been taken to ask for the *object* of science as that whatness which science appropriates and secures for itself; that matter which science subjugates and to which the speaking called science itself surrenders.

Whatness or nature so understood has been identified with the first things or firstness[2] and firstness has been conceived as the primary or first condition of subjecthood as the firstness of a species or concretum. The firstness of such a nature consists in the fact that in its subjugation, it licences and authorizes the speech which is directed to it; it forces that speech to answer to it. The firstness of the nature consists in its character as the object that rules speech and licences speech to speak in its name, and which excludes speech which fails to touch it as extraneous. This firstness is not like the material source or cause but is re-presented in speech as the essent.

From this view, what is Real comes to be that which is described by true speech when true speech is speech that conforms to the path laid down by the firstness of the essent. True speech is speech that qualifies, predicates, and explicates the attributes and relationships internal to the essent secured in its firstness, but the achievement of this securing as itself an instance of true speaking is suppressed.

In contrast, Aristotle's notion of whatness in general – of the whatness of whatness rather than the whatness of a being or subject – hints at another conception of the firstness of a subject; not the firstness of an appropriated essent but the firstness of arché (of the source and

[1] Aristotle, *Metaphysica*, book *Δ* 1014b, 16–5a. Also see L. Strauss, *The City and Man*, Chicago: Rand McNally, 1964.
'The idea of a thing is that which we seek when we try to find out the "what" or the "nature" of a thing or a class of things. The connection between "idea" and "nature" appears in the *Republic* from the facts that the "idea of justice" is called "that which is just by nature," and the ideas in contradistinction to the things which are not ideas are said to be "in nature."' (p. 120).
[2] Strauss, *op. cit.*

power of *Physis*)[1] as reflected in the true subject which itself grounds any conception of the essent appropriated in speech. This true subject could be designated as the Real as it could be said to differ from the ordinary conception of whatness as ruler to ruled, i.e., that the firstness of the secure essent or nature is actually derivative, or is an icon of that force which moves all things, of that which is at once genuinely 'first' and Real. Firstness as the Real subject, as the foundation or ground of arché is that which is critical, central and essential to speech. It is this subject which makes the appropriation of objects as subjected essents possible and intelligible. Whereas Plato glimpsed such 'whatness' through the metaphor of the Good, Aristotle tended to see it in terms of the methodic and conventional instrumentality of appropriation it-self and of the grammatical possibilities which ordinary language provides for speaking to appropriate.

The relationship between nature and Reality is complex. Guthrie claims their equivalence in his history of Greek philosophy.[2] Yet, this would mis-construe the conception of nature in Plato. Because thinkers *did* identify nature and the *Real* only within the context of their con-cretization of whatness as essent, this identification was most likely to occur within the tradition that treated nature as equivalent to the secure subject as it manifests itself in speech as the essent. In contrast, the conception of subject as itself an achievement or as a belonging to whatness invoked the idea of *Physis* which makes necessary reference to the grounds of authority as that which surpasses the concrete essenti; *Physis* reverses the relation between subject and whatness by asking not for the essence of subject but for how a subject essences.[3] *Physis*

---

[1] See Klein, *op. cit.*, p. 96.
'A most important passage in Socrates' account is the statement, almost casually made, that "all that comes into being is connected in kinship" . . . because without this assumption the entire account would not hold together. By virtue of this assumption everything, every bit the soul recollects can be understood as a "part" of the "whole" and can be traced back to a common origin. The word *Physis* is attuned to the assumption of kinship, of a common ancestry of all that is. This assumption makes the world a "whole."' (p. 96).

[2] W. Guthrie, *The History of Greek Philosophy*, Vol. 2, Cambridge: Cambridge University Press, 1965, pp. 351–352.

[3] For *Physis* besides Klein, *op. cit.*, and Guthrie, *op. cit.*, see N. Luyten, 'Matter and Potency' in McMullin, *op. cit.*, for the following:
'The fundamental problem faced by the early Greek philosophers was not so much that of matter as of nature. *Physis* was, indeed, the central theme of the speculation. Considering the world of their experience, they were struck by the fact of ceaseless changing; the spectacle of becoming and disappearing appeared to be the most all-embracing feature of reality. In a remarkable intuition they realized that this infinite variety and multitude could not be the last word about reality. Wherever they looked, they could see transition from one state to another . . . they decided that in a mysterious way every item in reality is somehow linked to every other, because one changes into the other. There must,

necessarily pointed to a higher reality and worked against the identification of nature and reality.

Instead of asking for the whatness of science, for the nature or 'essence' that science appropriates – a question that preserves both the security of science and of whatness – the question becomes, how does science belong to whatness? in the sense of how does science essence? How does science science?[1]

The objects which science speaks about presuppose that science *can* speak and thus fail to address the possibility of science, the critical existence of science-as-science. Again, when the subject of science is equated with the concrete source of intelligible speech – the agent – a material cause is equated with an analytic ground and cause is treated as a concrete condition of performance.

Aristotle's innovation lay in hearing the question which asked for the nature or (firstness) whatness of science to be asking 'how is science possible?' and his conception of possibility as the critical and decisive foundation eliminated both object and agent as extraneous vis-à-vis the foundational character of grammaticality, of rules and procedures for enabling intelligible discourse. In this transformation, Aristotle conventionalized the critical – the foundation – by translating whatness into the firstness of grammar (into what would later become a 'transcendental analytic' for philosophy, 'culture' for sociology, and variations like 'history' for radicals). Aristotle brought whatness down to earth by making it an object – subjected matter – for a science.

The alternative notion of how 'science sciences' transforms the meaning of science from the secure and fixed subject into the active subject which comes to be as an instance of coming to be. The question directs attention to the struggle of some-thing with no-thing (of Being and Nothingness) and at once differentiates science from Being and asks for that difference *qua* difference. Science sciences in the sense that science comes to be: science is not already here as a secure sub-stratum upon which attributes are added, but science appears as part of the force that moves and causes all things to endure and to be. Whereas the sciencing of science was a grammatical achievement to Aristotle,

---

therefore, be a fundamental kinship between things. The whole multitude of varied things, incessantly changing from one to the other, hide and manifest at the same time a more profound nature common to them all. This common . . . hidden fundament they called "*Physis*," which means: the nature, the profound and genuine reality, at the bottom of all reality, what in German would be called *Ur-grund*, i.e., the most genuine and deepest principle by which things are what they are, not in their ever-varying, rather superficial – since evanescent – aspects, but in their true – because permanent – essence.' (p. 103).

However, the most important resource is still Heidegger's various discussions in *Introduction . . . op. cit.*

[1] W. Marx, *op. cit.*

for Plato it 'appeared' as a disclosure of the omnipresence of Being.

The whatness that is the Real is then neither the whatness appropriated to a subject, nor the structure of appropriation itself, but is that to which the subject belongs as the true subject or as the only subject worth speaking. The firstness of this Real is not the firstness of a unity secured in intelligible speech – the communal discourse, nor is it the firstness of conventional communality itself – but rather, the primacy of the force in terms of which all being appears and comes to surface. How does science belong to whatness? as how does science science? then asks for how science surfaces, or better: how Being appears in the form of science? How does the intelligible form and appearance of science make reference to the firstness of Being?

Consequently, science sounds different than Being but it is not, for science essentially belongs to Being; yet, neither is science the same as Being, for in appearing, science is a bringing of Being to permanence and manifestation. Science is both different from and similar to Being, but these characterizations are empty masks for the relationship of belonging-together, for science is not a thing separable from Being, nor that which is 'similar' or identical to Being. Science is a *One* of the *Many* things that participate in Being and is both a One and a Many, but its Oneness is only intelligible as a Oneness that belongs to Being as *one* of its many possibilities. To conceive of science as different than Being is a mistake as is the conception of science as identical or similar to Being. Whereas Aristotle makes the first mistake, the sophists commit the second. Science belongs to Being and is owned by Being and shows how it belongs by making reference to Being.

II

Parmenides assimilated existence to Reality, not by identifying them, but by asserting the necessity of existence through its Rationalization, and thus, by stipulating the impossibility of conceiving non-Being (non-reality);[1] this implied that no difference could be Real, because difference would recommend the existence of Non-Being. Parmenides then disregarded all process as impossible.[2] The results of this formulation

[1] For Parmenides, Heidegger should be consulted, see *Introduction . . ., op. cit.*; also Guthrie, *op. cit.*, Vol. 2; F. Cleve, *op. cit.*; Cornford (ed. and translator), *Plato and Parmenides*, Library of Liberal Arts; H. Sinaiko, *Love, Knowledge and Discourse in Plato*, University of Chicago Press: Chicago, 1965, Chapter 4. However, at this writing the single most comprehensive and instructive source is L. Tarán, *Parmenides, A Text With Translation, Commentary, and Critical Essays*, Princeton: Princeton University Press, 1965.

[2] Tarán, *op. cit.*, p. 175.

were remarkable, for it suggested that everything that is, is, i.e., that everything is the same in the sense that everything intelligible must be Rationalized. For Parmenides

> A thing if it exists must have the characteristics established by reasoning, and if it fails to come to this level, it does not exist, since a thing either is or is not.[1]

Thus, mere existence is conceived and decided analytically, i.e., in terms of the requirements of an analytic; 'to exist' is 'to be' analytically (i.e., to be truly). Parmenides tells us that Being is the only subject, that Being is the critical subject because Being is the only thing that truly exists (that *is*) while other things merely exist.

To be is to be truly and not merely 'to exist.' To be as to exist is easy, for then Being only follows the distinctions made through speech. To be is not merely to be spoken, but to be spoken truly. But *what* is the status of that which is to be spoken truly? If 'to be' refers to the *what* that is spoken about, true and false speaking are then controlled by whether what they speak *about* exists; to speak truly would be to speak about some-thing that exists, and to speak falsely would be to speak about no-thing. Yet, if all speech is *about* some-thing (for even the no-thing spoken about comes alive within the 'thing' that is intelligible speech), false speaking can only be conceived as aberrant speech about phantasms, or as speech *about* the more or less; or else, false speaking could be seen as impossible and any speaking would be accredited as true.

If 'to be' is not merely 'to exist' then appropriated objects cannot be the critical subject; nor can the concrete conditions and agencies of appropriation; nor finally, can rules for speaking about what exists or about what is the critical subject because speech it-self merely exists and every course of speech is a demonstration of its subjectitude. Being is the only thing there *is*, though many things exist: Being is the only thing that is Good, though many things sound good. While many things appear *to be* to appear is to appear *as* (a disclosure of) Being what appears *is* only as a disclosure of Being and so Being is the only thing that is. Our every speech testifies to this and to deny it is to deny that our speaking derives from more than what is present to us (an impossible claim), i.e. it is to deny that speech is achieved.

Truth cannot be speech that is *correct* in terms of rational criteria of speaking (communal criteria) for then speech will not have an object (subject) which is external to its practice, and true speech will be equated with speech that speaks correctly within the limits prescribed by some context of authoritative, intelligible speech.

True speech cannot be speech which authorizes it-self as correct and

[1] Taràn, *op. cit.*, p. 135.

then conforms to such authorization for everyone speaks in this way. Such a notion of true speaking concretizes truth by treating it as empirically correct speech. Under the auspices of such a concretization of truth true speaking either becomes conventional or relative, and both options are nihilistic.[1] True speech cannot be speech which only conforms to its own standard of artfulness because such a standard is not external to the practice itself (it accepts the firstness of speech).

Parmenides' conception of 'all is one' makes reference to the unity of linguisticality as an authoritative unity outside of which there is only silence (the void). Yet speech only coheres with its authority insofar as it respects the possibility of silence as the condition of failure for speaking. True speaking is settled *within* this unity as speech which respects its authority as grounding the achievement of the Oneness of speech over silence as a wresting of Being from nothingness. 'All is one' means that true speaking speaks in the face of the possibility of silence on every speaking occasion and thus essentially shows unity where difference *appears*; the unity *as* the difference between Being and no-thing means that Being *is* this difference, and that the oneness of Being is this difference *qua* difference. In contrast, false speaking follows the path of difference laid down by the concrete predicative possibilities of speaking, and follows the appearances of the high sounding and impressive to create many things where there is only One.

True speech must provide for the re-experience of its unity with that which grounds all speech. Speech should not be spoken of as true unless it is true (faithful) to Reason. Parmenides helps us to see that true speech is not correct speech, but speech that is faithful, and the question of truth becomes the question of that to which speech must be faithful.

Parmenides could then assert that the speech which his predecessors spoke was an instance of their bewitchment, for the subject(s) of their speech only *existed* and to speak under the rule of these subjects is not to be faithful. Thus, he contrasted to Being, the empty names uttered by men in their conviction that they name Being, because since there is only Being (in the sense that the only speech worth speaking is that which shows its faithfulness to what owns it), speech which fails to show this says nothing (speaks about nothing). Since the opposite of Being is nothing (or Non-Being), false speech speaks *about* nothing. Whereas true speech shows Being *as* Being and Nothing (as a difference which is One), false speech speaks *about* Nothing as if it was *a* thing (as if it was Really true).[2] In the strict sense, to say nothing or Non-Being is then impossible, for every speech is (a disclosure). No-thing should not be confused with nothing. Speech is either faithful to what

[1] Rosen, *op. cit.*
[2] Taràn, *op. cit.*, pp. 124, 131.

owns it (to its true subject) or it disperses and distinguishes many things in an action which shows that it is not together with itself and that it is not ruled by any-thing worth its respect. Such speech *says* nothing and it can only pretend to say some-thing (such as Non-Being exists) when it mistakes that which it speaks *about* with that which it *says*.

> Since the object of thought must exist and Being is the only thing there is, Parmenides concludes that when mortals talk of coming into Being and perishing, of Being and Non-Being, of change of place, these expressions cannot refer either to Being (for Parmenides has shown that all these things are impossible, since they would amount to the assertion that Non-Being exists) or to Non-Being (for Non-Being is conceivable). Consequently, those names which mortals utter with the conviction that they are true are just names, i.e., empty names.[1]

Therefore, when men talk of Being and Non-Being, they do not use the words correctly (i.e., analytically), for properly speaking, men can only speak analytically. When men fail to speak analytically, though they make noises, etc., they do not really speak (speak analytically).[2] Note the parallel here with Heraclitus' notion of 'truly hearing' the Logos, i.e., when men truly near the Logos they do not merely listen, but are 'all ears,' etc.[3]

To say that false speaking is impossible is not to deny that it *happens*; it is to call attention to speech that does not address its Real subject. 'Impossible' does not mean 'cannot be done' because that usage treats 'possible' as 'can happen' or 'can occur.' 'Impossible' means: it is not true or faithful to analytic (rational) notion of speaking, does not re-cognize its critical subject; 'impossible' means 'is not analytic,' 'is not Rational.'

Parmenides reminds us that to speak *about* (either Being or no-thing) is redundant, since speaking-about as characterization is already an appearing of Being (as the difference *qua* difference, as the difference between Being and Non-Being). Thus, in its very occurrence, speech makes reference to the difference between Being and Nothing which *is* Being, and the attempts to characterize Being and Non-Being are false because speaking itself belongs essentially to Being. The falseness of false speaking consists in the fact that it ignores its togetherness with Being as a One, and that it misunderstands Being – as the difference between Being and Nothing – by treating this difference as if it was an analytic difference between two things rather than as an appearing of the Same. Being is a metaphor for the difference between being and no-thing.

---

[1] Taràn, *op. cit.*, pp. 131–132.
[2] Taràn, *op. cit.*, p. 137.
[3] See Heidegger's reading of Heraclitus in *Introduction . . ., op. cit.*; also Cleve, *op. cit.*; and G. Seidel, *Heidegger and the Pre-Socratics*, Lincoln: University of Nebraska Press, 1964.

The connection between sophistry and science becomes more intelligible. The sophists sought to preserve Parmenides' formulation in the form of the authority of self and science. They argued that since all intelligible speech is communal speech, and communal speech always has a topic or subject for itself, the idea of speech which speaks about no-thing (following Parmenides) is impossible because by definition speech has its subject. They drew the consequence of affirming as true any speech which speaks with the authority of its subject and thus, they returned the question of truth and falsity to the question of membership.[1] The sophists drew from Parmenides' maxim the lesson that false speaking is impossible because they understood 'possible' concretely; but, whereas Parmenides intended this as a critique of a member's conception of falseness vis-à-vis his conception of analytic speaking as faithful speaking, they treated 'possibility' as 'cannot be done.' They then used this maxim to justify any opportunistic speaking. Parmenides' notion that false speaking was impossible intended to remind men that false speaking had the analytic status of silence, that false speaking could not be faithful to Reason; but certainly men could concretely speak and show their silence. The sophists themselves exemplified this; they spoke about many things but said no-thing. Thus, to say there *is* only true speaking is not to assert that whatever is spoken is true, but that the only thing worth speaking is Reason; that the only kind of speaking that ought to be spoken is that which shows its faithfulness to Being. False speaking is not different than true speaking, but is a way of making reference to what true speaking has to say. False speaking as speech which has not understood itself or which does not know what it is, is not to be taken seriously (treated as 'incorrect' or 'wrong'), but as a reminder of 'that for the sake of which' speech speaks. The maxim 'all is one' then includes false speaking as part of that unity; because silence exists as a surpassed possibility within every instance of true speaking, false speaking is integral to truth; in that false speaking re-presents the unity of Oneness in its distinctions, every such re-presentation covers over the unity and truth which it *is*.

For Plato, false speaking is a movement internal to truth and thus, they are not two different kinds of speech, nor yet are they identical. To make false speaking a difference in kind from true speaking would be to accredit the Reality of nothing, of faithless speech, while to make them identical would be to accredit *any* speech which happens to be spoken as *saying* something. The difference between truth and falsity parallels the difference between Being and science with which we began.

This is to say that we want not the whatness of false speech, but rather, how falsity belongs to whatness. We want to know how falsity

---

[1] Protagoras' 'man is the measure' is exemplary here; see *The Theaetetus, op. cit.*

surfaces as the appearing of whatness. False speaking as difference appears as the difference which is One: in its dispersiveness false speaking covers over the unity which it is at the same time it disperses. If whatness captures the sense of true speech, then falsity appears through whatness and truth itself; though not the same, they are inextricably tied together, for truth and falsity are moments in that which comes to be. What is addressed is the way false speaking appears out of the Desire to speak truly (out of the negation of that Desire) and as its coming to appearance. The appearing of this otherness is the appearing of this Desire. False speaking then points to true speaking and in making such reference directs us to the union of speech with what owns it. False speaking has no resolve: it shows itself under the influence of peripheral subjects which it treats as Real subjects rather than as images of Being. Since it does not see a disclosure of Being for what it *is* its falseness resides in what it fails to see (not *in* the subject it sees); its falseness resides in its resting secure, in stopping too soon. False speaking does not seize the opportunity which is present (though concealed) to it and in this failure shows its participation in Being by not seeing itself as what it *is* – a disclosure of Being.

The faithlessness of false speaking is then not like deviance or the failure of a standard to 'take,' it is not a failure of performance, for in such a case true and false speaking would be two 'things' only related externally and concretely. On the other hand, the unity of true and false speaking does not suggest that we cannot tell them apart, for they appear as speech attracted by different music. False speaking is not the opposite of true speaking (like a separable thing); rather, it is inarticulate true speech, speech which in speaking what exists, covers over what needs be said.

False speaking as faithless speaking is speech which shows no faith in that which moves and summons all things and which causes all things to be. False speaking has no faith in that which it conceals and because of this, false speaking has no conception of what it is (i.e., it is false or faithless to a true conception of what speech is): if speech is essentially ruled and authorized by what owns it, then it belongs together with its author in a relationship which is anything but concrete. Yet, false speaking sees *this* relationship as a concrete demand, and consequently, false speaking shows that it misunderstands what it is (or, what speaking is). False speaking first concretizes that with which it belongs together and then, because of this very act of concretization, chooses to disregard it *because* of its concreteness. False speaking chooses another master and this is how it shows its faithlessness. False speaking is speech that is faithful only to it-self in the most concrete sense. The differences between true and false speaking dissolve when the resonances which false speaking conceal in its speech are disclosed. This disclosure is accomplished through the dialectic between truth and falsity personified as the struggle of speech to re-collect its source by showing the incompleteness of all collecting.

False speaking chooses to subject it-self to itself, to what *it* can speak, and it uses this conception of its speaking possibilities as that which authorizes it and to which it decides to submit. In this way, false speaking shows that it loses what it is in it-self. Yet, the unity of true and false speaking is seen in this loss, for what false speaking loses is the truth and it can only lose what it has. If false speaking forgets, it can only forget that which it once had and so, it always points to the truth.[1]

In this sense, false speaking is a speaking that turns away. From what does false speaking recoil? From that which would make it true; false speaking turns away from the only thing that could save it, or from that which could make it *say* rather than merely *speak*. False speaking turns away from that which is worth saying and thus, turns away from what it is, because that which is worth saying is that which *it* could say. False speaking is not a distinct category of 'thinking' or 'behaviour' different from true speaking as a rule violation differs from a rule; truth and falsity are not predicates attached to speech as a subject. False speaking is a different way of looking at true speaking, or to put it better, both true and false speaking are ways of making reference to the Oneness of truth. They are different ways in which this Oneness appears, and they are differences *as* this Oneness. As differences, true and false speaking belong together with this Oneness.

False speaking is then a turning away from what is decisive and essential, it is an attempt to live at the peripheries rather than in the centre. False speaking confuses the peripheral with the central because it does not face the relatedness of centre and periphery as a difference *qua* difference and as a difference-in-unity. This is to say first, that false speaking does not see the difference between centre and periphery in how the peripheral *covers over* the central – it does not see this concealment as a difference – and secondly, that it does not see this 'covering over' as a unity (a relation which is no-thing) in which the peripheral announces how the central lets it lie.

III

For Plato, problems unfold within the context of a (thinking) discourse, and each problem presents itself in the guise of names and descriptions

[1] False speaking is personified in the act of birth which alienates man from Logos and which brings him under the control of the eyes and ears (see Heraclitus' fragments). This is why theorizing becomes a preparation for death as in the *Phaedo*.

mouthed securely by men and repeated without thought.[1] The 'forms' or ideas which Plato developed were metaphors for making reference to the Oneness of Being that lay concealed beneath such mouthings and which, in its concealing, threaten to become lost from sight through the dispersiveness of these mouthings. It was *through* such ideas that one could come to re-enact the thinking experience, and through such a re-enactment could come to face that which thought ought to think. The bringing to speech of each idea and the making of these intelligible through speech then stands as an intersecting series of examples through which true thinking is pointed to as a dialectic between the secure and unthought and the thought-provoking which lies covered over. To treat the ideas as more than examples is to treat the dialectic concretely: to see ideas as composites of particulars, as hypotheses, as concepts, or as mathematical methods, is to misunderstand their exemplary function as personifications of the occasion of thinking.

The question 'what is knowledge?' is transformed into the query 'what purpose ought knowledge serve?' and in this way, such a question raises the possibility of something beyond knowledge, something that owns knowledge and to which it is subject. The question 'what is knowledge?' does not ask for a *description* of knowledge or for a *science* of knowledge, because the *is* in 'what is knowledge?' raises the deeper question of that to which knowledge ought be faithful *to be* (truly spoken of as) knowledge, rather than as other-than-knowledge (opinion). That to which knowledge belongs is neither a concrete entity or genus, nor a 'goal' in the conventional sense, but serves more as a needful concern to which the speaker is oriented and which he re-discovers on each and every occasion of authentic inquiry. What is re-collected is not a concrete datum nor yet a 'world view,' but is more like an abiding and enduring root which each occasion of inquiry can nourish, make manifest, and bring to light. All inquiries then serve not as solutions to problems, but as occasions of pointing to, and of making manifest that which lies covered over.

To ask 'what is courage?' 'what is virtue?' 'what is piety?' (what is its essence?) is neither to ask for some finite calculus of predicates nor for some concrete 'thing.' Rather, to ask for the essence of a thing is to ask for the idea of the thing in a particular way. The query after the idea of a thing is not the quest for an hypotheses or substance or category, but is instead the posing of the following question: what kind of excellence does the thing require? This kind of excellence is not a substance or hypothesis itself, but is a way of making reference to that to which the idea belongs. The excellence of the idea is typified in its

[1] The mouthings of men are repetitions of what they have heard or memorized, but not of what they have truly addressed. Men are ruled by what they have heard and their repetitions testify to the authority of this rule.

belonging together with that which moves all things. Consequently, to form the idea is to point to that which the idea covers over and since all ideas participate in this unity, each idea in-itself provides an occasion for glimpsing that which all ideas share. Plato speaks of such a unity as the Good. The excellence (*areté*) which each idea requires is its belonging-together with what moves all things and in this way the particular excellence specified in the particular idea becomes a method of making reference to the Good. Ideas are not external significations of the Good, but ways of making manifest Goodness itself, and as such, ideas 'appear' as appearances of the Good that are internal to it as a One.

Stenzel[1] (to take a typical example) and most, see the idea as a composite of particulars, and the instabilities recognized in the theory of ideas are generally connected to the changing conception of the relationship between universal and particulars. Thus, it is assumed that in the early Socratic dialogues a moral conception of the ideas as standards of excellence prevailed, but that under the pressure of science Plato was led to develop a 'theory of knowledge' which more adequately resolved the latent problem of the relationship between the idea and the particulars of sense. Thus, the method of division and collection in the later dialogues (*The Sophist, Phillebus*) is seen as Plato's way of handling the relationship between the one (the idea) and the many (the particulars) under the impetus of scientific (mathematical) cross-questioning which induced him to extend the ideas to objects other than moral objects (to all objects).

The Oneness of the idea is then seen as residing in the fact that it unifies (all ideas are unities), and its manyness is attributed to its character as a *composite* of particulars. Every idea is a One because its essence is a unity of diverse elements and it is at the same time a many because it comprehends a variety of lower species. However, this reading of the notions of the one and the many treats them in terms of the conventional imagery of whole and part; in contrast, it can be suggested that the unity of the idea resides in the fact of its bringing to speech the excellence which it typifies as a standard for using the idea, that its oneness consists in its belonging-together with its nature, and that its manyness consists of the participation of this unity (the unity called the idea) in the Good, i.e., that its manyness consists in the fact that the typification of the idea is one of the many ways in which Being comes to shine forth and to appear. The unity of the idea does not consist in its organizing potential but in its intelligibility as a discrete disclosure (a display); the manyness of the idea does not consist of the elements which it combines, but in its *exemplification* of the omnipresence of Being as one of the many possible exemplifications.

This is a crucial difference: the manyness of the idea does not reside

[1] J. Stenzel, *Plato's Method of Dialectic*, New York: Russell and Russell, 1964.

in its character as a composite of particulars (that it is a 'whole' with concrete 'parts'), but as a way of bringing Being to appearance – as itself an appearance of Being; the idea is a *part* of Being only in the sense that it typifies one possible disclosure of Being, and in this bringing of Being to unconcealment, shows Being through itself. The unitary character of the idea resides not in its capacity to *combine* particulars, but in the fact that it is spoken, and its manyness consists of the fact that in being spoken what it *says* is Being (if one takes the trouble to hear).

Plato's so-called problem is then only a problem for the mathematical theorist who formulates ideas as universals which collect the particularities of sense.[1] Stenzel says that the ideas were originally moral standards (in the Socratic 'period') and that they were treated absolutely; consequently, when the moral point of view was abandoned (and when Socrates was dropped from the leading role in the dialogues) ideas had to be freely postulated whenever a common name was applied to a group of objects. The requirement to accommodate the earlier notion of the idea as a moral standard to the changing conception of the idea as a class concept supposedly led Plato into a number of major adjustments. Stenzel insists that such adjustments are shown in Plato's pre-occupation with method in the later dialogues.

What Stenzel terms Plato's discovery of the concept supposedly arises at the beginning of his intellectual development as a result of the changing objects to which Plato ascribed ideas. The two periods depicted in Plato's development are characterized by Stenzel as: the moral period in which the ideas were conceived as having a transcendental existence (the existence of an *areté*) with each serving as a cause and an end, and; the period of theory and of natural philosophy in which the ideas or the class is defined by natural science and the method of division is introduced as a procedure for determining the ideas in order to bring individual reality within the grip of science. In other words, it is asserted that Plato became a mathematical theorist under the impetus of the growth of science and the awakened interest in the world of appearance, for it is only through such a new interest that Plato could come to find his dialectical theory inadequate.[2]

---

[1] The ideas might be exemplified through the image of intentional, extensional, attributive, *et al.*, relations, but only insofar as it is recognized that any such relationship is a *format* for speaking about the ideas and what lies beyond them, and is not a display of their analytic character. The trouble with all such formats is that they undermine the possibilities for beginning to address the ideas dialectically.

[2] Thus, accounting for Ryle's charge that Plato only became a philosopher in his later dialogues see *Plato's Progress, op. cit.* Also, see Ryle's essay 'John Locke on the Human Understanding' in C. B. Martin and D. M. Armstrong, eds., *Locke and Berkeley*, New York: Anchor Books, 1968, especially pp. 16–25.

The story goes: at about the time of *The Parmenides*, Plato realized that the dialectical conception of ideas was not elastic enough to accommodate ideas like horse, fire, mud, dirt, hair *et al.*, because of the rigid segregation of the intelligible from the sensible: thus, Plato was led to revise his conception of the ideas in an effort to integrate these two domains which his earlier dialectic had forced him to segregate. However, this is Aristotle's story. Plato's so-called separation of the intelligible from the sensible was a metaphor for the difference between Being and Non-Being (between the analytic and the concrete), and for the necessity of preserving this difference *qua* difference; thus, *things* like 'horse' and 'dirt' can be concretely spoken of in many ways, but they only acquire life as occasions for re-discovering the relationship in which they essentially participate. Parmenides' cross-questioning gave Socrates trouble because terms like horse and dirt did not conventionally and ordinarily provide such occasions: hair, horse, fire and dirt were not normally the occasions on which thought was provoked or which exercised and awakened the impulse towards true thinking. Plato was not interested in developing a comprehensive grammar for every imaginable term or name mouthed by men; he was not interested in developing a science of knowledge, or a grammar for categorizing the possibilities of 'mere existence.' Rather, his concern was to re-orient men to the Good, and he was prepared to use any particular concrete expression as an occasion for initiating such a movement. One could say that for Plato hair and dirt failed to exist not in the sense that he would have treated washing and combing as impossible because the matter which such operations acted upon 'did not exist,' but because hair and dirt were analytically 'nothing' (useless) for his purposes until they were assimilated into a critical conversation within the soul. This is not a principled objection because any-thing or particular becomes analytically relevant (something rather than nothing) when it can be employed as the example. Thus, the true mark of the sophist has always been that he is one who can raise problems out of the spirit of pure contentiousness without respect to the relevance of the problem for the occasion. In contrast, examples must come to light as part of a critical context and not as disputatious attempts to score empty verbal triumphs.

Whereas in Descartes, ideas depict objects entertained by the mind, for Plato, the Reality of ideas did not reside in *what* they depicted, or in *where* they originated (objects, mind), but in how they served to make reference to that of which they were icons. Since the essence of the idea is to point beyond itself, the idea is essentially a course of action, i.e., a pointer. This is not to say that the ideas are like dispositions in the way that the idea of theorizing is a complex of dispositions, e.g., solving problems, or arguing (this is an empirical conception).[1] Rather, the idea is typified as a kind of *areté*, i.e., as the hypothetical course of action of 'one in tune with' the Good. Consequently, the idea *makes reference* to the Good.

The Platonic ideas are only 'methods' in the sense that they are used *to make reference*; they are not systematic, planned projects. The idea makes reference as a course of action because the action typified by the idea always personifies the dialectic between true and false speaking. For example, Stenzel finds unclear Plato's frequent talk in the early dialogues about the unhappiness of the tyrant (e.g., even if the tyrant *thinks* he is happy, he cannot *be* happy because he is doing evil and no-one wishes to do evil, etc.) because Stenzel fails to realize that the happiness of the tyrant is a matter which Plato legislates and authoritatively decides on the basis of his commitment. In other words, there is nothing 'unclear' – as Stenzel suggests – about the authoritative decision to use an idea like happiness in a way which conflicts with ordinary usage if one decides to use ordinary usage as a beginning to be surpassed rather than as an authoritative standard.

If *areté* is the excellence which fits each conceivable thing to perform its specific function, the essence of a thing is included in its *areté*. This raises the question of the essence or particular excellence which fits the human to perform its particular function. This is Plato's version of the question – what is the *Sum*? Obviously, the *Sum* is the excellence shown in addressing the Good and in acting with reference to it. If all virtues are translated into a relationship to the Good, and if the human is typified through the excellence of addressing the Good, then the distinctive virtue of the human is seen in his effort to bring the Good to appearance. The particular excellence of the human is that he desires to theorize despite all obstacles. Yet, theorizing is not the end or *telos* of the human (that would make man a god and vanity the supreme power), but is rather, a method of serving the Good and of making it reveal itself in discourse.

To speak truly is to address that which belongs together – speech and Being – and to speak in such a way as to deny the vision of this togetherness is to speak falsely. Yet the questions of 'addressing' and 'denying' true speech are not empirical questions for which criteria can be furnished, for we can only understand what such questions raise when we re-cognize our speech to be 'in tune.' Stenzel shows a failure of analytic wit in his brief mention of the *Charmides*, for he takes the argument in this dialogue as showing Plato's early unreflexive theorizing, i.e., his failure to conceive of one's own consciousness as a topic. However, this is plainly muddled, for Socrates' complaint in this dialogue that one's consciousness cannot be a topic for the thinker

[1] This is Ryle's conception of 'theorizing' in *The Concept of Mind*, New York: Barnes and Noble, 1951.

78

shows that – analytically – self is not the same as subjectivity or as the empirical and concrete ego, but rather, is knowledge of the Good. Thus, the soul knows herself if she knows her essential nature, i.e., her excellence, but this is not the same thing as knowing oneself concretely. Thus, Socrates is far ahead of Stenzel (and of phenomenology) in his analytic conception of self-knowledge as knowledge of the Good. Rather than deny the possibilities of reflexivity, Socrates was repudiating a concrete and empirical conception of self as subjectivity in favour of a version of self as the particular excellence for which the soul is fitted. Thus, Critias' objection[1] is not 'thought to be justified' as Stenzel says, but should be repudiated on the grounds that it shows no Real conception of self.

Stenzel's interpretation of Plato's transformation is that as the range of ideas is extended, the problem of 'participation,' the one and the many, and the relationship between universal and particular become acute and demand resolution; however, this is intelligible only if we interpret Plato's ideas descriptively. If the ideas are icons of the Good, the question of the extension of their range is irrelevant. This transformation is only discerned on the grounds of Stenzel's imputation of mathematical interests to Plato as one who constructed ideas as *descriptions* of state-of-affairs. Thus, these interests supposedly led Plato to adapt the earlier 'ideal theory' to the requirements of a newer epistemology, and they were reflected in two inter-related trends in Plato's work: the extension of the ideas to everything that exists, and the re-definition of a thing's essence in such a way as to abandon the notion of value (of the excellence of a thing). However, we are saying that the first could never have been a problem for *Plato* (for Aristotle, yes) because the application of ideas to things was not *his* problem, and, that Plato could never abandon the distinction of (so-called) 'value' between ideas, because this would have been equivalent to abandoning the very conception of analytic theory in which he was grounded.[2]

Stenzel the mathematician then poses for Plato the problem of the later dialogues: how can what is a One (the idea) at the same time be 'in' the many? But this was no problem for Plato as seen in the fact that the one-ness of the idea can be read as referring to the vision of the unity which grounds the collecting of the essence and which inspires and organizes its coming-into-speech. For us, what is interesting to Plato is not the composite character of this idea, but the fact that as a bringing to speech it itself provides only a glimpse of the most perfect speech. It is not that the form is 'in' the particulars, but that Being is 'in' the

---

[1] See the *Charmides*, 165E.

[2] One who is interested in the detail of the historiography of ideas *could* read such changes but to what good would such a reading make reference? To the good of 'accuracy' and of 'setting the record straight'?

form. The idea is a many not as a composite of subordinate species, but as one of the many ways (many speeches) through which Being can disclose itself. Thus, ideas like courage, virtue, tolerance, and piety are to be understood as raising questions not of the essence of the ideas, but of how the idea essences. The Oneness of the ideas is seen in their status as exemplifying intelligibly distinct occasions of essencing, but their manyness consists in the fact that in essencing they personify the struggle between Being and Nothing, and thus, they each in their severalness disclose and bring to unconcealment that struggle as the dialectic through which what is, is.

In Plato, the analytic status of manyness is not *having* parts but being a part, if we understand 'part' metaphorically. In this sense, the Good is not a many (though it can be spoken of as a whole composed of ideas which belong to it essentially) because the Good is not a part; on the other hand, the idea is a many because it is a part only in the sense that it is one of the many ways in which Being is announced. But it is better not to speak of parts in this sense. Manyness then means analytically, the capacity to be an icon of a higher whole, to be subject to what owns. Mathematically, manyness means *having* parts and in this sense both Being and its appearance may be said to constitute a many (this is what is meant by calling them 'concepts'). Plato desires to make the distinctions analytically because he wants to differentiate appearance from Being while preserving their essential togetherness; to make the distinction concretely is to treat Being as another idea, this idea as a 'universal.' In contrast, to understand the idea analytically is to comprehend it as one of the many because it belongs together with what moves all things; if the idea is analytically understood as one of the many, then the One to which these many essentially belong is a One that appears *in* the many.

The dialectical conception of science as a many means that science is conceived as an appearance or showing of Being, as one of the many ways in which Being is announced. The idea of science is not seen as having parts (even though many concrete types and degrees of science can be spoken and named), but in its appearing as one of the many forms through which Being announces itself. To say that science is one of the many is to say neither that it is a composite or a 'part' of a composite, but that it is a way of making reference to that which owns it and to which it belongs.

IV

The problems which Plato's commentators have expressed concerning the status of forms revolves around the conception of 'participation' as a metaphor for the relationship between form and particular. Most assume that participation is a concrete relationship rather than an iconic reference; most model participation after 'predication' rather than on the relationship of 'belonging-together' in which a something which cannot show itself announces itself through something which can show itself.[1]

As some exigetes have shown,[2] the relationship of an icon to original is not a relationship of similarity (but neither is it a relationship between two different 'things'), and it is 'causal' only under the constraint of Plato's notion of cause as Reason. The problem which commentators have expressed is then: either original and the copy are similar or different; if different, they require a standard (a third term, a third man) in terms of which they are brought into relationship (for one begins with the idea of their relatedness) and if such a standard is introduced, the possibility of infinite standards is created. On the other hand, if they are identical (in kind) and differ only in degree, their relatedness as universal and particular is guaranteed, and particulars are formulated as a deficiency of the same kind as the form which they particularize. If different then a third is needed and a fourth to ground the third, a fifth to ground the fourth, etc.: if similar then they are not analytically distinct and to relate what is the same is nonsense.

In other words, to make them analytically different is to ground them in concrete similarity in the sense that there will be no internal solution to the problem of their belonging together (no principled solution, infinite regress, etc.). On the other hand, to make them analytically similar is to use the most concrete distinctions of generality-specificity to discriminate them (given that they must be discriminated). So the problem starts from the recognition that form and thing must be discriminated and given this requirement, the problem of re-establishing

---

[1] See Heidegger's discussion of appearance and phenomenon in *Being and Time*, pp. 51–55.

[2] Plato's 'problems' of universals and particulars, participation and predication, and the third man, are discussed with admirable clarity in Stenzel, *op. cit.*, see his discussion of the 'emergence of the four problems.' Unfortunately, these are only problems for a theorist constructed to meet the specifications of a mathematical interest. See also, the essays on ideas, the Third Man Argument, and participation and predication in G. Vlastos, ed., *Plato: A Collection of Critical Essays I: Metaphysics and Epistemology*, New York: Anchor Books, Doubleday & Co., 1970. The only reading in this volume to which we could begin to speak is R. E. Allan 'Participation and Predication in Plato's Middle Dialogues.'

their unity is recognized as one that can only be resolved externally and concretely.

The relation of icon to original is a difference *qua* difference, a relation of difference that belongs together. The original and the icon differ and belong together: while they differ as the concrete differs from the analytic, they belong together as both the concrete and analytic belong to Being. The belonging together of form and particular is not a relation of similarity and is consequently not based upon a 'standard' of similarity because their relatedness is grounded in Being. What is spoken of as the third man is a concrete version of Being and to speak of Being as a third man is ludicrous, faithless.

The relationship between form and particular is not analytically crucial to Plato because their separation was never a problem. The *problem* is that men speak unthinkingly and such unthinking speech shows itself in discourse through the many and dispersed distinctions that are produced. The problem is to move concertedly to address and to re-collect the resonances which these many mouthings cover over, and thus the discourse is led to anchor itself at stable and secure points. By keeping these points in mind and by not losing them in the face of impressive and high sounding pressures towards fragmentation, men can come to re-cognize what these points and their many exemplifications in discourse cover. These points and their exemplifications 'belong together' in that through the mouthings – as dispersed and as fragmented as they are – the points are made to show themselves.

The mouthings of men show themselves as appearances, which is to say that the focal points of discourse (the forms, the ideas) announce themselves through these mouthings and from these mouthings men seek to disclose the points which are announced through the mouthings but which are hidden until the mouthings bring them to life through the conflict of discourse.

Yet, these points are not themselves the phenomena, for the appearing of the points in discourse is itself a re-minder of that which is hidden by the discourse and by all of its characterizations and distinctions. Thus, the exemplification of the idea in discourse, instead of appearing as two things – the idea and the particular – is a One – an-exemplification-of-the-idea – which is itself an exemplification, icon, or re-flection of something which does not show itself but which *belongs* to the exemplification-of-the-idea which does show itself and which 'belongs to it so essentially as to constitute its meaning and ground.'[1]

If phenomenon is a disclosing or bringing to light and its counter-concept is 'covered-up-ness,' that which is covered up belongs to that which shows itself by constituting its ground even though that which

[1] Heidegger, *Being and Time, op. cit.*

is covered up does not show *itself* but announces itself through that (phenomenon) which shows itself and which in such a showing 'indicates' that which does not show itself. Thus, so-called form and particular become a One phenomenon which in showing itself points to the 'covered-up' with which it essentially belongs. The *telos* of the discourse is directed towards making manifest that which lies covered over and is not directed to the development of a science of predication.

The notions of form and particular are metaphors for the relation of showing to hiding as this dialectic occurs in discourse. These metaphors should not be taken predicatively, descriptively, or concretely; they are not intended solutions to the mathematical problem of the one *in* the many generated by the requirements of a science of discourse: they are pointers to the essential dialectic between the showing and hiding of Being which every phenomenon itself shows. Seen in this way, the relationship of 'belonging together' as a difference *qua* difference should become more transparent.

In this connection, note how Plato often speaks of ideas such as beauty as beautiful, or of justice as just. Commentators have seized upon this as an instance of self-predication[1] and thus, as a fatal flaw in his work. Yet to say, e.g., that justice is just is not to do self-predication for it is not a *description* of justice: rather, it is to say that justice *ought* to be formulated as a belonging-together with its nature (with what owns it). If this *what* owns justice – its nature – is seen concretely as another idea or form or as the essence of justice, Being is again treated concretely. What owns justice is Being *as* the difference between justice and nothing as this difference announces itself in the 'idea' of justice.

Thus to say that justice is just and that an act is just is to say two different things; to say justice is just is not to describe justice, but is to address that which justice covers over; to say that a concrete act is just is to use justice concretely. The distinction parallels the so-called contrast between theory and practice and in Plato one starts with practical interests shown by speeches such as 'this man is just,' 'this action is just,' etc., and moves to address the question of how justice could be seen as just, of how justice justs. Thus, Plato preserves the distinction between these usages as icons of different points in the movement of inquiry that is personified in discourse; but in distinguishing them, he recommends their deep unity in the one service they provide of directing the discourse to the *Physis* in terms of which (the justing of justice is made transparent) justice is wrenched, and through which its concrete dispersion in speech becomes possible.

---

[1] That is, that in speaking of beauty as beautiful, beauty is transformed into the concrete exemplar of the beautiful thing.

V

When a commentator reads dialectic as consisting of three methods, e.g., collection, division, and questions such as 'whether A can be truly predicated of B' and vice versa, his scholarship might be commended, or conversely he might be seen as a dupe of his own authoritative version of reading.[1] Similarly, when someone extracts Plato's literal definition of the Dialectician in *The Sophist* as Plato's analytic conception of dialectic,[2] he might be commended or pointed to the *Seventh Letter* in which Plato says the following:

> One statement at any rate I can make in regard to all who have written or who may write with a claim to knowledge of the subjects to which I devote myself . . . such writers can have in my opinion no real acquaintance with the subject. I certainly have composed no work in regard to it, nor shall I ever do so in the future, for there is no way of putting it into words like other studies. Acquaintance with it must come rather after a long period of attendance and instruction in the subject itself and of close companionship, when suddenly, like a blaze kindled by a leaping spark, it is generated in the soul and it once becomes self sustaining.[3]

The Sophist is an attempt to clarify the status of true thinking and its essential relation to false thinking through the example of Non-Being. That is, since true speaking can only be understood through its essential togetherness with false speaking and since members only comprehend thinking predicatively, Plato uses the resources of predicative speaking to make reference to the ideal of Logos which was personified in the earlier dialogues in the character of Socrates.

Plato seeks to conceptualize false speaking as speaking about that which does not exist. However, he uses the language of reference and predication not because nothingness is something to which predicates are applied, but because the language of reference and predication is the only idiom intelligible to his audience. To speak about nothing is not to speak about that which is concretely absent, but is more like speaking in an empty, vacuous, and irrelevant manner. To speak about nothing is to show through one's speech that one is not alive to Being, i.e., to the belonging-together of speech and Being. To speak falsely is to show that one does not understand what speech is. Thus the central topic of *The Sophist* is not even Non-Being, but language itself, i.e., the relations of saying, displaying, and hiding which constitute language.

[1] A. Wedberg, 'The Theory of Ideas' in Vlastos, *op. cit.*, p. 50.
[2] Stenzel, Chapter VI, *The Dialectician Defined: Sophist*, 253D.
[3] Letter VII to 'Friends and Companions of Dion' in the Bollingen edition of *Plato: Complete Works, op. cit.*

84

The first tactic Plato used was to change the sense of 'to be' from the complete or substantive use as a one-place predicate to its incomplete use as a two-place predicate.[1] Thus, he could re-cast his examples into the subject-predicate format. While, as Owens has showed, he could use Non-Being as difference rather than as negation, this use itself showed that analytically Non-Being *is* negation (non-existent), and that otherness or difference is just a device for making intelligible reference to this. For example, Owens says that to re-write 'A is not a greengrocer' as 'A exists as a non-greengrocer' is to the point because it avoids 'the absurdity . . . of suggesting that A's failure to be a greengrocer is a sort of non-existence for A.'[2]

Yet, it is just this 'absurdity' which we want to preserve; it only becomes absurd for one who cannot recognize the analytic character of 'does not exist.' Analytically, the fact that A is not a greengrocer is equivalent to saying that A is nothing, that he does not exist. While we all know that A concretely exists as flesh and blood, as other than a greengrocer, this is not the issue. Analytically, if 'being a greengrocer' is the only speech for addressing A, to call the speech 'wrong' or 'false' for Plato meant that as a speech it was not thought provoking, i.e., calling A a greengrocer is equivalent to saying nothing about him. It is misleading to say that the predicate does not apply (that it misses, or fails to correspond), for what the speech shows is that the speaker is not thinking truly about A, that he is not reflecting truly on what A truly is. What we should say is that it is not possible for A to *be* a greengrocer though he *exists* as a greengrocer. Although this might appear 'absurd' to the philosopher, it is the most critical way of conceiving of being human. Whether A is or is not a greengrocer is strictly speaking nothing because to say *that* about a man is to say nothing. It is not a true way of speaking about a man; it does not formulate him critically, it fails to touch him as a subject. It takes what appears to be as what is. The question of *The Sophist* – how can one speak and say nothing? How can one speak and be silent? – points to the relationship between showing and hiding as the relationship that *is* language. To say that A is not a greengrocer is to speak rather than to say A, but in so doing it is to show the speaker as an instance of that which comes to be; though it is *both* true and false, what is false about the speech is not its accuracy in depicting A's occupation, but that in so speaking it shows the speaker as one who covers-up the possibility of saying through what he speaks.

The same comments apply to the familiar example of 'Theaetetus flies.' This is interpreted as false speaking because flying is not predicable of Theaetetus, or because 'flying' is other than Theaetetus, etc.

[1] G. E. L. Owen, 'Plato on Not-Being' in Vlastos, *op. cit.*

[2] *Ibid.*, p. 236.

However, in the context of this proposition what Plato means is that the speech 'Theaetetus flies' says nothing because as a speech it leaves Theaetetus untouched, it does not clarify him, it does not use him as an occasion to address what man really is. In this way, the incomplete use of 'to be' cannot be regarded as different from the complete or so-called existential use, and Otherness or Difference does not transform the sense of 'what is not' as negation because the analytic use of otherness as difference is always grounded in the grammar of Negation. To speak falsely as to speak of 'what does not exist' is the only sense of false speaking unless one treats non-existence referentially (and in this work that is a concrete treatment). The problem might be put as follows: to think *of* nothing is to think like a nothing, it is to speak in such a way as to show oneself as saying nothing, i.e., of thinking of nothing that is worth thinking. What is worth thinking is Being, and so, to think of nothing is to think of anything and everything but Being: to think of everything other than Being is to think of 'nothing' since it is only thought that thinks Being that can be said to truly think of some-thing.

The comparison of flying and sitting is used by Plato because members tend to grasp speech referentially and to be most at home with conceptions of truth that are furnished and grounded by concrete standards of similarity between rank ordered things. It is easier to isolate the properties of true speech when it is exemplified in contrast to a concrete specimen of false speech.

Most can only understand false speech concretely as lying. So, Owen says of Theaetetus flying: 'If I tell Theaetetus he has taken wing, I speak of a non-existent flight, but not of nothing. . . .[1] In false-hood the speaker does not touch anything; where there should be the flight ascribed to Theaetetus, there is no such object for the words to hit. . . .' (Or '. . . the suggestion that the false statement says what-is-not about something implies that what is missing is the flight.')[2] Such readings have disastrous implications; Plato could not invoke that kind of correspondence version of truth and be the Plato we want to resurrect. To speak falsely is not to lie, nor to speak about a non-existent some-thing, it is not to fail to touch 'things' with words; it is to speak *as a nothing*, it is to make speech which comes out of a body rather than a soul. To speak falsely is to speak in such a way as to show that *one is false* and that one is other than his speech, that one is not alive to its grounds and possibilities. What is false about false speaking is the soul of the speaker, for he is one who shows through his speech that it is guided by the impressive and high sounding, i.e., by no-thing to speak of. To speak falsely is to speak in such a way as to show that one is

---

[1] *Ibid.*, p. 244.
[2] *Ibid.*, p. 245.

false (false to oneself and consequently to Reason). One could be most accurate about Theaetetus – about the body that sits there – and still be faithless to reason (in fact, this is the ground for Kierkegaard's characterization of the level of conversation of his day as much information but little truth).

In *The Theaetetus*, Plato uses the example of 'Theaetetus flies' and 'Theaetetus sits' as exemplars of true and false speaking. What is usually taken as the difference between the two is the fact that the predicate 'sits' is applicable to Theaetetus where 'flies' is not. However, 'Theaetetus sits' is just as much a falsehood *even though Theaetetus does sit*. 'Sitting' does not say anything essential or initiate any essential type of thinking about what the idea of Theaetetus covers over, for it merely reports or describes something he *happens* to be doing. What does 'sitting' *say* about a man as a way of addressing what he truly is? To speak of a man that he sits is not a more successful declaration than to say he flies, even though he actually does sit and does not fly. The advantage of saying 'Theaetetus sits' is that it provides some information about Theaetetus and perhaps some information about the sorts of activities which an entity like Theaetetus can perform, but it is only a start, for it must yet begin to initiate discourse.

Though in ordinary social intercourse we must speak this way and our everyday joys and sorrows are integrated into the fabric of such talk, theorizing ought not re-produce our everyday mode of conversation. This is not to demean that mode, but is to discriminate it from the theoretical life as it is personified in the existence of inwardness exemplified in speech.

When might 'Theaetetus sits' be relevant? Perhaps, if we enter a room with two persons inside, one standing and one sitting; we then ask, 'which is Theaetetus?' and we obtain the answer that he is the one who sits. Certainly this is useful information, and it is correct, for if we were told that he is the one who stands (and if he was not) this answer would be incorrect. But these are concrete senses of 'true' and 'false' and unless they get taken up for discussion and become weaved into the fabric of discourse as an occasion for surpassing, they *say* no-thing. In this context, it is correct to speak 'Theaetetus sits,' but such an assertion says nothing until it begins to orient one to that which is essential about Theaetetus – to that which he truly is – and beyond that, to that which is essential to man, and beyond that, to that which is essential to essentiality.

Why then, does Plato use the example? In forcing the reader to consider the difference between the two predicates as differences between speaking truly and falsely, he alerts them to the fact that the difference is somehow grounded in something covered over. He is willing to concede the 'correctness' of 'Theaetetus sits' as a way of inducing reflection upon the question – what is Theaetetus? What is man? He uses the mundane examples of 'sitting' and 'flying' because he assumes that we find it difficult to relinquish the truth of our correct speaking standards as near-at-hand-truths. Thus he attempts to sensitize his Other to the fact that it is not the 'sitting' *per se* through which the proposition acquires its truthfulness, but in the relationship between the predicate and the idea or form of Theaetetus, and to the possibilities for re-forming an idea from speech about Theaetetus which the proposition covers over. Yet, even this relationship serves as a mere occasion for inducing men to relinquish their concern with the predicates altogether, so as to re-orient to the idea-*qua*-idea as a showing of that which it hides. The example is employed in order to induce us to *begin* to think truly. Thus, to speak any of these things about Theaetetus is to say nothing.

Therefore, the differences between the two propositions and between 'flying' and 'sitting' can be taken as differences between speaking about something and about nothing if the example is seen as an icon; in the context of a quest for information, one proposition is like speaking nothing while the other speaks some-thing; yet, from an analytic perspective they both say nothing, while collectively showing that to which they belong.

When the two propositions are considered comparatively as they are in the example, some movement is generated. The comparison provokes thought about the idea of the man; and through that, about other matters; it would not be as successful an example if each proposition was used separately because then it could merely be affirmed or negated and let go, our souls remaining untouched. When they are used comparatively as in this context, men are forced to consider how it is that one can be intelligibly called 'true' and the other not, and thus, are induced to enter into serious thought about the covered-over that the ordinary idea of truth announces. The focus is upon the ways in which ordinary speeches about a man provoke thought concerning whatness; sitting and flying becomes a medium for the activation and exercise of thought. Perhaps 'Theaetetus sits' is a better example than 'Theaetetus flies' and this accounts for Plato's decision to call it 'true.' 'Theaetetus sits' is assertive information about Theaetetus that we might accept with some uneasiness, for we can see how it might apply concretely without provoking us. It is the kind of example that forces us to admit 'yes, it is accurate to say that he sits, but that doesn't say anything about the man . . . it is linked to what he is doing here and now, in this place and time, and it does not say anything *essential*. . . .' The use of 'Theaetetus flies' then serves the function of isolating the accuracy of 'Theaetetus sits' and in so doing, in showing that accuracy is not sufficient; the example of flying alone would not provoke thought because a correspondence theory would dismiss it as self-evident. Similarly, the sitting example alone would only provoke the sort of thought that would reinforce the correspondence theory; considered together the relative truthfulness of sitting vis-à-vis flying can lead to a movement to address the question of whether this kind of concrete correctness is what ought to be shown by the idea of true. What we are led to consider is how the first subject underlies these ordinary matters which are themselves correct or incorrect but not central or critical. These speeches say nothing because they make no difference; they do not make a difference between the extraneous and the essential; these speeches are false because they make no difference and the men who speak them do not show a Desire to make a difference.

Thus Plato moves through this example, by starting from and terminating with the conventional conception of true and false as better and worse, as accurate and inaccurate, as present and absent, i.e., with the conventionally rank ordered differences through which truth is typically shown. Yet, this example is not a description of true and false speaking in the same way that Plato is not the Stranger; both example and stranger are used to point to the hidden.

Falsity resides in the character of speech which is not faithful (true) to that for-the-sake-of-which it speaks; it is speech that does not listen to what it says, or that does not use itself to make reference to its essential togetherness with Being, but instead refers, predicates, and qualifies under the illusion that this is where its truth lies.

Speech is then false when it fails to see its subject as itself an image or icon, i.e., when it fails to treat itself as covering over, or its terms and assertions as images of that which it covers over. False speaking does not treat speech as an image but as trustworthy, and thus fails to see the objects depicted in speech as icons, instead, securing them as trustworthy objects. False speech is speech which shows no analytic relation to speaking, it is speech which does not grasp the covered-up-ness of speaking in the dialectic between showing and hiding. Not to treat speech as an icon is not to see the differences of speech *qua* the originals which it reflects, and is thus, not to appreciate the community between image and original (the difference *qua* difference), between showing and hiding, as a unity wrenched from Being. False speaking in treating its subjects as subjects – as the critical subject – fails to see that which it subjects as the icon of a foundation.

Yet, although false speech can be seen as speech which understands itself concretely, such a 'failed' understanding is still an instance of true speaking. This is clear from Parmenides maxim: if all is one, the falseness of false speech does not reside in *its* existence or non-existence because the false speech occurs as a disclosure of Being. This is how Parmenides can say that strictly speaking, one cannot say Not-

Being; for all speaking is deeply a saying, a disclosure. All speaking is true to Being in *that* sense because All Is One. Yet this fact (the analytic character of speech as showing) is not understood in speech that speaks *about* as if it was a saying, and consequently, it is false because it does not understand the character of true speaking; false and true speaking belong together *and* they differ according to whether or not they show this belonging together as a respected constraint and condition of discourse.

The truth of false speaking consists in the fact that what it subjects is a disclosure of Being and thus, it (its subject) belongs-together with Being as one of its manifestations. Because false subjects participate in Being, their falseness resides not in what they are (not in *them* at all), but in how they are taken. What is false is the speaking that forgets its grip in the hand of Being by losing its head to *what* it can create (appropriate). False speaking is thankless: it loves it-self because it can create; by situating its subject(s) in the objects it creates or in its own mode of creative appropriation it is essentially self-centred. False speaking exemplifies the art which forgets that it is a work of art itself. It formulates its whatness – its nature – in terms of its own genius. In forgetting that it it-self is a work of art, false speaking detaches itself from that which creates it. False speaking as faithless speaking shows no gratitude.

When Aristotle then sees Being as a genus, he does not see their differentness in the way that the most inclusive categorization differs from that which grounds and animates all categorization and speech; and, at the same time, he fails to appreciate their Oneness which the difference covers over in the relationship of 'grounding.' He fails to see how 'genus' belongs to Being in the way that all things belong to Being, but that genus is still not Being in the way that two things are similar. Thus, he does not understand Being as the relationship of belonging together, as itself and in-itself a belonging together which grounds all unification and distinction. He does not appreciate either difference or similarity because he loses sight of how difference and similarity belong to Being: he uses difference and similarity as resources to 'explicate' Being, but he does not address the difference-in-similarity that *is* Being.

Thus, Being is either abstracted as the most general and inclusive category, to which things phenomena, and appearances externally relate (as particular to universal, as indicators to concept), or else, Being is identified with the fullness and detail of concrete characterization, the substance that underlies all predication. In either case, everything that Being is, is withdrawn from it and converted into an environment external to Being itself. That is, the appearances, things, and phenomena (the particulars and predicates) which are used as external 'reflections' of Being are not things external to Being, for these are the ways in which Being announces and presents itself, the ways in which Being emerges, abides, and shines forth.[1] Being discloses itself through itself and through what belongs essentially to it, and *Physis* as the power that emerges marks appearing as the making manifest of Being.

Appearance which usually is related to Being as a sign is related to what it signifies, must be re-experienced as belonging to Being and the difference between appearance and Being is re-experienced as a difference that is One. The question of science is the question of how Being emerges and endures in science, how Being in shining forth through the appearing of science announces its presence. This belonging together of science and Being requires any formulation of science to address its source, and to speak in such a way as to make reference to the sciencing of science. Thus, the idea of a first science or of a science of Being can only occur upon the scaffolding of a notion that has already secured a segregation between Being and science: the idea of a science of Being (as compared to a science of some other thing) can only occur with the segregation of Being from science; and the idea of a first science can only occur when the unitary idea of science is detached from that which owns science, thus creating many sciences. The idea of a first science can only become intelligible when science has been watered down to refer to what men speak of as science, and the notion of a science of Being can only occur when Being has been concretized to refer to the limits of intelligible speech which are personified in a common subject.

There can be no first science because firstness points to Being and the *only* science worth its name is the science involved faithfully in Being. The idea of *a* science of Being re-presents the notion that one particular science takes Being as its object, that one science subjects Being as its matter. This profanes the notion of Being. The only way there can be a first science is to conceive of firstness concretely – whether as object, material cause or agent, or as grammaticality. Then, we could generate first sciences like sociology (which deals with the most inclusive object or matter), like biology or psychology (which deals with the most incorrigible agent), or like linguistics, philosophy, theology, or history (which deal with the most comprehensive concrete causal sources of mere existence).

If science essentially belongs to whatness, the conception of *a* science *of* whatness impoverishes both science and whatness by treating their relation as external and concrete. Thus, Aristotle's conception of science is only intelligible *given* his understanding that science does not essentially belong to whatness – an understanding based upon his observation and description of the concrete practices and usages of

[1] Heidegger, *Introduction* . . ., pp. 92–93.

scientists. In allowing the community of practical men to limit and authorize inquiry, Aristotle turns away from the experience of Being on the grounds of its impracticality. Aristotle converts whatness into a member's problem, and thus succeeds in producing a radical transformation of the Desire to theorize.

VI

'We agree' makes reference to the limits of intelligible speech which *we* (ought) elect to follow. The critical limit is that subject to which we claim responsibility. In this sense, 'we agree' means: we agree on what is first (that speech is first, that there is nothing other than speech because there is no-thing other than speech and no-thing is nothing).

A difference between Plato and others can be discerned in their alternative conceptions of firstness. For Plato, firstness was the Real (or critical) subject – that to which speaking is subject and so, firstness was understood not as the first element in a series contrasts to the subsequent, but in the way that the central contrasts to the peripheral. Firstness pointed to that which acquires its status at first because it includes all others. In contrast, was the idea of firstness as *being first* – as one of the many, a primary element in a whole. Whereas the Good symbolized Plato's notion of firstness (because he understood the first as the 'all'), other notions of firstness were represented in the idea of the 'what' that comes first (thus, identifying firstness with temporality).

The dialectical character of Plato's conception of firstness comprehended in its occurrence the difference between centrality and peripherality (as the difference between Being and nothing) as the critical condition of dialectical limitation. The difference between the same and other was addressed as the difference which is central (critical, first), as the essential.

In contrast, other notions of the criticalness of the first are linked to a conception of firstness as that condition which makes things happen, which make things appear. The first is the thing which makes an other thing appear. Because this idea connects to a concrete notion of action as the appearing of an appearance which is independent of that which it is an appearance of, what is first is the thing that produces the apparent as an independent event. Such a first thing tends to be located in human agencies, methods, or histories which enable concrete events. Man as grammatical possibility, as mind, or as history is the critical subject and that to which man is subject – the Reason of theorizing, the Good – is detached as an irrational fancy.

Moderns limit their speaking in such a decisive way because their use of 'we agree' expresses their commitment to the imperativeness of agreeing itself as the warrantable ground of intelligible speaking. 'We agree' to submit to the requiredness of organizing this very agreement as a communal product; 'we agree' to speak in such a way as to make this organization enforceable.

'We agree' because we need to agree and to affirm this agreement is to appropriate subjects which are likely to mobilize our agreement. What we agree *on* then, is our concerted solution to the problem of the first subject (the subject which is firstness) as the first *topic*. 'We agree' to treat firstness as the topic with the greatest organizing potential; 'we agree' to substitute for the critical subject a topic or discursive theme.

'We agree' then points to our decision to orient thinking to a standard furnished by the conversation (not within the soul) that is concrete social inter-action. We decide to model the thoughtful speaking that is theorizing after inter-action and not the inwardness of what Kierkegaard spoke of as Real action. That to which Aristotle's use of 'we agree' points is the decision of thinking to allow itself to be ruled by a standard of communication. After Plato, thinking thinks of itself as 'communication' and the problem of knowledge becomes a problem of reconciling difference through social interaction as a solution to a *social* problem. To know is to create concrete communities and the science of knowledge is the method of unification. The science of knowledge desires to make community as a concrete product, a complete speech.

'We agree' then makes reference to the requiredness of terminating any possibility of inwardness and faithfulness, a requirement necessitated by all standards of adequate communication. This agreement first shows itself in its limitation of what is critical and first – its delineation of the 'nature' that is first – to that which it can appropriate as a speech, either matter or rules for appropriation themselves.

It is assumed that Socrates was Plato's *description* of the theoretical life and that he served as such 'matter' to re-present Plato's notion of rational discourse as the concrete exchange spoken of as 'dialectic.' A concrete reading of Plato locates his theoretic interest to be in that kind of *method*. Yet, thinking as a conversation within the soul (not a conversation between the two of us) was the faithful inwardness exemplified by the theorist who sought to make his authorial existence answer-to the togetherness of speech and Being. Socrates is an aesthetic metaphor for this togetherness and for the resolve and Desire to address it: the fact that Socrates denigrated writing is as irrelevant as whether Theaetetus sits or flies, for we have to account for Plato's decision to write as a Rational decision. The disparagement of writing put into the mouth of Socrates by Plato the writer is an attack on the kind of speech that is ruled by communicative standards and Socrates is used to symbolize the Desire and truthfulness for which critical speaking aspires. The dialectical character of the Socratic exchange is a metaphor for the contest within the soul called thinking, and it is not a description of a method of communicating. The discourse which Socratic dialectic exemplifies is the discourse of inwardness existing subversively and ironically within the common language, the limits of which this very existence seeks to unmask. Socrates points to the tension and truthfulness of such an existence, rather than heralding the appearance of a new science of communication. His existence is actually used to testify to the extinction of inwardness by any such science.

In Plato, discourse always makes reference to the conversation within the soul. The inwardness of that conversation is dramatized (not described as) through the icon of innumerable mundane social exchanges. The contests personified in such exchanges between Socrates and his interlocutors are icons of the Rational movement of mind as it aspires to display its togetherness with Being in thoughtful speech. Because this movement is not linear all of the interlocutors in the dialogues serve to re-present pressures to which thoughtfulness is always vulnerable and thus, they re-assert the integral connection between true and false speaking as moments in the career of thoughtfulness. Critical speaking is dedicated to *showing* that which is hidden – could bring to bear upon one-self as tests of the Rationality of faithfulness. Critical speaking is dedicated to *showing* that which is hidden – the belonging together of language and Being – and in its very occurrence the writing that is critical aspires to show itself as an instance of the (internal) dialectic between concealment and disclosure which is thoughtful speaking.

Inwardness is the existential correlate of incompleteness (of the otherness of Being to speech) and irony is the method whereby the illusions of the drive for completion are unmasked as the root of every positive speaking claim. In such an unmasking the truth of inwardness is itself proclaimed by showing the self deception of men who in trying to speak like gods forget their humanity. The truth of inwardness is exemplified in such reminding.

4

Ethics/Grammar

I

Science has to be made to confront Nothingness because if science is to be formulated essentially as an instance of firstness, the first is only comprehended dialectically as the contrast between some-thing and nothing. If the sciences are made to differ from one another, they then achieve their analytic character on the basis of what they have in common, and are limited by what each of them generates. In such a conception of science, there is no surpassing.

On the other hand, if science is formulated on the basis of what makes science science – through comparison with non-science – the range of intelligible usages is surpassed through the idea of *Physis* in terms of which science's sciencing is conceived. Thus, the hierarchy of sciences in any but a metaphoric sense is an uncritical convention because it uses the external differences among sciences as a way of addressing what science *is*, instead of seeking to personify this 'is-ness' in the icon of science as the re-presentation of the conflict between thinking and the unthought. A hierarchy of sciences can only be a metaphor for the conversation within the soul that is thinking and not a description of different concrete sciences.

Following Plato, it can be suggested that a science which does not address Being is really no science (although it can facilitate the development of knowledge by drawing the mind away from the concrete).[1]

---

[1] For example, any discipline which forces the thinker to 'exercise pure thought' (see the *Republic*, *op. cit.*, 524b–526c) and to free himself from material objects is to be employed, and the mathematical discipline encourages such a liberation. So, the comment by Socrates in the following exchange is apropos.

'Take our perceptions, then. I can point to some of these which do not provoke thought to reflect upon them, because we are satisfied with the judgement of the senses. But in other cases perception seems to yield no trustworthy result and reflection is instantly demanded.' (*op. cit.*, 521c–531c.)

In other words the mathematical discipline can provoke one to begin to think; this means that those of us who do not recognize the compelling need to reflect upon the unthought are most likely to be aroused to reflectiveness when the senses produce disparities.

Whereas Aristotle formulates science by differentiating the sciences, in doing so he makes the question of Being a question that science can choose to ignore. Since the sciences can only be differentiated by describing them concretely, to differentiate the sciences is not to address a critical conception of science because science is not seen in terms of its firstness or centrality against what is other than science. Concretely the sciences might differ in terms of the subjects which they appropriate, or even in terms of the methods of appropriation, but these distinctions only mask the unity of science with Being, i.e., the belonging-together of science with what is first. Whereas Aristotle sees the similarity of the sciences to lie in the fact that they expose different variations in the achievement of 'common' grammatical possibilities; this is to treat their similarity as a relationship of predication rather than as iconic disclosures of Being.

The descriptive use of the hierarchy of sciences obscures the experience of true thinking which is pointed to in the question – how does science science? – a question that can only be faced by re-thinking science as the re-collecting of itself in itself with what owns it and against the dispersiveness of that which is other than science.[1]

Any notion of science as *how* the sciences differ among themselves hides the authentic unity in which science as a One participates. An analytic notion of science draws an essential contrast between science and non-science as its ground: if science belongs together with what owns it, all ways of depicting science are ways of addressing the question of how science sciences, of how science appears as a manifestation of coming-to-be and as a decision against the dispersiveness of not-science (nothing), or of what is other than science. Science then, ought to be a metaphor for theorizing whereas Aristotle uses it as the *matter* which is a project or method of appropriated speaking.

Aristotle's characterization of the sciences does not formulate science as belonging to Being, it does not formulate science essentially, but

---

'If unity can be satisfactorily apprehended, just by itself, by sight or any other sense, as we said of the finger, then it will not have the quality of drawing the mind towards reality.' (*op. cit.*, 524b–526c.)

The reason why an idea such as 'unity' is important has nothing whatsoever to do with the possible predicates of the idea, or with the ways in which the idea resolves the problem of the one and the many (the particulars to which it relates), but is instead seen in the fact that 'unity' is the type of idea that can 'draw the mind towards reality.' Unity as an idea provokes thought.

[1] See Heidegger, *An Introduction* . . ., *op cit.*,

'Because of this relation between being, unconcealment, appearance, and non-being, the man who holds to being as it opens round him and whose attitude toward the essent is determined by his adherence to being, must take three paths . . . he must bring being to stand, he must endure it *in* appearance *and against* appearance, and he must wrest *both* appearance and being from the abyss of non-being.' (p. 93.)

rather accidentally, in terms of the concrete differences among concretely existing sciences which are then re-grouped as differentia within
a common field. This is to say that to formulate science is to make
reference to science as a One which differs from Being and in this sense,
the formulation addresses the contrast between Being and Nothingness
as a feature of *its* very being.

If an analytic formulation of science addresses how science sciences
(how science is some-thing rather than no-thing), then any formulation
of science raises the question of the essential conflict between science
and non-science. If science is formulated in terms of the subjects it
secures in speech, then what science *is* is formulated concretely rather
than essentially (in terms of what is second rather than first) and the
dialectic between science and non-science (between Being and Not-
Being) is suppressed. What science *is* is then conceived as what these
different sciences – in their concrete differentness – have in common
after Being (their belonging-together with Being) has been revoked.

In Plato, science is addressed in terms of its essential contrast to
what is other than science and science and non-science become metaphors for knowledge and ignorance, i.e., science differs from what is
other than science as thinking differs from the un-thought. Plato's
formulation of science personifies the dialectic between true and false
speaking because everything that is non-science is the un-thought
struggling to think truly. For Aristotle, this dialectic is hidden precisely
because science is formulated in such a way as to be analytically
indistinct from what it is not. Instead, what science *is* is secured and
assumed and within this limit, distinctions and characterizations are
added; but these distinctions never touch what science *is* (what science
ought be to be truly).

Whereas Plato's conception of science is personified in the surpassing
of the un-thought by thought which seeks to enact this Desire,
Aristotle's conception itself personifies the un-thought, since its
formulation of science as concrete difference does not address the
grounds of science itself. While Aristotle's scale of knowledge – as the
movement from sensation to knowledge of causes – *does* make reference
to the grounds of science, this movement is not personified in the
organization of the sciences themselves.[1] In Aristotle, science is a mode
of being that institutionalizes one conversational possibility provided
by the culture, by prescribing a project for appropriating, subjecting,
and unifying through speech. Science uses language to control, rather
than let itself be used by language to show its togetherness with Being.

[1] That is, the organization of the sciences impersonates the movement within
thought; the social organization of the sciences as a system of relating disciplines
is a metaphor for the idealized character of thought as it is depicted in the
movement from its origins in the unthought towards its aspiration to think truly.

Theorizing is a way of speaking that conforms to the requirements of a particular project, a particular method of appropriated speaking. Each science has a form of theorizing appropriate to it and each science then idealizes a mode of appropriated speaking as a standard and intelligible method of subjecting through speech. Yet each method is only constructed on the basis of how it answers-to the particular domain; yet the particular domain (science) is only constructed on the basis of the principles which regulate its (subjected) matter; yet, this sub-jugation can only occur through theorizing; yet . . . underlying all of this is the notion that gets it rolling: the idea that the speech called theorizing can only be constructed on the grounds of a grammar (a sense of intelligible speaking possibilities) and though this grammar is ultimately re-presented as yet another object in the form of categorizes and logic, such a re-presentation never touches what the grammar is.

The implications for the first science are obvious: if metaphysics is (despite its differentness) a science nonetheless, then it participates in the unity of science with that to which it belongs and by contrast to that which is other than science. Yet, to make the topic of whatness the special consideration of the first science is to treat the first science as other than science. With an analytic conception of science, the first science can only differ through its personification of ignorance; since this is not a rational reading of Aristotle, the conception of the first science only shows the pre-supposition of rank ordering the sciences which in itself makes reference to the empirical rather than to the essential character of science. If metaphysics is the first *science* it belongs to the idea of science and to Being as do the other special sciences, they belong as a One; then its characterization as the science which attends to what the others fail to heed is the most concrete kind of characterization, for in principle metaphysics as self-conscious science – as the science of self – only *happens* to be the first science because science has not been formulated as a One. Such a first science can never surpass the concrete limitations of the sciences and must accept as its limit the communal characterization of science. Consequently, the very idea of firstness loses its power because metaphysics is first only in the most concrete sense. Firstness is that which is common to the sciences after Being has been withdrawn. Firstness then means the conscious-ness of what is first, where this 'object' becomes the author-ity of grammar (of the permutational possibilities for intelligible convincing).

The first science is first because it appropriates firstness as its sub-jected matter. Firstness is then concretized to become another object, a common topic. Firstness loses its connection with Being, it is no longer *that* kind of firstness. Science is then concretized because it becomes a way of speaking that lawfully appropriates, it becomes a method for communicating rather than a metaphor for thoughtfulness.

Science loses its connecting to Being. Theory is concretized to become the handmaiden of a particular communicative project as that which conforms to the rule of the method, that which answers-to the sociable impulse of the project. Theory loses its connection to Being.

II

In the opening passages of the *Physica*, Aristotle says:

> When the objects of an inquiry, in any department, have principles, conditions, or elements, it is through acquaintance with these that knowledge, that is to say scientific knowledge, is attained.[1]

That is, that the *objects* of a study *have* 'principles, conditions, elements' raises the question of this relationship of 'having.' The objects *own* principles, conditions, and elements and thus, the objects *are* these principles, conditions, and elements. This is how he can say that it is through 'acquaintance with these' (principles, conditions, *et al.*) that knowledge is attained. In other words, one does not know the objects directly, but only through these principles, and yet 'direct' and 'indirect' are misleading, for in learning these principles one learns the object. The object is not separate from the principles, conditions, and elements like things different in kind though related; the object *is* its principles in the sense that the principles announce the object and belong together with it. The principles, conditions, and elements *show* the object in the sense that through them the object comes to shine forth, they stand in a relation of belonging-together.

If the idea of the object is the idea of what it has or can have, what the object can have is itself authored by a conception of what the object *is*. Consequently, the 'acquaintance' with principles that is attained as knowledge is less the discovery of something new, than a re-constitution of what is there all along, for the principles, conditions, and elements lay within the original conception of the object as its essential possibilities. Though this sounds like *anamnesis* in that the object is *given* as in Plato, it differs in the sense that it is given as a 'what' (as a concrete subject) which has principles, conditions, and elements. This relation of *having* expresses the way in which the object belongs to its nature. The 'whatness' of the objects consists of these possibilities, its 'whatness' is its grammaticality, that it can be intelligible and distinctly characterized as 'principles' 'conditions' and 'elements.'

[1] *Physica, op. cit.,* 184a.

99

To know is to attain an acquaintance with what the object owns (its principles, conditions, and elements) and not of that which owns the object. But the knower is also owned by the object in the sense that his knowing can only follow a path laid down by the object (by what there is to be known as principles, conditions, and elements). Yet if the knower follows a path laid down by the object (by what the object *is*), it is the knower who creates and constitutes the object through his understanding. That the knower is owned by the object as his creation means that the knower is ruled by him-self, for the originary conception of the object makes reference to the limits of intelligible inquiry as furnished by the inquirer him-self. That is, though the inquirer begins with the object to be known as the object upon which theorizing will reflect, this very beginning is an achievement of theorizing itself. Aristotle's programme of theorizing will re-capitulate the history of his theorizing; but instead of recognizing this *anamnesis*, Aristotle speaks of his programme as 'serious' while collapsing this history under the conventions of the 'we agree.'

Because the knower cannot know *more* than what the object owns (i.e., the very notion of 'more' is external to the domain of the object), what the knower attains will be what *he* authored: he will acquire an acquaintance with self as the source of the object. Thus, one could say that we learn to know the objects or the principles only superficially, for what we display through an apprehension of the principles is a re-cognition of self. Only superficially do the principles constitute the medium for apprehending the *object*, for deeply, the principles *qua* object constitute the medium through which the self of the inquirer comes to appear. Yet, this risks overlooking the fact that both author and object are creations of grammaticality, that the author re-discovers the object *in* 'principles,' 'conditions,' and 'elements' of the combinatorial possibilities of a grammar. It is the achievement of the grammar that the 'we agree' masks and it is this achievement which his writing ought to re-create as an achievement by evoking the contest within the soul to which it makes reference in what he writes *about*.

The object is conceived as a determinant whole and what is given is the object as a determinant whole with knowable features (principles, conditions, and elements). What this relationship *says* about the object is not knowable in the sense that the very conception of the object (as a determinant whole with knowable features) is already a bringing to appearance of the relationship between knower and that from which the object is wrested (Being). The appearance of the object makes manifest the belonging together of thought and Being and this is what the object shows; yet, what the object shows (says) is covered over in our haste to acquaint ourselves with its features.

For we do not think that we know a thing until we are acquainted with its primary conditions or first principles and have carried our analysis as far as its simplest element.[1]

These principles, conditions, and elements now appear as primary (first) and simple. Their simplicity resides in their firstness. *They are the first principles in the same way that metaphysics is the first science.* Their simplicity consists *not* in the ease with which we can re-discover them, but in their unconditioned character (that they are not derivative). There are many icons of the first principles, but the first is that which cannot be an icon; although this relationship holds *within* the special sciences, when the sciences are related to one another their respective 'first principles' all become icons of 'firstness-in-general.'

Thus, 'we think that we know a thing' when we are acquainted with these (primary, first) principles and conditions and 'have carried our analysis as far as its simplest elements' could be construed as Aristotle's comment upon an opinion: we think we know a thing when we are acquainted with its first and simple principles – but how wrong we are! But plainly, 'we think' serves not as an ironic contrast but as an authoritative proclamation: 'we think we know a thing' means 'we agree that we know a thing . . .' where 'we agree' serves to root our beginning. Thus, the power of the 'we agree' becomes even sharper. 'We agree that we know a thing . . .' as irony would provide the 'we agree' with the function of segregating 'they' from 'me' through the descriptive character of 'we agree.' As ironic contrast this use of 'we agree' parallels the inventory of opinions and by intending itself descriptively, it differentiates what *they* do from what we ought do. On the other hand, the present use is not ironic, for it solidifies 'they' and 'me' in a unity that is sanctioned as authoritative. In this case, the device is rhetorical since if it actually depicted *what we do in concrete cases*, he would have no need to write. In this case, 'we agree' speaks of what we do as seen from the vantage point of one who grasps the Logos, it idealizes what we concretely do as a Rational typification and imposes this structure upon the work as an authoritative assumption and starting point. This assumption concealed by the 'we agree' is not a neutral limitation or 'premise,' but is an authoritative declaration of a direction to follow concealed as an 'assumption'; what the assumption does say is that we would (should, ought) agree if we grasped the Logos of theorizing as the author does. So in the present case, the status of knowledge as being acquainted with primary conditions *et al.*, could describe the ordinary opinion of the many as contrasted with Aristotle's position and the 'we agree' would be principally critical; yet, he uses the convention to typify the unity between the many and him-self as the only Rational starting point; so it is not a description of this unity

[1] *Ibid.*, 184a.

as much as a way of making reference to a typical authoritative programme. The use of 'we agree' cannot be both descriptive and include Aristotle because that would leave him without a Reason for speaking (he would be a parrot of common sense) and consequently it would not provide for the primordial distinction between convention and knowledge. 'We agree' is Aristotle's device for *leading* men to re-collect the unity which their mouthings cover over by forcing them to start with what he knows, or to believe and trust what he knows. This use of 'we agree' is an appeal to faith and a stipulation for suspending disbelief; it essentially says, withdraw doubt at this point and trust me. This is after all, the deep structure of the notion of an 'assumption.'

Aristotle's theoretical programme, like Plato's and in contrast to that of Descartes and the modern tradition, begins in faith and trust; this trust is suspended on the classical ground of the authoritativeness and responsibility of the teacher as a speaker. In Plato, this trust is used as a resource for deepening and re-surrecting the notion of trust itself; whereas for Aristotle, this trust is secured as a point from which to begin, but is never itself re-explored or deepened. Trust becomes a conventional resource for Plato in his examination of the grounds of trust itself, while for Aristotle trust becomes an 'assumption' both secure and authoritative. It is only with Descartes that this trust becomes radicalized as itself the authority for the programme, thus re-presenting the loss of any opportunity to re-constitute trust as an authentic unity.

> The natural way of doing this (inquiry) is to start from the things which are most knowable and obvious to us and proceed towards those which are clear and more knowable by nature.[1]

'The natural way' could be heard as a critique of the natural way, but this would obscure its analytic character: since the natural way is to proceed in this way, let us follow the natural way; let us think in a way that conforms to the natural way (to the way we think empirically, conventionally). Since the way we think is by starting with what is obvious and clear *to us* and by moving to what is clear and obvious by nature, we move from what is obvious to what is remote and hidden. Since the remoteness (of nature) of whatness has already been identified as the 'primary and simple,' we move from what is obvious to what is primary and simple. We move from what is later to what is first, from what is peripheral to what is central. Thus, the simplicity of the primary cannot reside in its obviousness but in its underlying and indivisible character, though primary and simple, the first is hidden. The way we think is to move from the obvious to the covered-over, so let our programme re-present this movement, i.e., let it facilitate our search

[1] *Ibid.*, 184a.

for the simple which lies covered over by the obvious. Yet as we have said this is 'the way we think' as formulated in terms of the Rational interest of the theorist and *not* as a re-production of the ways in which members characterize their thinking. That this is the 'natural' way we think means that it is the only way to think – the primary and first way – and even though it is the primary and first way, it is hidden from 'us.' It is hidden from us but not from 'me.'

> So in the present inquiry we must follow this method and advance from what is more obscure by nature but clear to us, towards what is more clear by nature.
> Now what is to us plain and obvious at first is rather confused masses, the elements and principles of which become known to us later by analysis.[1]

Thus, in an important respect the unity of Plato and Aristotle can be discerned in *both* the notion of knowing as a kind of *anamnesis*, and in the character of *anamnesis* as a critique of what is at first 'obvious and clear' to us through a search for its origins which lie covered over. But, this conception of knowing itself covers over the two contrasting possibilities which we come to understand as Plato and Aristotle. Aristotle's reason for following this method is its conformity to 'the way we think' and therefore, it acquires its rationality as an instance of communal practice. Yet there is an ambivalence, for what is clear and obvious to us is (at first) 'confused masses' and so, what is clear and obvious is really confusing. If what is clear and obvious to us is (really) confusing, then we make the mistake of confusing the confusing with the clear and obvious. Thus, *we* are only metaphorically used as a standard, for *we* mistake the 'confusing mass' for the clear and obvious: obviously analysis (as sanctioned by this programme) will seek to re-construct what *we* start with (the clear and obvious) by showing how – in its clarity – it obscures the intricate and covered-over. *We* take the remote for the obvious because we do not have the programme, we do not know how to distinguish, sort, and reduce. The task of analysis is to reduce and clarify 'confused masses' by making transparent the relationships which it covers over.

That what we treat as 'clear and obvious' is *not* clear and obvious is only possible through Aristotle's differentiation from the 'they'; *they* treat as clear and obvious what is (really) 'confused masses,' and it requires 'we' to recognize their treatment for what it is. What 'they' regard as obvious – as trustworthy – is something other than it appears for one who adopts the attitude of the programme. Not that what they trust – these objects – are untrustworthy or are to be doubted, for the objects are trustworthy; what they trust is them-selves and *they* are

[1] *Ibid.*, 184a.

untrustworthy as witnesses because they do not have the programme. What is required is not distrust of the object, but a distrust of self and a transfer of authority to the programme.

The programme will allow *them* to see the object not as spurious, but to understand their conceptions of the object as icons or reflections (re-presentations) of the Real object (its first principles, primary conditions, and simple elements). *They* see confused masses because they do not treat the object as an icon of those principles, or better, they do not see their object as a reflection of the theoretic object. Note then, the use of *anamnesis* in Aristotle: to initiate his programme, he has to assume principles as icons of original objects, while theorizing begins with the re-cognition of the object as an icon of its principles; thus, to become acquainted with the principles is to 'know' the object of which the principles are icons, and this pre-supposes the capacity to treat the object as itself an icon of first principles. When one grasps the principles, one re-collects the object as the relationships between simple elements.

The ideal of 'grasping principles' as a goal of theorizing radically differentiates Aristotelian and Platonic uses of *anamnesis* because such a 'grasp' points to the capacity to complete a synthesis in speech. To grasp principles is to be able to satisfy one-self through a communicative method, to be able to communicate to one-self, to convince one-self ethnically. To grasp principles is to assimilate objects to a law, to be able to stand with the objects under the law (to understand). Although all theorizing seeks to convince itself (and therein lies its rationality), to grasp principles is to be able to grasp the way in which an object is organized in discourse, it is to be able to convince one-self *as one would an other* by totalizing the speech as a distinct and discrete object, it is to be able to fit the object into the categorization nexus of grammar, to adapt the object to grammatical possibilities. If *anamnesis* terminates in the 'grasp of principles,' such a grasp says nothing less than this: that the goal of theorizing is to produce commodities. *Anamnesis* in Aristotle is mathematical, for the idea of limit contrasts 'principles' from what is other than principles on the basis of what we can productively speak: the limiting character of a principle is provided by the organizational capacity of speech to combine and de-compose in a way that is intelligible and agreeable to all, in a way that satisfies conversational standards of adequate communication. The firstness of this kind of principle is equivalent to its concreteness even though its achievement is an 'abstraction' and all of Aristotle's 'abstractions' are essentially concrete.

The task of analysis is *not* to radically question these principles (the object itself) or the understanding on which it is grounded, but by beginning with this understanding, to explicate and reduce it. To question the understanding itself is really to show no sense of moderation, it is to seek to argue endlessly.

> For just as the geometer has nothing more to say to one denies the principles of his science – this being a question for a different science or for one common to all – so a man investigating principles cannot argue with one who denies their existence.
>
> We physicists . . . must take for granted that the things that exist by nature are. . . . Moreover, no man of science is bound to solve every kind of difficulty that may be raised, but only as many as are drawn falsely from the principles of the science.[1]

The principles are then secure and to question the principles radically is to fail to respect the limit. However, if metaphysics is the science which legitimately questions principles, the 'metaphysical passage' interspersed between these comments shows the same respect. For example, that 'the principles in question must be either . . . one or . . . more than one,' and the discussion which this entails, recommends that Aristotelian metaphysics accepts the limits of an apparatus for generating intelligible questions, i.e., that these questions (one vs. more than one, finite vs. infinite plurality) are only intelligible for members. Note in this respect, Aristotle's critique of Pamenides:

> The same kind of argument holds good against Parmenides also . . . the answer to him being that '*this* is not true' and '*that* does not follow'. His assumption that one is used in a single sense only is false *because it is used in several* (my italics).[2]

What is 'false' about Parmenides here is his 'assumption' that one is used in a single sense and its falseness lies in the fact that one 'is used in several senses.' This comment treats Parmenides as if he was concerned to describe or re produce ordinary usage: as if Parmenides *assumed* that one is used in one sense (whereas in contrast, he proclaimed that it *ought* to be used in one sense). The falseness of Parmenides is located in his failure to conform to ordinary usage, but this standard itself is never questioned. Thus, Aristotle says of him:

> His conclusion does not follow, because if we take only white things, and if 'white' has a single meaning, nonetheless what is white will be many and not one. For what is white will not be one either in the sense that it is continuous or in the sense that it must be defined in only one way.[3]

The only arguments which Aristotle can bring to bear on Parmenides are arguments from ordinary usage: that what is called 'white' by the many recommends that white cannot have a single meaning. Further-

[1] *Ibid.*, 185a.
[2] *Ibid.*, 186a.
[3] *Ibid.*, 186a.

more, Aristotle says that because whiteness differs from 'what *has* whiteness' as the analytic differs from the concrete, Parmenides' notion that there is only whiteness overlooks this distinction. On the other hand, because Parmenides' distinction respects this difference as a difference *qua* difference (as a belonging-together of being with Being), it is Aristotle who treats the concrete difference as analytic and Parmenides who sees through this with his striking metaphor. Again, Aristotle's objection that whiteness *need not* be defined in only one way mistakes Parmenides' speech for an empirical description of usage in exactly the same way that Thrasymachus takes Socrates' conception of ruler (and in the same way that Aristotle himself re-interprets the Socratic notion of pleasure, Plato's idea of form, and just about everything else Plato spoke). Aristotle wants to protect the resonances of common culture by preserving them in a speak-able format and thus, he licences himself to re-form the Desire to theorize into a communal resource. Therefore, the unity between Plato and Aristotle differentiates at precisely these points: that Aristotle conceives of *anamnesis* concretely as an analyst's completion of the looseness of speech which is conceived as incomplete because it is inexact, and that the 'critical' character of this re-construction is displayed in its impulse to replace the 'confused and obvious' with explicit re-statements of the relationships between simple principles, conditions, and elements which the 'confused and obvious' cover over. Yet, this impulse to correct the conventional is essentially an instance of the conventional itself, for the re-statement is controlled at every step by the constraint of 'what is clear and obvious to us,' only the typical 'us' is the rational member who commands the intelligible possibilities of speech re-viewed as a calculus.

III

The symmetry between the theorizing depicted in Aristotle's programme and the experience through which the programme becomes possible is seen in the following way: if a grasp of the object *as* its principles constitutes inquiry, then Aristotle's programme requires grasping the object as the icon of these principles. The programme is not merely secured by the ontology, but the ontology is an achievement of the programme. Aristotle is then teaching the programme to those who do not know the ontology and consequently *must* induce the suspension of disbelief. Yet his students are ignorant of the ontology only in the sense that they are not acquainted with its primary principles, conditions, and elements, for they live within the ontology and trust it, even though upon inspection it (would) appears to them as 'confused masses.' To teach them the ontology pre-supposes then, a grasp of his programme and to teach them his programme pre-supposes their (theoretic) grasp of the ontology (which secures the programme). They must be forced to accept the ontology rather than the programme on faith because the ontology cannot even be faced without mediation through the programme and such an attempt to face the ontology 'directly' could not even be comprehended because ontology can only be faced through speech. Thus, the programme acquires primordial relevance, in that through its mastery one comes to exemplify the ontology; the programme is designed to exemplify the ontology, for the ontology provides its support.

Therefore the experience of learning to theorize must exemplify the re-experience of the achievement of the ontology. Aristotle's programme assumes the security of the ontology and that men are regularly deflected from interrogating the ontology through the convention of the 'we agree' on the grounds that movement through the programme will re-enact the achievement of the ontology. This achievement is then a promise which the programme holds out, and it is only in this sense that a programme succeeds; the success of the programme lies in its capacity to re-produce the experience of the achievement of the ontology on which it is grounded as an instance of the selfsame ontology. The success of the programme does not lie in its accuracy or fidelity in speaking 'what exists' because all such descriptions only re-affirm the authority of the ontology as secure and limiting. The success of the programme consists in its making reference to such authority as a typical instance of the programme itself.

Thus, Aristotle's ontology of objects *as* principles, conditions, and elements is itself the securing of an object – the object *as* principles, conditions, and elements, is the object which Aristotle secures. When masked under the 'we agree' or when concealed as an 'assumption' or as 'a matter of faith,' *this* object can only be 'confused masses.' Yet, since submitting this object to 'analysis' only re-capitulates the programme licenced by the selfsame object, *this* object does not have to be isolated for analysis because any object will do. So *this* object is not made transparent by speaking about it or by making it a concrete subject. Rather, to make this object a subject is to treat every inquiry as a way of referencing this object as that authority which every inquiry affirms.

However, since such affirmation can never do more than re-assert the authority of this object, unless it impersonates the experience of this object as an achievement it can only re-affirm the authority of the ontology. Aristotle's object-and-principles as his primordial object is according to his own programme the 'confused masses' of an original object which re-flects and re-presents *its* primary principles, conditions, and elements (where these principles, conditions, and elements are a metaphor for Being), Aristotle's ontology is itself an icon of an 'object' (a theoretic object) which it covers over. This is to say that the object called 'Aristotle's ontology' is – on his own programme – a re-presentation of what is authentically 'first' (either as 'first object' or as its 'primary conditions, first causes, and simple elements'). Yet, his programme of inquiry fails to treat his ontological object in the way that he recommends objects be treated – as an icon or re-presentation of what lies covered over.

Thus, Aristotle's ontology as itself an 'object' is treated as if it is not an icon, as if it is the unconditioned first, as if *it* was the Good. Aristotle treats his theory as it was Being, Aristotle the genius treats him-self as God rather than as a man. Consequently, Aristotle invokes the convention of the 'we agree' whenever the iconic character of his object (his 'theory' as an object) is introduced into discussion as a possible topic. Because Aristotle silences such a concern, he can only treat his ontology as secure and authoritative and his programme as descriptive; consequently, Aristotle's students are prevented from re-experiencing his monumental achievement of wresting his object (ontology) from Being as the experience which underlies his speech as the only experience worth speaking. As Aristotle insulates his students from that which is worth speaking – from the re-experience of *Physis* through which Aristotle's very intelligibility and authority comes to be – his programme at every instance suppresses this experience.

Note then, it is not being said that Aristotle fails to *describe* his ontology, or that he fails to engage in self-characterization, for such exercises only preserve the authority and sanctity of the programme under the auspices of which his description and self-characterization become intelligible. It is not that Aristotle fails to be 'reflexive' as that term is used by moderns; reflexivity as description and self-charac-terization only 're-flects' the authority which licences it to reflect. Rather, Aristotle does not use his speech to re-enact and to impersonate the experience in terms of which his very authority is authorized. Aristotle must show in his writing the achievement of the 'grasp of principles' which constitutes his theory; or, he must show how his theory as the ideal 'grasp of principles' finds itself in its movement from original 'confused masses' on every occasion of its use.

Aristotle shows how science belongs to whatness and his notion of whatness is an achievement of science; Aristotle then shows how science belongs to itself. In the idiom, Aristotle identifies whatness with his concrete ontology and thus, in showing how science belongs to whatness he shows how science belongs to his ontology. Therefore, Aristotle shows how science belongs to him-self; such a demonstration amounts to showing how Aristotle (as whatness, ontology) belongs to science in the sense that whatness in the form of ontology (as Aristotle's ontology) can only be transformed into 'world view', 'weltanschaaung' or 'perspective.' Aristotle does not provide for the re-experience of this unity between science and 'weltanschaaung' as itself a bringing of whatness to appearance, because that would point to a firstness beyond science, ontology, and weltanschaaung, to an authentic whatness which this conventionalization conceals. Aristotle's notion of whatness can only transform Being into the epistemological conception of self-consciousness, or into the sociological idea of 'weltanschaaung,' world view, or common culture. Note for example, how Aristotle's very conception of the modalities of change – as seen in the *Physica*[1] – is grounded in his understanding of the possible patterns of predication and of the 'ways in which we speak.' For example, his notion of change as being *from* something *to* something is itself based upon the way in which we speak. His rationale for deciding upon his various types of change such as qualitative, quantitative, and local, i.e., alteration, diminution and growth, and locomotion, is based upon an analysis of language, or as he says, upon 'how we speak.' Though his notion of 'how we speak' masks his ideal, this ideal is never extra-ordinary (it *looks* extra-ordinary only because of the density and concreteness of the distinctions which his grammatical method generates). Aristotle's commitment looks extra-ordinary because his method is so productive and therein lies its ordinariness. Aristotle never touches the Real and critical simplicity of firstness, of whatness.

Aristotle consistently begins with 'how things are said to be' and his *Physica* is an explication (rationalization) of our ways of speaking. To rationalize our ordinary speech is to limit our attention to the rules and procedures of speaking. Thus, he provides for ordinary language analysis by refusing to transcend the limits of ordinary language. Therefore, although he is not doing science, he provides the grounds for all of the sciences.

Since all of Aristotle's distinctions are controlled by how we speak – 'what we say' – he is not describing, but rather, explicating our speaking practices in his various descriptions. He multiplies distinctions without listening to what the speech says. This is how 'scholarship' gets started: the differences he locates do not resonate; rather, he displays intelligence as a mind that can grasp most of the distinctions and inter-relations recognized as intelligible in an ordinary language. Intelligence comes to be synonymous with the competent use of the resources of history and culture, i.e., the member who can generate 'data.' Consequently the *Physica* is just as much an icon of his conception of theorizing as is his logic: both are based upon his conception of Rationality as the explication of ordinary discourse, as the science of discourse.

[1] *De Interpretation*, I.

In Aristotle's world, there are types of objects and co-responding principles, conditions, and elements. Although objects and principles are One, it is only possible to speak *about* objects through principles and they are discriminated for practical purposes. The types of objects or natures or things are conceived as substances, and he elects to identify three principle types of things (which conveniently provide for three 'departments' or fields of study). Since each type of thing owns its distinctive special principles, conditions, and elements, and since these co-respond or answer to the type of thing to which they belong, each field (and thing) is identified on the basis of principles, conditions, and elements which follow the sorting principle for things. Things have their *own* principles. Since the things exist, these principles are icons of things in that they re-produce links among the phenomena of nature.

To find the causes – the primary principle – for each type of thing is to re-discover the thing. Yet, one requires some medium for mediating the relationship between self and thing – the relationship called 'knowing' – and this relationship is depicted in the matching of speech to things through reasoned discourse about principles, conditions, and elements. Such speech makes reference to knowing because knowing is an increasing acquaintance with causes and principles and this 'acquaintance' is *shown* in speech about causes, principles, conditions, and elements. Analysis is the reasoned speaking of conditions, elements, principles, and relationships where 'reason' refers to statements of relationship between terms and combinations of terms that are assumed by fiat to exemplify formal relations among items of nature (the relations among elements, conditions, and principles internal to the thing). The links within speech are designed to re-produce the links among items of nature not in the sense of 'assumptions,' but as a sanctionable normative order of speaking to which speech is required to comply. This normative order of correct speaking crystallizes in three different ways (i.e., makes three contrasting sets of speaking demands) depending upon the type of thing (and principles) that are being spoken about. Each of these normative orders is organized around a different conception of adequate demonstration and proof as a different conception of relatedness between elements.

The ontology then generates types of things, types of causes, and criteria of necessity, i.e., types of things and of their relationships, and is grounded in the sub-position that controlled discourse will re-produce the primary and natural relationships internal to a thing through relationships between elements of discourse; the connection between things and speech is then guaranteed through the rationalization of speech as an idealization of the relationships internal to things.

Yet, the relationship between speech and things is mediated by thought.

Spoken words are the symbols of mental experience and written words are the symbols of spoken words. Just as all men have not the same writing, so all men have not the same speech sounds, but the mental experiences, which these directly symbolize, are the same for all, as also are those things of which our experiences are the images.[1]

Although he concretely discriminates between thoughts, speech, and writing he uses speech as the decisive and critical paradigm of the conversation within the soul. This is to say that Aristotle conceives of the conversation within the soul as concrete speech rather than speech's way of evoking its essential secondness.

If we treat speech generically as speaking *and* writing, we see that despite the differences in speech, it nevertheless re-produces a unified mental experience. That is, speech re-produces thought, and thought re-produce things, i.e., speech-thought-things stand in a relationship of icon to original. Certain consequences then become apparent. Speaking *about* causes and principles is speaking about things and ways of speaking are tied essentially to kinds of things. The kinds of things tend to be known (through sensation or laid down) and the act of producing kinds of things as known and their possible principles is not a topic for the practitioner but is shown through speech. Furthermore, thoughts depict things (standardly, without interference) and speech orients to these thoughts and is thus controlled by these thoughts. Speech which orients to thought is speech which *says* what is because the ideal course of thought is thought which is at one with things (not as a goal to be achieved but as a given). Thus, though Aristotle starts with the idea of speech relating to an ideal course of thought, because this orientation can only be spoken in certain standard ways *thought must come itself to orient to these standard speaking possibilities*. This is one sense in which thinking subjects itself to grammatical requirements. The notion of critique in this programme is then reflected in the attempt to subject this grammar itself to analysis; yet given the notion of analysis it can only become another subjected (matter) object.

That is, while the image of the relation of speech to thought to things suggests that speech is under the control of thinking, note in his quote how he standardizes the experience of things and thought, while locating the crucial source of variability in speech (writing and speaking

[1] For a nice discussion of the differences between the logics of Plato and Aristotle, Cornford's translation of *The Sophist* should be consulted, especially 253c–254b; and for just the opposite – a conventional and concrete conception of Plato's logic – see the standard history of W. & M. Neale, *The Development of Logic*, Oxford: Oxford University Press, 1962, pp. 17–23. Imaginative discussions are contained in the following two books: E. Kapp, *Greek Foundations of Traditional Logic*, New York: Columbia University Press, 1942 and R. E. Allen, *Plato's 'Euthyphro' and the Earlier Theory of Forms*, London: Routledge & Kegan Paul, 1970, see especially Chapter 3, parts 1, 2, 3.

sounds vary from man to man). It is speech that must be controlled and error and inaccuracy (false speaking/false thinking) can only be attributed to the fact that our speech has not been submitted to Rational control. But, this control will not be provided by thought, for thought only thinks within speech itself: consequently, speech must be rationalized to meet the requirements of an authoritative notion of true speaking. The reform is internal to speech itself. Speech which is an icon of thoughtfulness (of the thoughtful grasp of things) is oriented to as that which is first. Speech becomes the critical subject, the foundation or firstness. The question which will differentiate Aristotle from subsequent thinkers despite their common subjection of speech as the first will articulate in their different formulations of this subject.

The rationalization of speech then occurs in conformity with the authoritative programme for rationalization sanctioned by the project. That is, speech itself must be 'analyzed' as a thing with its distinctive principles, conditions, elements, and types of demonstration and proof. So, instead of asking how do we know if thought de-picts things? in the sense of 'are we certain?' (for we can never be certain since no test for things independent of thought exists), we then ask the following question: given this unity, can we make it intelligible and speakable? Consequently, an authoritative standard of intelligible speech comes to rule. In contrast an alternative query might ask: given that we *can* speak about this unity (about things) is this worth speaking? Does our speech (about things) belong together with the Desire to speak truly? or, does it deny and cover over such a possibility? In neither case, is it questioned that speech re-produces things (this is a modern tactic) but rather, we either seek to rationalize and solidify this unity through a science of discourse (Aristotle), or we seek to make it transparent as a negation of Desire (Plato). It is the relation of speech to what is other than speech that ought to be the concern and not the relation of speech to things or of thought to things (which are relations between speeches). We want to accept the relatedness of speech to things (or of thought – re-presented in speech – to things) as a necessary condition of our humanity.

Given that thought de-picts things, what kind of speech will rationalize this relationship? It will be speech which typifies rational thought (the thought which is at one with what it thinks, with things). The syllogism re-creates this unity of thought/things in discourse (speech). The syllogism preserves this unity by making it explicit and intelligible; it makes manifest what one is talking about from within the limits of this unity. Discourse mirrors thought, which in its turn mirrors things, and the science of discourse will re-produce the science of things. Yet, this science still treats discourse as itself a thing (the science of logic), for it does not provide for the re-experience of the unity between thought and things as itself an achievement. Furthermore, it secures this unity (as in the 'we agree'), and within its terms treats speech as a network of determinant assertions. Discourse is then treated as itself an object (the kind of thing that is an assertion) with its internal principles, conditions, and elements (i.e., with its words in isolation and combination, its categories, terms, premises and conclusions), and with its own conditions of necessity and relatedness. Aristotle has to destroy the thoughtfulness of speaking in order to produce a science of speaking.

Thus, discourse as an object is formulated in terms of the kind of thing that is an assertion, with principles, conditions, and elements that make reference to terms, categories, and propositions, and with conditions of analysis and necessity that are specified by that which a syllogism and deduction recommend achieving. The logic which is developed as a method for proving, enumerating and describing what the ontology lays down as a problem is actually developed within the limits of the ontology and only demonstrates and describes elliptically because it is an instance of the ontology. The logic is not a method independent of the ontology which is *then* applied to it; but it re-presents the further extension of the ontology to discourse as a topic. Thus, if the main problem is knowing, knowing is only de-picted within the world of the ontology and the re-experience of the *ontology* as itself an instance of knowing is suppressed.

To make the ontology an intelligible topic is to address it to the science of discourse (and it is to be a user of such a science), and yet the ontology itself (the ideas of substance, types of things, types of principles and causes, of what there is) is developed through an analysis of discourse (a notion of intelligible, relevant speech). The science of discourse re-presents a re-construction or formalization of ordinary, communal discourse as description and proof – as analysis. Thus, the topic of the science of discourse is ordinary discourse considered as a thing (and not things and principles external to speech) under the assumption that speech re-produces (thoughts of) things.

The syllogism does not exemplify the movement within the soul because it does not exemplify the achievement of the unity between thought and things upon which *it* depends. The syllogism *shows* through its every move its security in the grip of the ontology. For example, the notions of identity and contradiction upon which the syllogism rests, and of the subject-predicate unity, raise the problem of how terms belong together, i.e., of belonging-together in speech. The syllogism hides the experience of the original gathering and disclosure of the unity between thought and things upon which it is based. This is not to say that the syllogism fails to prove or describe this unity, but rather that it 'hides' the experience of this unity by continually re-asserting and re-affirming this unity behind the mask of discovery and demonstration. Rational thought is thought which permits itself to be ruled by the science of discourse. Thought submits to the project of rational speech rather than vice versa. Since the project of rational speech is based upon the ontology (which in its turn is grounded in the conventional and ordinary forms of understanding), thought is ruled by the conventional understanding which is masked in the science of discourse. Thought is responsible for making it-self intelligible in terms of this understanding and thus, thought is segregated from that which this understanding covers over. Thinking and Being are divorced: thinking only thinks what it allows itself to be authorized to think, i.e., thinking only thinks the range of intelligible possibilities sanctioned by communal linguisticality. Thinking cannot think beyond this because the very notion of *beyond* (intelligible possibility) is un-intelligible (impossible). To say that rational thought respects its ontology (in this way) is to say that 'rationality' is an achievement of the kind of thought that exemplifies the highest development of the conventional understanding of speech and discourse. Adequate thinking is that which exemplifies adequate communication. Rational thought is self-conscious in the sense that it is conscious of where it is (it knows its environment and limit, it knows its place), i.e., it is conscious of its position (its status as a re-presentation of common culture). Rational thought *knows* that its success in speaking under the auspices of the science of discourse serves to re-enact the success of the science *and* of the understanding (culture) on which it is based. The achievement of this rationality is an affirmation of common membership.

The science of discourse re-duplicates the vague and confused communal conception of the world (the conception that produces the ontology – things, principles, conditions, elements, etc.), but in a sense, this is misleading because the ontology is actually quite sophisticated. It is better to say that the science of discourse is there all along co-existing within ordinary thought and providing for the ontology itself as a possibility, for the ontology *has* to be a result of the science. How is the science of discourse possible? asks how its re-statement in the *Analytic* re-presents its original achievement? How does discourse (reflect upon) speak about itself in order to generate the science with which it begins? Discourse discourses (about itself). The question asks not for what is the essence of discourse as assertions, terms, categories, propositions, syllogism? But, how does discourse essence? An answer to this question cannot be the recitation of causes or principles because in the absence of these causes and principles discourse does not dissolve into nothing (into chatter). Thus, Aristotle's science of discourse does not even address what discourse *is* and how it comes to *be*, but differentiates correct from incorrect speaking within a universe of discourse sanctioned by an unexplored conventional conception (of grammaticality) of the limits and possibilities of discourse. What discourse *is* is then identified with his version of correct discourse. The problem is to make reference (in his very science of discourse) to the way in which his science surfaces (discourses) through its essential struggle with what is other than discourse (chatter). The science of discourse should show how it emerged out of the ordinary resources of linguisticality as violent struggle: if there was no struggle, then he had the science all along, but since this is impossible he had to actualize the possibility by wrenching it from the ordinary notion of discourse. Again Aristotle hides his achievement under the mask of genius. Thus, the ordinary notion is *essential* to the achievement of the science because they belong together and together they contrast with chatter (with non-discourse).

Note in this respect in the first section of the *Physica*[1] how Aristotle's conception of speech provides for a notion of the field, and though he takes the object for granted, the object appears already as the result of analysis. Thus, the science of discourse must show not only how it speaks about things, but how it produces things to speak about, and thus, how in its speech *about* things (analysis) it makes essential reference to the thinking experience which produced the things.

Its speech *about* must use that which is spoken about (the object or subject) as an icon of the experience which resulted in its achievement (the achievement of the object). Consequently, its speech *about* should make reference to how the speech wrenched it-self from the unity of linguistic possibility. This is what is meant by the question – how does discourse discourse? Aristotle's failure to face such a problem results from his subjectitude to a rational standard of communication derived from an external image of relations among different men rather than from the *experience* of theorizing.

IV

The possibility for the relationships among the sciences are more transparent. We suggested that the special sciences relate to the first science as parts of speech relate to the whole or complete speech, or in general, as self-conscious discourse stands to discourse which is un-thought. If 'self-conscious' is understood as the 'attitude' of theorizing it would include every kind of philosophy yet invented.

[1] See the discussion of types of change in *Physica, op. cit.*

We have also suggested by implication that these very relationships – between self-conscious and un-self-conscious discourse – are rooted in Aristotle's conception of subject-predicate relations where the special sciences relate to the first science as predicates relate to an underlying subject (or as particular to universal). Now, we have further pointed out that the special sciences relate to the first science as the 'confused masses' of the original object (known or trusted by us) relate to the first principles, primary conditions, and simple elements of which they are icons. Consequently, the relationship between the special sciences and the first science deeply exemplifies the movement of theorizing from the obvious to the hidden and covered over.

Yet, if the formulation of science is itself an icon of the activity of theorizing, the description of science should impersonate that experience. We have tried to show how any description of science in terms of the differences among sciences actually conceals that experience. Instead, Aristotle provides us with a characterization of what these different sciences have in common *after* this experience has been revoked, i.e., after the unity of the sciences as an appearing of Being has been withdrawn. Consequently his characterization has to locate what is common to the concrete practices of the sciences. The commonality shared by the sciences is their attempt(s) to speak intelligibly, so the *fact* of their speaking is taken as their commonality and the criterion of correct speaking is imported as that to which their speech ought be faithful. The power of this 'ought' resides in its status as a theorists' re-construction of what they actually do.

Thus, self-consciousness deeply differentiates the first science from the special sciences and this self-consciousness means: consciousness that the part of speech is a partial speech (a perspective) which is re-cognized from the perspective that the collection of parts completes speech (making speech first). To be self-conscious about speech is then to be able to distinguish between speech as an object known to us (as 'confused masses') and speech as a theoretic object (as primary conditions, first principles, and simple elements). To be a theorist is to be able to treat the partiality of speech as if it could be completed, i.e., to have in hand a science of discourse which provides for the intelligibility of discourse as a *thing* with its distinctive principles and types of demonstration and proof.

To be a theorist is to have the science of discourse and the achievement of the science is a result of theorizing. The origin of the science of discourse is buried in the experience of achieving it, for neither Aristotle's statement of the science, nor his exemplification of it in various inquiries serves to impersonate the experience of its achievement. Whether future generations accepted the details of Aristotle's science of discourse or not, they all converge in their conception of theorizing as the self-consciousness which is manifested in a distinctive attitude towards rational discourse as a normative order, as communication.

Furthermore, the normative character of the science of discourse requires that the authority of true speaking be lodged in standards which are re-constructed from the concrete speeches of competent members as a limitation and constraint. The power of the science of discourse lies in its ability to at once preserve, protect, and re-construct these speeches: the science retains the authority of communal usage by re-constructing that usage in terms of the requirements of a Rational speaking project that is generated from a perusal of this selfsame communal usage.

We have argued the ambiguity of using a science of discourse to resolve the problem of science on the grounds that any science of discourse is a re-affirmation of the authority of the selfsame conception of science by which it is licenced and that consequently, the most rigorous and methodic discourse only affirms its subjectitude to an unexplored conception of science. That is, that the science of discourse must exemplify the sciencing of science and not the security and authority of science, that the science of discourse must make its authority transparent *not* by characterizing or describing this authority, but by displaying its authorization in its very discourse. To treat a science of discourse as *the method* (as a solution to the relation between thought and things) is to treat discourse as itself a 'thing,' i.e., as a further exemplification and extension of the authority of science.

Speech is treated as first because it is the method which completes the relation between the internal (thought) and the external (things) where both thought and things are formulated as other speeches. It remained for others to revise this view of the firstness of speech by unpacking the relation that is speech and by conceiving of speech as vocalization they reinterpreted externality as the interiority of the speaker (i.e. his unique and incorrigible relation to his voice).

Yet, the alternative to Aristotle's science of discourse itself remains hidden as long as discourse is treated as an occasion to further extend the 'science' rather than as an occasion for questioning the very authorization of science and of any idea. Discourse then becomes the 'object' for a science (and a resource for the conduct of science) and as an object for science, it is conceived as a thing with its principles, conditions, and elements. Given the character of the 'elements' as categories and of propositions constructed from them, they can only 'relate' in terms of principles which govern the 'participation' of predicates in subjects. This notion of participation is controlled by Aristotle's conception of the structure of things which in its turn is grounded in his conception of the structure of discourse; so his science of discourse re-presents his (unanalyzed) re-construction of an original conception of ordinary discourse of which it is the transformation (and one that preserves the character and authority of ordinary intelligible discourse). Aristotle's science of discourse never addresses its own possibility since it presents itself as a beginning that is differentiated from ordinary discourse through the grace of Aristotle's individual talents, his genius. To face the relationship between the science of discourse and the original possibility of the science which is concealed in its beginning would be to address the science of discourse in terms of the question, how does discourse discourse? This question would then force a re-thinking of the relationship between subject and predicate as that which grounds the science of discourse; that is, it would 'take up for discussion' this relationship as-a-relationship in a way that his writings obscure.

Aristotle's science of discourse does not clarify his science; it extends that science by exemplifying it in 'discourse.' Thus, Aristotle cannot address the resonances of discourse – what discourse is – because discourse like science has been segregated from whatness. The whatness of discourse is identified as the being that discourse has – the intricate relationships of assertion and predication – and the question of this relationship *qua* relationship is hidden. The question is: what is the whatness to which the whatness of discourse points?

That the elements of assertions 'relate' under the auspices of principles and conditions in the way that all 'things' relate is itself an occasion for beginning speech. That the 'relationship' depicted here is the relationship that *is* discourse is itself an instance of an unthought beginning. It is this reading to which Plato's conception of form and particular is held accountable and it is through this conception that Plato's notion of participation is seen and reviewed. How speaking 'participates' in its authority is the interest which exercises both Plato and Aristotle and through his ontology, Aristotle created the opportunity for a radicalization of the Platonic notion of participation as concrete predication rather than as the iconic relationship of appearance to Being. Aristotelian predication fragments into two what is One, and then rank orders the two in an authoritative series where the authorization for the series is never put in question.

V

Despite their differences Plato and Aristotle share a decisive unity: theorizing as a kind of *anamnesis* or re-collecting is a movement from what is obvious to men to what lies hidden and covered over, and as such it is essentially *critical*, i.e., it orients towards firstness (though Aristotle saw firstness as an other speech). Whereas they both recognized that the decision to theorize was a commitment to something beyond that which is present, those after them tended to deny this distinction and so, to refuse to accept responsibility for their speech. Furthermore, as an achievement of theorizing, any description of science conceals the experience to which it points, where this experience is the ground of any conception of the sciences. This experience itself – the experience of theorizing – is a metaphor for the relationship between man and whatness and can only be grasped and learned through discourse. It is through speech that men relate to whatness but this relationship is not completed under the auspices of an other speech.

To be aware of *this* and to command the resources for displaying this awareness and for articulating it is what it is to be conscious of oneself; self-consciousness in this sense means knowing what belongs to oneself in an essential way – to the distinctive excellence (*areté*) of the human – and by acting with reference to this excellence (by displaying it). This excellence acquires its virtuous character only because it 'announces' man's Desire for whatness, his longing to integrate with Being. Thus, to be self-conscious is to be aware of man's place in the cosmos which pre-supposes a Rational vision of cosmos, of man, and of man's relationship to cosmos (and of the relationship 'internal' to man between pleasure and Reason within his soul).

To the Greeks self-consciousness was not consciousness of what one *is* in the empirical sense, or consciousness *that* one is in this sense. To be self-conscious was not to be conscious of self as an object, but was to re-cognize the part which the human (speech) plays in what is. To be self-conscious was to be much more than conscious of self, for it was to be conscious of the place of self in the whole, to be conscious of 'all-in-one,' and to love and desire *this* object of consciousness as that which essentially belongs to one by nature.

Self-consciousness as neither self-love, nor self-congratulation (i.e., neither 'insight', 'introspection,' 'reflexivity,' or any of the narcissisms invented by modern man) is that to which self essentially belongs, and is shown as the love of that to which self belongs – the Oneness in which 'all is.' So, even the self-consciousness of the first science of metaphysics (like the science of dialectic) is grounded in the conception of the distinctive excellence of the human as a given. Self-consciousness as consciousness of the distinctive excellence of the human is conscious-ness of that to which the human ought be directed, it is consciousness of the ideal of humanity as understood by those who glimpse the Logos.

Self-consciousness does not then imply the empirical study of 'human nature' or the concrete characterization of what that being 'man' *does* (his behaviour, or characteristics) as these interests become articulated in their great modern offshoots, epistemology and sociology. Rather, it is the given authoritative declaration of the distinctive virtue of man and as such, it grounds all human projects by proposing that they can only acquire a Rational (excellent) character when they are designed to accord with the excellence of man. Thus, all human projects like science serve to exemplify the concerted achievement of virtue: science is only science – thinking is only thinking – when it provides a direction for the attainment of the right order, the Rational order, the order that is in tune with the distinctive excellence of the human. The right order is the order which maximizes human virtue and excellence by 'announ-cing' the omnirelevance and omnipresence of Logos. The right order is not the order that liberates men from concrete 'mistakes,' or which ensures the accuracy of their assertions. In fact, this order is evil insofar as it deflects men from glimpsing through their projects their distinctive virtue. *These* orders put men to sleep and draw them away from what they Really are and from that with which they essentially belong.

Yet, despite their rootedness in the classical ideal of knowledge, the right order can only be anticipated by Aristotle in the vision of a science of discourse, and Aristotle re-interprets man's faithfulness to Reason as obedience to the law (*nomos*) of correct speaking, where the law is itself an icon of convention and common culture. That is, the authority of the science of discourse is granted by an authoritative, conventional conception of ordinary usage as both constraint and limit.

Consequently, Aristotle's first science and all of the possibilities which it generates will not be a true science of whatness because it will not concern itself with how science belongs to whatness, and instead shall mark off a part of whatness-as-a-genus and will explore and investigate. This first science will take as its concern the similarities between the special sciences and it will conduct it-self as an instance of the very common understanding which these similarities express. The first science will be yet another science, only it will be first; and this 'firstness' will not point to Being but to the common. The first science shall appropriate to itself metaphysics and logic because these subjects express the most common character of the special sciences as a gram-matical possibility and this kind of first science will create the opportunity for its re-invigoration as epistemology and ultimately, as sociology.

Aristotle's project collects both the concrete speaker or agent of speech and the subjected matter appropriated as an object of speech through the notion of a grammar. The firstness of speaking is seen to consist of its grammaticality and the method(s) of appropriation through which grammaticality becomes concretized as performance. Aristotle's science of discourse is an inventory for re-presenting and codifying the critical subject of speech as grammar. Yet despite this innovation Aristotle still treats his subject – grammar – as a method for completing speech, and he still leaves unspoken the source of his very achievement suggesting to those who followed him that this very achievement points to a firstness beyond speech. The moderns asked for the authorization of grammar it-self, but not as a disclosure of Being: they required a justification of the achievement as a truly and radically common achievement and not as the product of genius.

Thus, metaphysics is the first science in the sense that it proposes to take as its subject firstness itself, on the grounds that what is common is first, and what is common as the most concrete commonality is self-consciousness personified as the rationality that is grammaticality, or, the complete speech about the essential partiality of speech; the common nature of grammaticality consists in the fact that it re-flects a solution to the problem of reconciling difference – of bringing men together – by re-orienting them to that which they can commonly subject. Firstness as a topic is nothing other than the grounds of concrete communication and no longer the source of what is. The firstness of communication is to be sought in those conditions which ignite intelligibly as a performance. By equating the intelligible and unintelligible with similarity and difference, Aristotle introduced the commonness of culture as a grammar. Those who followed him – the moderns – situated their subjects in the conditions common to every intelligible expression, in the concrete invariants of 'experience' whether of 'self' or 'history' (which are merely surrogate expressions for the concrete agents of speech), or they sought to introduce new developments in the grammatical metaphor which he began. The moderns wanted to formulate such a comprehensively common subject that would guarantee even the differential achievement of the formulation itself.

VI

Aristotle's conventionalization of whatness – through its equation of firstness with grammaticality – successfully suppressed the needful relation to Being as the critical experience. From that point on thinkers had to orient to the Aristotelian tradition – to its formulation of first-ness as grammar – and Plato's Socrates became an historical curiosity (whether 'gadfly' or 'monstrosity,' first 'moral philosopher' or 'pre-historic' logician). The *problem* of Socrates could not be re-experienced because the experience of Being – the irony, solitude and inwardness of that experience – was detached (at best, an 'object' for theology) or forgotten (at worst, an 'irrational' obsession, an example of the bewitch-ment of 'essentialism' and of linguistic pathology).

Aristotle's grammar as the law for the production of intelligible speech was inspired by an image of thinking as a rational communica-tive exchange, by a 'social' metaphor which in its very organization was *designed* to repress the inwardness and tension essential to theoriz-ing as a mode of existence. This grammar was developed in response to an authoritative standard of reconciling difference as an ethically binding maxim for regulating the production and organization of intelligible speech, and in forcing men to comply with it it guaranteed an intelligible community of speakers – of men who were articulate (intelligible to an other), who were capable of using the resources of their language to speak with clarity and weight, of men who had the same idea of the weight of words and of the importance of having the same idea of the weight of words. The grammar intended to formulate one resourceful use of ordinary language as it *could* be employed to create agreement and in this sense, it imagined what was possible in an inventory of possibilities. Since to see the possible in the actual (ordinary) was to 'go beyond' the actual (ordinary) it-self, the achieve-ment of the grammar had to be extraordinary and could rest on no claim which identified its achievement as ordinary, as an achievement that could be included as an ordinary instance of what it formulated.

The grammar authorized it-self on the basis of its claim to re-surrect ordinary language as a rationalized system, and critical attention was directed to the congruence between the system and the mathematical properties of organization which were stipulated as ruling any rational system. The strength of the grammar lay in its claim to bring to appearance an image of a rational system and in *this* sense the grammar was a work of art, for it only required of itself that it be at one with the form which ruled it, that it could be seen as the image of such a form.

Because the grammar could not move outside of the form and could not address the grounds of the authority of the form in anything but a grammatical way (because the boundaries of the grammar were stipu-lated to be the boundaries of intelligible speech), the authority of the form was authenticated through its use of the grammar as a method for producing speech which satisfied the very conditions which the form stipulated as satisfactory.

The formal authorization of the inventory – its Rational character – had to be accepted as a 'fact,' as an object in the environment of knowledge because the contours of its Achievement as a progressive Rational surpassing of thoughtlessness were never made to appear. While the grammar could be used as a resource to speak about many things – even about speaking and thinking itself – all such speech only re-asserted and extended the law in terms of which it spoke. The grammar could speak and convince (justify, prove) through its products, but these products (which were treated as new and independent creations of the grammar) only affirmed their unity with the grammar as belonging-together with the very authority that they were designed to 'test.' The ultimate justification of the grammar rested on its ability to induce respect for the Rational authority of its law by making products that could affirm the organizing capacity of that law. A principal modern objection was that 'organizing capacity' was still an instance of faithful rather than true speaking and that it easily degenerated into the formal aestheticism of a closed system which was grounded in nothing other than a conventional stipulation. This was one view of classicism.

A problem raised by the grammar was then: if it was designed to produce (as its justification) *appearances* of the organizing capacity (and hence, Rationality) of its law, it was designed to produce that which was apparent only to a member because to *see* the organizing capacity of the law was to see it as a member of the selfsame organization. The grammar could not produce membership it-self as an achievement and hence, the theorist's formulation is outside of the scope of the grammar. The law organizes insofar as seeing it as organized is the kind of organized seeing which affirms just this organizing capacity. The achievement is outside of the system he creates; the theorist is not a member of this organization.

If the production of the grammar is worth saying then its Rationality cannot consist in its capacity to organize because the very achievement of producing it – as extra-ordinary – denies the organizing capacity. The organizing capacity of the grammar cannot organize the act of theorizing itself.

The theorist must live in the discontinuity between the claim of the grammar to be first and *his* externality vis-à-vis the grammar. For, if he remains external, his very achievement cannot be exposed and the grammar touches everything extraneous to the theoretical creation itself. The grammar is clearly second to his genius. If he is grammatically formulated his achievement becomes a topic for the grammar in a way that leaves open the question of what organizes the grammar, showing again that the grammar is second.

The grammar claims that it is first but its very achievement shows it to be second. To attempt to eliminate this discontinuity by making the grammar re-formulate its concrete origin (in the act of theorizing) rationally is to so generalize and rationalize the achievement as to divest it of its extra-ordinary character. In the first case, the discontinuity is accredited as an analytic difference in kind, while in the second case, the discontinuity is normalized and treated as a concrete difference in degree. Both options must affirm the firstness of an extra-grammatical achievement; they announce the secondness of speech.

Because the grammar claims to be a rationalization of the common, whatever grounds it must be a comprehensively common inspiration. Because any such inspiration is only formulated through the grammar itself, any such condition is a matter subjected after the achievement of the grammar. The grammarian must re-cognize and live with the claim of the grammar to be first even though the very achievement of the grammar (as *his* particular achievement) shows that it cannot be first. The moderns recognized that the only way for the grammar to be (second) an intelligible achievement and *not* a product of (personal, inexplicable, irrational) genius was to see it as a concrete description of some nature that was first. But if this nature was first, its firstness had to reside in its commonness (its apparency to all) and such a conception denied the very claim to knowledge embodied in the act of writing. The only way to normalize the discontinuity between the achievement of the grammar and its claim to be first was to convert the theorist into an ordinary observer who was only explicating that which exists (first) and common. To make the theorist as ordinary as those to whom he spoke by ignoring the differential claim entailed by the rational act of speaking.

If it is accepted that the difference between author and reader is analytic because of the essential meaning of authorship as a claim to authority – as making a claim to know – then any formulation of the achievement of authorship (which is a particular and extra-ordinary achievement) insofar as it makes authorship rational and intelligible (ordinary) denies this difference and the ideal of the authorial claim loses its weight. The author has no moral mandate for speaking.

Moderns recognized that the grammar cannot be both first and extra-ordinary but they wanted to preserve its achieved character (as second) by concretizing firstness as yet another speech. They did not see – in the same way – that the grammar cannot be both second (which it is) and ordinary because any such formulation would have to re-assert the inexplicability of the achievement (would have to *show* its extra-ordinariness). A theorist can show how his theory provides for him-self (he can describe himself within the terms of the theory), but any such normalizing enterprise still leaves the question of the possibility of the

theory as an achievement unexplored because the formulation merely
extends the authority of a theory already achieved.

In this sense the moderns recognized that there was a discontinuity
between the achievement of the grammar as a particular and decisive
performance and its claim to be first. They saw that such a discontinuity
could only mean that its formulation was an achievement of genius –
that genius suited the achievement of the grammar and that the claim
of the grammar was denied by its very genius. They saw that the
preservation of discontinuity in this relationship recommended the
fortuitous, inexplicable and contingent character of the achievement
as reflected in the metaphor of genius.

The moderns knew in this respect that what the grammar answered
to was not common, but the most personal. The problem of this lay
in the fact that the claim of the grammar to produce unity and relatedness among men – through its equation of adequate speaking with
communality – was itself a product of idiosyncrasy and caprice. Though
designed to produce community, the very creation of the grammar was
a result of all that is antithetical to the very agreement which it
desired to produce – of difference, particularity. Though designed to
quiet passion, the grammar was achieved as a monumental act of
passion. What Aristotle failed to recognize was that while the grammar
cannot be first, to invoke the firstness of genius is self-centred; what the
moderns failed to recognize was that while the grammar must be
second, to formulate its achievement grammatically was to invoke the
firstness of an inspiration so common that it failed to differentiate
theorizing from anything else.

The difference between Aristotle and Plato is striking here. Both
recognized the discontinuity, Plato by living within it and affirming his
faithfulness to this difference as itself First and Real. The discontinuity
is Real because it shows that what is first is neither law nor genius,
but Being (or, no-thing). Aristotle's recognition of the discontinuity –
that his communicative ethical ideal or law could not be first – meant
that what was first was his own artfulness or genius as that which
instigated his achievement. For Plato the authoritative commitment
of the speaker to his differentness from the reader which was entailed
in the Rational notion of authorship was an analytic difference in the
sense that the speaker had faith (had a direction) and was speaking
under a mandate to show the goodness of that to which he was faithful.
Plato's attempt to make the source of faithfulness a subject could not
appear as a formulation of the object of faith because to formulate the
Good was to concretize it as another speech and faith was not shown
in *that* kind of speaking relationship. Neither was faithfulness shown
by ignoring the discontinuity because that still preserved the authority
of an inexplicable achievement and was faithless. Faith was shown by

exposing the discontinuity as origin-al, by re-affirming the extra-ordinary committed character of writing; faith was *shown* by preparing one's speech as a demonstration of the Rational *and* objectively uncertain character of that which the faith served.

Aristotle's refusal to make the discontinuity a continuous subject of theorizing re-asserts the authority of his genius. His silence *says* that the achievement is inexplicable (not because it shows the difference between man and God, between beings and Being, but) because it is *his*, since that which is inexplicable must be due to *him*. Since that which is inexplicable cannot be explicated by the very grammar he develops, the most decisive experience is precisely the experience which is excluded as a subject for the grammar.

Aristotle knew correctly that his achievement was not formulable by *what* he achieved because what he achieved was an inventory and the source of his achievement could not be spoken in terms of the conditions stipulated by the inventory. Instead of re-cognizing a problem in a method of theorizing that could not answer-to the funda-mental experience that inspired it, he avoided facing the experience. His silence toward the experience had the active implication of trans-forming Being into genius because silence towards Being only re-asserts one's authority as the unformulable but awe-inspiring authority of creative genius. By avoiding facing the discontinuity as an original difference, he avoided facing the difference between him-self and Being and he effectively said – what is first is genius (is Man).

Plato did not suffer from the tension between the communicative claim of a grammar and the uncommunicative source of its achieve-ment because he dwelt in that creation itself as an existential oppor-tunity to re-affirm its firstness. The discontinuity as an origin-al difference pointed to the firstness of the Good and had to be exemplified as that which is Good, on every occasion of writing. Such an exemplifi-cation struggled as an evolving 'contest within the soul' as the author sought to make that difference his subject (to subject his writing to it) by re-creating it as an experience on every occasion of writing. For Plato, to ignore the discontinuity as Aristotle did was to re-assert the self-centred claim of privilege and genius and by disregarding the difference between Being and being was to treat one-self as a God. On the other hand, to seek to normalize the discontinuity (as the moderns attempted) by making the achievement continuous with its source was to withdraw any moral purpose from speech and by identifying what is first with what is common and apparent only succeeded in making theorizing the most concrete kind of speaking (speaking which *says* no-thing, which has no reason to speak).

It should be clear how the solution of grammaticality to the problem of firstness is an *ethical* solution and how the notion of adequate speaking as a 'competent grasp of principles' is an ethical standard. The authority of grammar is ethical, its medium an inventory of possibilities, and its conception of theorizing as legislating and law-abiding is essentially constitutional.

Whereas Kierkegaard often spoke against the twin icons of modernity – the ethnical and aesthetic modes – in ways that tended to obfuscate their rationality, what becomes clear now is that the ethical mode shows it-self classically in the grammatical conception of theorizing and in the normative rationalization of mathematical features of relatedness as morally binding. Grammar emerges as an ethical solution to the problem of difference by seeking to enact speech under the auspices of a moral standard grounded in the image of inter-action as a concrete relation between difference and unity.

Eventually aesthetics – through the icon of description – seeks to authenticate the experience of the inter-action that inspires authoritative speaking by re-constructing the relationship that is experienced as one between the speaker and that which is most immediate and apparent to him. In this way, aestheticism produces epistemology, empirical philosophy, and those great modern disciplines, art, history, and sociology. In this sense, the modern tradition of theorizing is the aesthetic tradition, one which emerged principally in response to the ethical character of Aristotelian classicism. Grammar stops by conceiving of the whatness of speech to reside in its status as a method for exemplifying its own possibilities of artfulness (legality) whereas æsthetics locates this whatness in the most concrete interior relation presupposed in the very fact of intelligible vocalization.

Aesthetics complements grammar by explicating the radical and incorrigible firstness (first relation) that animates speech as the relation between the speaker and his 'voice' (a relation symbolized as 'experience' or 'intuition'), a relationship essentially interior and uncontaminated by contingency, facticity, or sociality. Yet by converting externality into interiority (as the necessary and indubitable primary relationship) rational speech has to be identified with the facticity of empirical speech in order to overcome the necessary isolation required by the aesthetic stipulation of interiority as first.

5
Aesthetics/Description

I

Because grammar begins with a stipulation its authoritativeness is not self-evident – apparent and immediate – to a reader (or potential user). It must be accepted on faith, which is to say that one must willfully submit to the authority which it expresses by suspending disbelief. Because a suspension of disbelief that is essentially willful and passionate underlies the acceptance of such a programme, moderns wanted to develop a plan of speaking that would create in the reader no other option than assent. Because such assent is not an act of passion but is a direct response (imitation of) to what is immediate and apparent, this new programme was symbolized in the ideal of a passionless science.[1]

The notion that the grammar was an achievement of genius (was rooted in a past that was inexplicable) led to an interpretation of its achievement as passionate. The modern interpreted genius as an expression of will, and possibly pride. Genius symbolized passion and the prideful refusal to examine one's origins, where these origins were conceived by moderns as apparent and common property and not the hidden and idiosyncratic resource of a privileged one. Descartes prepared the transition from ethics to aesthetics, from grammar to description, from one standard of heroic excellence – the prideful law giver (Aristotle) – to a modern variant – the tribal administrator.

Descartes prepares the ground while operating within the horizon of classicism because his method still preserves in some form an ethical ideal (a grammar of rationality). The Cartesian distinction between appearance (opinion) and Reality (knowledge) reflects this tension inasmuch as the distinction itself is fundamentally classical while the grounds for its re-statement are aesthetic. The fact that what is Real is that appearance which is present and immediate meant that what is Real is an appearance; this aesthetic grounding denied the classical

[1] For the usage 'passionless science' see L. Strauss, *The Political Philosophy of Hobbes*, Chicago: Phoenix Press, 1963.

conception of the distinction it-self by identifying the lawful and desirable with the apparent.

The moderns desired to address the tension between the a-sociality of the achievement of the grammar and the sociality of its communicative (and descriptive) claim as authorized by its lawful standard of knowledge. The inexplicable genius which roots Aristotle's achievement is self-centred because it is a-social; it claims the privileged immunity of private property. Because the experience is *his* he authoritatively exempts it from the very communal review which his theory desires to produce. *He* is not provided for by his theory; *he* is outside of his theory. The moderns posed the question – how can the achievement be socialized? How can genius be democratized? How can the theorist be incorporated into his theory as an instance of it? They attempted to transform the idea of genius as private property into common experience.

The achievement ought record the memory of its occurrence as an organized public document. The record must preserve in memory the essential universality of that which inspired it; it must record its very construction – its becoming – as it proceeds. The achievement will record itself by preserving in memory that which it speaks about and what it speaks about is this very achievement. The achievement will constitute it-self essentially as memory – as a record of the memorable – and what it re-members (puts together) is the comprehensive sociality – the commonness – of that which inspires it.

To radicalize Aristotle's notion of genius as private property is to seek to locate the commonest experience from which genius derives on the grounds that despite the inexplicability of genius, it owes its life to the commonness of its humanity. The moderns want to locate a metaphor for man's decisive and critical *experience* of him-self as a human actor – as one who actively re-enacts his humanity. This decisive metaphor will be experience and the task of theorizing is to re-produce the history of human experience as a record, to re-produce the organization of experience as memorable (as history) by re-organizing it as a record.

To re-organize experience as a memorable organization is to have in-hand a notion of what is worth preserving. It is to have a grammatical understanding. What is worth preserving is that most common experience that underlies speaking, where the commonality of such an experience is required by the need to convert it into a topic. This standard leads to an identification of the most common (concrete) experience as the first topic and the record seeks to rationalize the discontinuity between subject and its achievement in a formulation by treating the creation of the idea as the most communicable method of naming and characterizing the experience from which the idea evolves.

What the record records is the career of common experience as it is re-membered by the creator of the record.

What is memorable about common experience is that it is creative, that it can be *used* to construct a record (a common document detailing its very transformation). What is memorable about common experience is that it can be spoken about (this is what 'history' is). The memorability of common experience consists in this record-ability, in this creative potential. The record is the authoritative tribal document and its authoritativeness consists in the fact that as a product it records the creativity of common experience through its mere production. The authority of the record consists in its preservation of common experience and the firstness of common experience consists in its primacy as material for creation of the record. Thus, the record stands to description as the inventory stands to the grammar; where the grammar is authorized *ethically* as the image of a rational and legal association, the description is authorized *aesthetically* as the preservation of a common experience.

Moderns then devote themselves to the development of methods for transforming common experience into histories (records), but to the extent to which every such development *claims* to be more than a banal paraphrase of the common experience (and as responsible speech it *has* to make such a claim), then it re-asserts the inexplicability of its achievement (which is it-self extra-ordinary rather than paraphrase) and re-introduces the immunity of genius. Aesthetics seek to avoid this dilemma by denying to be more than a paraphrase of common experience and by construing this denial as an affirmation of its rationality; by morally legitimating the most concrete speech, aesthetics sacrifices rationality to destroy genius and in such a sacrifice creates speechless speech (speech that says no-thing) as the adequate speech.

The topic for moderns becomes creativity itself – how common experience is transformed into record – and the difference between science and everything else is a difference in degree (whether or not this topic is 'oriented to'). The study of creativity is the study of (action, *praxis*) anyman because common experience is first for all. In creating his own record (transforming common experience into record) the theorist records the common creativity, the artfulness, of anyman. The record records (common experience as commonly experienced) that which is (first) only because the record constitutes itself as an answering-to what is (first) where first is that which is commonly experienced as the common experience).

Aesthetics and not ethics is concerned with certainty because while grammar is concerned with presenting an image of an ethical 'grasp of principles' re-presented in a possible society (that is productive and inter-related), description is concerned to preserve what is present to all by showing it has the force and immediacy of that which is present to a one. To say that description preserves experience means that describing answers-to an authoritative notion of inwardness which is that feature that *my* speaking shares with all speaking. This feature is that *I* listen to what *I* say in the way that all men listen to one another. The difference between *me* and *all* is that I am closest to what I say. Inwardness is reformulated aesthetically as *immediacy* and the task of theorizing (as description) is to transform what is immediate to me into what is apparent to all by pre-serving the force of this immediate presence (for me) as a presence which is immediate for all.

What I hear my-self speak (my voice) must be converted into something which all can hear. I must permit all to be present to (privileged to) what only I am present to. The commonness of what *I* am present to is affirmed when it can be converted into what is present for all.

I own my experience and must allow all to be present to it. To achieve this requires that I exploit that common resource in which my experience participates. Since I am closest to my voice, speech allows me to communicate to all the immediacy of that which is present to me by divesting the experience that is mine of the element that is me. Since what is present to me is authentic because it is immediate and mine, the task of theorizing is to preserve this immediacy as a demonstration of the irrelevance of it being mine; to make its presence lie in its immediacy and not in its being mine. Aesthetic theorizing records the (desirable) growth of share-ing and it is rooted in the grammatical stipulation that the authentic common experience is the one whose immediacy is apparent and present to all as a demonstration of the fact that it is not the private property of a one.

Theorizing describes how inwardness as the immediacy of what is present to a one breaks down, how the privileged access which one has to what is present to *him* declines: theorizing describes the decline of the private property of one's presence – the property that is private for a one – and the growth of sharing. How one sacrifices his possession – what is immediate and present to him – by converting it into what is present to all. This is the real sense of possessive individualism – that what an individual possesses as his property is what is present to him – and while its decline is the topic of theory, aesthetic theory it-self exemplifies that decline in the wholesome and virtuous product called a description.

The theorist shows what he shares with all men by exemplifying what he writes about in his very writing. His writing about this sacrifice is constituted as a sacrifice; his difference consists of his recording in the form of a sacrifice – the description – what all men do.

Because the decline of this kind of possessive individualism is the topic of theory, his very writing is designed to preserve and commemorate that decline. His very writing shows in its evolution and construction the self-same decline that his writing registers. The theorist administers the commemoration and differs from the ordinary member only in terms of his ritual function, that *he* makes the sacrifice public and memorable by preserving it in the record. He is the administrator for the tribe.

The theorist destroys the discontinuity between the achievement as a differentiated performance and the claim of the theory to unify what is common because he personifies the administrative expression of ordinary artfulness. His 'theory' is also a result of relinquishing what is private and present to a one and he 'justifies' this by recording that process of sacrifice as it occurs in a way that answers to the decline of possessiveness it-self.

Theorizing then celebrates ordinary artfulness and creativity – the artfulness that is common – by making a product that meets all of the requirements of artfulness it-self. Theorizing justifies itself on the grounds of its claim to re-produce as a product (a record) that which it records (the growth of sharing) as the same kind of thing (as an instance of sharing).

II

The description displays the artfulness of sacrifice as a product, as it-self an artful product, as a work of art. The success of the description depends upon whether it produces it-self artfully (whether it describes artfulness artfully) and the ability to show this *is* its artfulness.

The grammar displays an authoritative standard of speaking as a rational order and it succeeds in terms of whether it produces the appearance of comprehensiveness and consistency.

A description shows that it is share-able when its production can be commonly experienced, when its production (which rests upon the commonness of experience) can be an object *of* common experience. In withholding *that* claim a grammar seeks to overcome inarticulateness by idealizing an organized exemplification of articulateness not as an object of common experience, but as a direction for faithful speaking. The grammar depicts men *as if* they were rational, while the description describes men *as if* they were in the same place (and that is its image of rationality).

By ignoring its achievement – by treating its lawfulness as self-evident – grammar accepts the discontinuity between its own occurrence and the possibility that it creates (which excludes this occurrence) as a showing of genius.

In creating its achievement as ordinary – its fateful commitment to becoming as a Good – description denies the discontinuity between its own occurrence and the experience which it records (which is assumed to include this occurrence) and shows it-self as speaking which is speechless (which has no-thing to say). Since aesthetics only denies its genius at the price of nihilism, rational aesthetics must re-assert its genius and thus, must come to exclude its own achievement from the programmes it creates.

Both grammar and description are interested in method, but the method of grammar is re-flected in the analysis which is grasping principles, surveying, limiting, composing, de-composing, deriving and relating: the method of description is re-flected in the analysis which seeks to preserve the sense of presence and immediacy while divesting it of its privilege; grammatical truth is reflected in the certainty which is a grasp of principles, while aesthetic truth is re-flected in the certainty which is having the same experience. The grammatical notion of unity is the social relationship of understanding, of having the same linguistic opportunities, while the descriptive notion of unity is the social relation of being co-present to the same experience (hearing the same sound, seeing the same sight); while members of the ethical society occupy the same position vis-à-vis the law, members of the aesthetic society occupy the same position vis-à-vis the concrete experience. The respective metaphors for the two societies are mind and body and while grammar ultimately turns to description to confirm the legality of its law as a possible aesthetic experience, description ultimately turns to grammar to overcome the perspectiviality of immediacy (yet all along, the grammatical conception of possibility is aesthetic and the descriptive notion of actuality is ethical). These are differences in degree and not in kind.

Depending upon the discipline, ethics accuses aesthetics of empiricism, romanticism, naturalism, and aesthetics accuses ethics of formalism, rationalism, classicism, aestheticism. Dialectic accuses both ethics and aesthetics of concretizing speech, of ideologizing, of nihilism, of egocentric and self-centred speaking, of ir-rationality, of disrespe ct Dialectic finds both ethics and aesthetics self-centred and artful.

Subsequent thinkers tended to explore the various permutations involved in the relationships between dialectic, grammar, and aesthetics. Rousseau, Kant and Hegel attempted in their various ways to arrest the aestheticizing of modern thought by showing the essential self-liquidating character of aesthetics. To the extent to which these attempts succeeded at *that* purpose, they failed to handle the problem of their achievements as other than achievements of genius.

Whereas Kant sought to show the universal grammatical roots of aestheticism to lie in an inventory of mind, his achievement of the inventory – like the Aristotelian achievement – could not stand as an appearance of that which it surveyed. In his grammatical reconciliation of grammar and aesthetics Kant produced mind as a mathematical metaphor for *law*. Kant invented the law which we now understand as modern science.

Hegel sought to temporalize the relations between aestheticism, grammar, and dialectic by seeing the movement between the apparent, the lawful, and the Good as a nesting and interpenetrating 'conversation within the soul.' Hegel's attempt to organize these relations around the metaphor of development led to the possibility of a solution concretized in the grammar of history. Yet, sympathetic dialecticians could claim that Hegel's use of history is iconic in the same sense that Plato's use of Socrates' exchange is iconic and that what appears as a grammatical solution is really a showing of the Rational character of the Good (the absolute). In the same way, sympathetic dialecticians could read Kant's grammar of mind not as an inventory but as an icon of 'fundamental ontology.'

III

The modern thrust was directed not to challenging the classical tradition of grammar in the name of dialectic; rather, the inventory was not considered sufficiently rigorous; this was because its method of constituting it-self as an appearance could not be shown to answer to the (most apparent) common experience which should be its only authentic foundation. It could not show it-self as ordinary. Thus, the moderns could only begin from the recognition that the origin of the passionless science lay in passion and their first concern was to convert this primordial origin in passion into an experience that was sufficiently universal and indubitable to warrant speaking of it as a fact (as an experience) rather than as a passion. To say that the origin of the grammar was passionate was to say that it was extraordinary, i.e., an act of genius and will. In contrast, their idea of a passionless start was that of a beginning so comprehensive that it would transform the inexplicability of will into the intelligibility of commonness. In other words, their interest was to locate a passion which, when realized, would arouse only the passions of assent; and the passion so constituted satisfies the requirement of being passionless.

Grammar started from hypotheses laid down or given, and aesthetics desired to radicalize this beginning. The beginning must itself be apparent and present rather than remote from immediacy; the beginning must be experienced rather than forced. Aesthetics desired to re-experience this beginning not on the grounds that by concealing resonances it closed off intellectual possibilities, but on the altogether different grounds that its achievement was secured by legislation whereas it should be authentically re-experienced as what is apparent and immediately present.

Thus, the Aristotelian assumption that speech re-produces thoughts which re-produce things – the assumption that planned speech re-produces things because the plan is grounded in the structure of things – was put into question. But, its foundation was not questioned; what was questioned was whether this relationship was authentic, i.e., whether it could be converted into some-thing that is present to all. That is, in the Aristotelian science the relationship between speech and thing – mediated by thought – was a relationship opined rather than certain. There was no independent test of this relationship. Yet, because the relationship could not be *tested* in a way that was free from the conventions of speaking (thinking), it had to be re-experienced and re-created within speech. To re-experience this relationship was then not to challenge the idea of the relationship, nor its place in inquiry as a support, ground, and resource, but was to adopt a different attitude towards the relationship. If one could re-experience that about which speech speaks *as a clear and certain experience*, one would succeed in re-constituting the origin as authentic. Authenticity rather than legislation was the new criteria because legislation masked the genius of will whereas authenticity revealed a common experience.

Since wise men had always spoken in different ways, either the plan does not re-produce things or men do not know how to integrate the plan into their speaking. Speaking differences are either due to the hollowness of the plan or to the imperfectability of man as a rule follower (a user of the plan).

Thus, the desire is to re-lay the grounds of the plan by re-experiencing the correspondence between speech-thought-things which the plan recommends in order to guarantee that speech re-produces things rather than opinions (thoughts which do not reflect things). The attempt was to certify this convention that both Aristotle and Plato had accepted as given. Of course (they would say), speech re-produces things in the sense that speech speaks about that which *exists*: to Plato this connection was not worth certifying, and to Aristotle such exploration meant the construction of an idealized standard of grammaticality as a mathematical system for generating discourse. The modern options were to either re-experience the correspondence between speech, thought and things, or to prepare men to execute the plan which formulated this relationship, through his speaking experience. Yet these options inter-relate: for the best grounded plans amount to no-thing if they are not realized in the speaking of men where realization as execution shows itself in the overcoming of speaking differences, but such unity is itself nothing unless it is supported by a grounded and authenticated plan which guarantees that the object of agreement *is* in the strongest sense.

The ground of the grammatical tradition must be re-laid so as to provide for its authenticity as an experienced fact and an experience-able possibility for users of the science. The ground must be re-laid in a way that co-responds (or answers to) to that which is most immediate and present to the human. The grounding of grammar in presence will transform it into a memory of the human race the very production of which will itself become memorable, i.e., an object of common experience (an object whose apparency and immediacy will be present to all because its production only recapitulates that which is present to all).

The universality or indubitality of the experience upon which the method rests guarantees the persuasiveness of the method. This is to say that while Aristotle ignores the impressive and high-sounding by segregating it from his programme as a nuisance, moderns attempted to re-constitute and solidify Aristotle's science by providing for the re-experience of its 'call' as itself an instance of the high-sounding and impressive. They designed their method to accord with an experience so incorrigible and powerful that it would essentially be both true, and impressive and high-sounding. The moderns attempted to bring the impressive and high-sounding and the correct into an essential relationship (a relationship that had been severed in different ways by the Greeks), and this essentiality was grounded in an experience the 'truth' of which guaranteed its appeal (its impressive and high-sounding character).

In fact, in their very re-experience of the 'given' which the science of discourse covers over men will make themselves masters of the given. The notion of *praxis* signifies the re-constituting of method in experience *as itself* the method, in re-experiencing the method, men will become users *of* the method. In this sense, the method will come to fruition through its use (it will come to *be* through its use) and it will be used as it is itself re-created, re-experienced, and re-constituted through the re-laying of its grounds. To re-lay the grounds of the grammar will be to (re) create the grammar within the lives of men as authentic and common experience under the condition that the re-laying of the ground answers to a notion of that which is most present and immediate to the human.

The grammar recommends that the origin of discourse is to be located in rules of speaking. Yet, the agent as the source of speech precedes the creation of rules and method because the agent is the first subject. The agent is the one who speaks. To re-experience that which grammar covers over is to provide for the re-experience of the subject which means: to provide for the subject's re-experience of himself. This

136

aestheticization of grammar says that the subject's experience of him-self is the primordial experience from which discourse emerges, because the authentic subject to anyman is that which is closest. Descartes' re-laying of the grounds means that the subject will re-experience him-self as a subject and that all subsequent speaking will be controlled by that experience, because it is only through that experience that what is Real (authentic, common) can be discriminated from what is not.

The task is to begin a-new. The weakness of classical thought (mean-ing the classical thought that is the science of discourse) is that it does not reflect upon thinking; it does not reflect upon its authentic begin-nings. For moderns, the true *arché* does not point to the Good, but to the presence of speech to the speaker as the most apparent (and thus, first). This is to say, that the beginnings of the science of discourse in convention, stipulation, agreement, and belief are not firm; they need to be solidified and certified. To say that the conventionality of the beginning must be subverted is to reject the dialectical claim that the beginning is essentially conventional; in contrast, the beginning must be secured not as a limit which is laid down, nor as a starting point for thinking, but rather, as one's indubitable and incorrigible experience of self as a fact. *This* experience as a beginning then serves as a model and control for all subsequent speaking because every occasion of speaking will re-enact and re-exemplify this primordial experience as a condition for its facticity.

IV

> The end of study should be to direct the mind towards the enunciation of sound and correct judgements on all matters that come before it.[1]

The intention is then to create a practical actor, i.e., a one who can de-cide on what he faces (on what appears before his face). Whereas the end of study for Plato is to make us better, the Cartesian *telos* of inquiry is to prepare us for sound and correct judgement. To 'direct the mind towards the enunciation of sound and correct judgements' re-presents a conception of mind as possibility which includes sound and correct judgement. Since the mind is the medium of study, the mind must direct itself – it shall receive no external support – towards the judgements of which *it is* essentially capable. The safest judgement (most common, first) which mind (man) can make is to judge what is apparent and present to him. The mind directs itself to perform in

[1] R. Descartes 'rules for the direction of the mind' in *The Philosophical Works of Descartes*, translated by E. Haldane and G. R. T. Ross, Cambridge: Cambridge University Press, Vol. 1, p. 3 (rule I).

accordance with its nature; the mind urges itself onward, cajoling itself and disciplining its march, guiding itself to perform as it ought. The goal of this march – an uphill struggle against the forces of dispersion and destruction which have to be overcome – is enunciation, the mind will guide itself to *enunciate* its nature (its capacity for sound and correct judgement). The ground is laid in the conception of the mind's nature as its capacity for sound and correct judgement and mind lays down this path for it to follow itself: the path terminates and the project is *realized* with an (enunciation) announcing of this nature; this nature will be *announced* through 'sound and correct judgement,' i.e., sound and correct judgement will *announce* the bringing of the nature of mind to appearance. Sound and correct judgement is the discoursing which shows the nature of mind which cannot show itself, but which appears through sound and correct judgement. In this discourse, mind shows itself as one with itself, with its nature. Thinking shows its truthfulness by making sound and correct judgement on what appears most immediately to thinking itself.

> Only those objects should engage our attention to the sure and indubitable knowledge of which our mental powers seem adequate.[1]

The only thing to speak is that which we have the capacity to speak: mind can lead itself to fulfil itself in an announcing of itself only if the 'objects' on which mind reflects are objects which are at one with its possibilities. As such a possibility mind is the kind of thing that can only 'decide' on what is present to it and thus, the objects which engage mind's attention are those sorts of appearances. Mind can announce itself through sound and correct judgement only if it reflects upon that which can be soundly and correctly judged. Yet, that which can be soundly and correctly judged can only be disclosed through mind itself and so, if the adequate performance of mind pre-supposes that which can be soundly and correctly judged, mind is grounded in that which it aspires to produce. Both mind and that in which it is interested share this: that they are immediate and graspable presences.

That which can be soundly and correctly judged as objects of mind is that to which (our mental powers) mind seems adequate, and that to which mind is adequate is that which mind can soundly and correctly judge. Since mind judges itself – it evaluates it-self – that which mind can correctly and soundly judge is that *part* of it-self about which sound and correct judgement can be developed. Towards what part of mind can sound and correct judgements be directed? Such a *part* of mind will be an object for mind (mind as an object for it-self); it will be mind as an Other for itself as that part which is 'present,' which 'appears.' We have the beginning of the modern notion of reflexivity: to seek to make

[1] *Ibid.*, p. 3 (rule II).

sound and correct judgements about that 'object' which is the source of sound and correct judgement is to treat thinking as the most immediate presence for it-self. This part – the self as the judging and deciding *part* of mind – will be treated as a descriptive topic for mind itself; self will be the object for mind.

Self is the kind of object of which we are capable of sound and correct judgement because self is the object for which 'sure and indubitable knowledge' seems adequate. There is no object surer and more indubitable than one-self for one-self.

If (sure and indubitable) knowledge is *announced* through sound and correct judgement, sound and correct judgement is itself enunciated in speech *about* that which is sure and indubitable. The sure and indubitable object which is used as the medium for the sound and correct judging that announces knowledge, is the object of one-self. In speaking of Hobbes, Leo Strauss notes:

> Generally stated, we have absolutely certain or scientific knowledge of those subjects of which we are causes, or whose construction is in our power or depends on our arbitrary will. The construction would not be fully in our power if there were a single step of the construction that is not fully exposed to our supervision. The construction must be conscious construction; it is impossible to know scientific truth without knowing at the same time that we have made it. The construction would not be fully in our power if it made use of any matter, i.e., of anything that is not itself our construct. The world of our construct is wholly unenigmatic because we are its soul cause and hence we have perfect knowledge of its cause. The cause of the world of our constructs does not have a further cause, a cause that is not, or not fully, within our power; the world of our constructs has an absolute beginning. . . . The world of our constructs is therefore the desired island that is exempt from the flux of blind and aimless causation.[1]

The notion of self as an object for mind, as an object to be described, marks the emergence of the modern notion of epistemology. Self appears as the primordial object – both as that which is to be experienced and brought to speech through description, and as that which is the source of all experiencing and speaking. There is no standard or ideal – no transcendental order – beyond self (or if anything is beyond it is a concrete and mechanistic notion such as 'god' for which the primordial object itself cannot provide).[2]

The idea that such a primordial object – as a topic of description

---

[1] L. Strauss, 'on the spirit of Hobbes' political philosophy' in K. C. Brown, ed., *Hobbes Studies*, Oxford: Basil Blackwell, 1965, p. 6.

[2] Or as in Hume, on the grounds of the consistency of the programme, God is recognized as another production of self – another idea – and its indubitability and authority is then challenged.

and experience – is more of an achievement than an indubitable, or that its very indubitability expresses the Good through which it appears and which *its* appearance discloses, is not taken seriously. In the act of segregating mind from self-as-other (as a descriptive topic) the unity of thinking is shattered, and self is treated as a Real thing – an apparent object is mis-treated as Real – external to mind as another object. Consequently, description can only re-late these two 'things' concretely and externally.

To describe one-self as an Other is to ignore the unity of a Real self as a unity that belongs together with that which owns it and to which *it* is subject. Furthermore, to describe one-self as Other is to show that one does not understand what speech is, since the very action of intelligible speaking makes essential reference to that which is being described as its concrete source of intelligibility. Description masks the unity of that which is shown in the very conception of the possibility of discourse; because description pretends to 'discover' what is there all along, it can only be understood as a re-affirmation of the authority which it expresses, rather than as a creation of 'fact'. In masquerading as such a 'creation' description persuasively argues on empirical grounds for the authority which licences it and thus, strengthens its claim; if it is seen as affirmation rather than discovery, what description 'finds' becomes a metaphor for the standard in terms of which it speaks. 'Description' then covers up the authority of which it is an icon – description is both a showing and a hiding – and in so doing it serves to reinforce that authority instead of 'taking it up for discussion.' Description never 'takes up what it describes' for discussion; description is anti-dialectic.

Consequently, the modern notion of reflexivity which originates in an effort to re-lay the ground merely re-capitulates and re-affirms grounds that have already been laid. The modern attempt to escape rhetorical and passionate speaking identifies the primordial experience with the high-sounding *and* true experience in an identification that can only be seen as an instance of passionate speaking. The modern re-formulation of thinking re-assimilates rhetoric into the science of discourse by grounding itself in an experience which is designed to rhetorically reconcile all of the differences that a rhetorical interest generates. The rhetoric of human nature, the conventional, and the empirical – of common experience and of immediate preserve – is used to destroy rhetoric itself; the persuasiveness of the new mode wrests upon the indubitable persuasiveness of the common experience of one-self.

V

> Science in its entirety is true and evident to cognition. He is no more
> learned who has doubts on many matters than the man who has never
> thought of them; indeed, he appears to be less learned if he has formed
> wrong opinions on any particulars.[1]

Science is true and evident cognition: since 'cognition' depicts the
(natural) way we apprehend, science is formulated naturalistically.
However, science is not any apprehension, but rather, that apprehension which results in 'true and evident' cognition. That is, we
distinguish science from non-science through the certainty of its
apprehensions. The difference between science and non-science is the
difference between having no (few) doubts and having many doubts
(or between having right opinions and wrong opinions). The scientist
exemplifies the fearlessness and courage of one who does not doubt;
in contrast to the scientist, Socrates must only appear as an ignoramus.
Note the difference between scientific knowledge as the faith that is
certain opinion and Platonic knowledge as the faith that is loyalty to
the Good.

Therefore, to say that one should 'not occupy oneself with objects
of . . . difficulty' (objects for which we cannot distinguish true from
false, objects which do not assuage our uncertainty), and that we should
'trust only what is completely known *and* incapable of being doubted'
is to propose that the scientist occupy him-self with objects which he
can know (which means objects that he cannot doubt). If the scientist
is to have no doubts, he is only to interact with objects which he can
trust. Other objects – objects which yield contrasting possibilities –
cannot be trusted. Science requires as its foundation a trustworthy
object. The scientist can only trust objects which are present to him;
the scientist can only trust that which is most immediate – to himself.
The scientist should only *trust* such objects and therefore the legitimate
object(s) of inquiry are objects that can be trusted, of which the
primordial object is one-self (one's self). Science personifies self-interest
and self-centredness.

But if this is what science requires, it is an ideal (a notion of what
a good or perfect science needs in order to sustain itself), because
actually and empirically 'there is scarce any question occurring in the
sciences about which talented men have not disagreed.'[2] Yet, this can
only be a problem if disagreement between men is taken as a sign of
the untrustworthy character of the object (about which they disagree).
However, this is not the case because 'wherever two men come to

[1] Descartes, *op. cit.*, p. 3.
[2] *Ibid.*, p. 3.

opposite decisions about the same matter one of them must certainly be in the wrong . . . for if the reasoning of the second was sound and clear he would be able so to lay it before the other as finally to succeed in convincing *his* understanding also.'[1] This is what is meant by the essential persuasiveness of the object (experience). The most persuasive object is the experience immediate to all men because the immediacy of this experience is guaranteed by its concreteness and commonness.

The two speeches (judgements, decisions) about the object (the same object) do not announce the complexity of the object, for it is *given* that any speakable object carries within it its one true speaking possibility. Consequently, where there is disagreement, one must be wrong (there can neither be many speeches nor many objects); the source of disagreement lies not in the object but in the speech.

The disagreement announces the very opposite of what sound and correct judgement announces: disagreement as unsound and incorrect judgement announces opinion rather than knowledge; and opinion announces a doubtful rather than a sure and indubitable object. Disagreement announces a doubtful object and yet, the doubtfulness does not reside in the object but in the mind. So disagreement announces opinion which in its turn shows a mind clouded with doubt. Behind all of this, a trustworthy object stands; it has just not been grasped in a manner adequate to its character, because mind has not functioned in a manner adequate to its capacity. The mind must lead itself out of its sloth.

The enunciation of sound and correct judgement will simultaneously announce the One judgement the soundness and correctness of which is displayed in the impossibility of doubting what it recommends. The sound and correct judgement is essentially persuasive, and its occurrence entails the assimilation of all possible objections. The sound and correct judgement imperialistically collects as a oneness the universe of intelligible judgement, it collects this togetherness within itself as a unity outside of which there is only silence (opinion, will).

The sound and correct judgement is then the perfect instantiation of the art of Rhetoric: its announcing is a persuading, and in its announcing it is a collecting of the many unto itself. Note, that the essential persuasiveness of the sound and correct judgement is grounded in the *method* followed in its production because that method is (re) constituted out of that which cannot be doubted (out of the primordial, common experience).

Apparently then, it is not the object that is untrustworthy but the mind. Perhaps Descartes' problem can be put as follows: for those objects which are trustworthy ('of which our mental powers seem to be adequate') there should be one judgement (one speech) because this is

[1] *Ibid.*, p. 3.

142

guaranteed by the conception of the object as trustworthy. If there is more than one judgement, the judgement is a mere opinion, while if there is only one, the judgement is knowledge. How we secure the object as trustworthy is another matter (presumably *this* question is one for which our mental powers are not adequate). Thus, given such a secure object, the appearance of many speeches is a sign of the failure of mind to realize itself in enunciating a correct judgement about the object, whereas the mind realizes its perfectability in correctly judging the object.

We betray the object, we are not faithful to it. We trust the object and the object trusts us to show our faith; but, we betray this faith by not disclosing what the object is. We show our faithfulness to the object by disclosing what it is and this is what it trusts us to accomplish. Yet we fail, and if our failure cannot be attributed to the object, where can responsibility be lodged? Obviously *we* fail, the failure is ours; what is it about us that makes us fail? We apparently fail because we do not have a method (a project or plan) for directing our mind towards those (objects) feats which it is capable of performing. Thus, mind and object are bound together and belong together in a perfect unity; pure mind (rationalization) is mind at one with things. This unity is given. But the unity of mind and things is the unity of rationalized, idealized mind and things: given speech's control by mind, speech that is out of touch with mind, testifies to mind that is out of touch with things. Since the source of this dispersiveness can be neither in things nor in speech, it must lie in mind. That is to say that the source cannot lie in speech because speech follows mind, and it cannot lie in things because things are trustworthy.

How can we ever succeed? Since the two ways in which we arrive at knowledge are experience and deduction and since deduction cannot be performed erroneously by a rational inquirer,[1] the source of our failure is not to be found in faulty inference (which is what Aristotle called 'ignorance'), but in that material upon which our inferences reflect. Our mistakes 'are caused merely by the fact that we found upon a basis of poorly comprehended experiences, or that propositions are posited which are hasty and groundless.'[2]

Thus, we fail because we allow mind to outrun our control. Mind has to follow the path which it lays down for itself, and must not outstrip or deviate from this path. Mind must not rush to concern it-self with that which the immediate covers-over; mind must not think, it must work. Mind must begin carefully at the beginning and this is only guaranteed when it has a path to follow. Without such a path, mind disperses and divides itself from itself, it posits and comprehends hastily

---

[1] *Ibid.*, pp. 4 and 5.
[2] *Ibid.*, p. 5.

rather than respectfully, and thus it fragments the unity of itself with itself. The task – for success – is to ground discourse, i.e., to replace its hypothetical, arbitrary, and conventional origins (what Aristotle called a 'lying down' through sensation or by hypotheses) with a beginning that is determinant and trustworthy. Such a beginning is the old beginning of Aristotle – the conventions of the trusted limitation – re-constituted as an experience for one-self as Other.

> For if we are without the knowledge of any of the things *which we are capable of understanding*, (my italics), that is only because we have never perceived any way to bring us to this knowledge, or because we have fallen into the contrary error.[1]

That is, we either lack a method, or 'we assume that what is false is true.' But, these two reasons are really one because the method should 'explain(s) how our mental vision should be used, so as not to fall into the contrary error, and how deductions should be discovered in order that we may arrive at the knowledge of all things.'[2] The re-cognition of the method will guarantee our avoidance of the error of 'assuming what is false is true' and in facilitating such an avoidance, it will bring us to knowledge, i.e., it will bring us to develop our mind in a way that is faithful to its nature (where such a nature is announced by 'never assuming what is false is true').

Descartes then attempts to orient us to the grounds (reason for accepting speeches as true and for deciding among true and false speeches) by preparing us to use a method which in its very use will guarantee our concern with grounds. This method is an account that underlies knowledge and that grounds it, and the rule *of* method describes the intellect which *is* (essentially co-terminous with) the possibility of perfect knowledge. This is how he can say that 'to locate the rules we should study the world.'[3]

That is, Descartes accepts the classical notion of knowledge as infallible (as distinct from fallible), the distinction between perfect knowledge and probable opinion, between the eternal and the variable: Descartes accepts the distinction between appearance and the Real, and that he retains the classical vision of an ideal for thought to follow even though the ideal is spoken in such a way as to deny its extra-ordinariness suggests his essential classicism. The account which knowledge gives of itself is then a description of how pure mind operates – as a set of rules or methods to follow in the performance of thinking; the capacity to provide an account grounds claims to know and the account as a method is a product of pure thought. The possibility of

---

[1] *Ibid.*, p. 9.
[2] *Ibid.*, p. 9.
[3] *Ibid.*, rule VIII.

grounding knowledge is not put into question and the problem becomes one of technique. The authoritative technique is a re-description of how mind functions as maxims of conduct when all of the intervening and extraneous 'passions' are controlled. Thus, the new ideal is perfect-grounded-knowledge just as in Plato, except the notion of 'grounding' masks their radical differences. Here is the supreme nihilist who recommends a method which denies his very achievement of it (for the method is not an apparent and immediate 'object') and who then exempts himself from having to face the question of the responsibility of his speech.

VI

... our inquiry should be directed, not to what others have thought, nor to what we ourselves conjecture, but to what we can clearly and perspiguously beyond and with certainty to do. . . .[1]

But what the other knows has to be tested for oneself; what we believe has to be certified. One must experience for one-self which means: one must re-experience what discourse is about as an Other engaged in apprehension that is 'undoubted' and attentive. Such an (re) experience is called intuition: it typifies the primordial experience of speech for the speaker. Intuition refers to an undoubting conception (a conception that frees us from doubt in the very act of conceiving), and is distinguished from deduction which is a movement within the limits of principles already secured. Though what is intuited can be re-constructed as deduction, deduction is a concrete movement in time that is self-correcting and self-organizing, the certitude of which is conferred by memory; whereas intuition secures the beginning in an action of clear apprehension, deduction preserves the beginning as memorable while exploring its consequences. Intuition stands to deduction as the deed stands to the word.

Intuition personifies the speaker's re-experience of what his speech recommends as *praxis*. Intuition is the primordial action. Thus, Descartes' programme for the creation of a practical actor (a sound and correct decision-maker) begins by instructing men into the primordial experience of intuition. Intuition is an action, the original creative action or *praxis*.

Deduction stands to intuition – word to deed – as organization to action. The world is founded and grounded on action, and deduction as organizing and preserving only organizes and preserves the possibilities internal and essential to this primordial action. The method is

[1] *Ibid.*, p. 5 (rule III).

designed to enable men to create intuition through action and it is designed to enable them to bring this action to speech and to preserve it in speech as memorable.

Properly founded intuition is essentially persuasive, so that it only need be brought to speech to authorize itself. Yet, speaking disperses and covers over the action of intuition because speaking is guided by the passions. Speaking must be controlled only and exclusively by the organizational requirement of preserving the intuition. Thus, organization both makes intuition possible as a speakable experience (the organization of the mind), and it preserves the authority of intuition as the persuasive action.

There is a need of a method for finding out the truth.[1]

The method must be a procedure for reconciling deed and word, action and memory. The method lays down a path to follow in speaking about our intuition; at every step, we adapt our intuition to the requirements of deduction, while submitting our every (deductive) inference to the control of the intuition. Without deduction, we would be uprooted amidst a plurality of segregated 'clear and distinct' intuitions – we would never move – and so, deduction furnishes us with a sense of history as an organization for integrating intuitions into extractable and memorable speeches; deduction enables us to preserve intuition as memory, as the historicism of a record. Yet, without intuition, our record would be an empty canvas which rests upon the doubtful and untrustworthy. Both intuition and deduction must be co-ordinated.

Thus, deduction serves to convert intuition into an extractable and persuasive speech. Deduction invests intuition with its persuasive character by explicating that which lies within the action, in assertions which can be judged and decided. Deduction exemplifies the art of rhetoric vis-à-vis the primordial action of intuition, by recording this action as the memory of a common experience. Yet, intuition is grounded in the rhetorical aspiration to experience and speak that which is un-doubtable.

Method consists entirely in the order and disposition of the objects towards which our mental vision must be directed if we would find out any truth.[2]

To say (as in rule V) that the method consists 'in the order and disposition of the objects towards which our mental vision must be directed if we would find out any truth' seems to identify the method with the objects. Note though, that the method consists in *that* to which we direct our mental vision – a 'conception of the order and disposition of

[1] *Ibid.*, p. 9 (rule IV).
[2] *Ibid.*, p. 14 (rule V).

146

objects' – by what is this *conception* given? Neither by intuition nor deduction, but by what we require 'if we would find out any truth.' Yet, since this requirement is itself indubitable (and not to be doubted) the method lays down a path for thought which wants to think truly and this path is itself a result of the method. In other words, the method is itself apprehended through intuition and consequently what the method *is* (a programme for integrating intuition and deduction, or a programme for explicating intuition persuasively) is an intuition to which his various rules relate as deductions. That is, his rules constitute his way of making the intuition which *is* the method 'clear and distinct' for others, his rules constitute his way of providing for the re-experience of the method as the action of intuition. The rules are then neither 'discoveries' not 'derivations' as much as icons of the experience of intuition. Such icons re-assert the authority of the method-as-intuition rather than pointing to or showing that which the action of the intuition (the method) covers over. The rules move the reader further away from what the method *is* by re-capitulating what it is as secure – as that which does not hide resonances.

Thus, the method *is* the rules (in the way that original stands to icon) and the is-ness of the method is secured through the action of apprehending the method as trustworthy; the rules (taken in isolation) stand as deductive steps secured upon the foundation of this intuition. Thus, what Descartes *speaks about* is mirrored all along in his speech. The rules used in speaking *about* theorizing, conceal in their very speaking the experience of theorizing to which they refer. The method *is* the rules and the rules make reference to the method, but the rules can only re-flect the method's understanding of itself; though the rules ought to belong together with the method as appearances of it, they do not provide for the achievement of the method as an action.

The method announces itself through Descartes' rules which stand to the certain intuition of the method as inferences and deductions. Descartes' very format of writing personifies the method in the sense that *The Rules, Meditations* and *The Discourse* each exemplifies the inferences and re-statements which grow upon the foundation of the intuited experience of the method. The 'introspective' character of the writing exemplifies that which the writing is about: since the writing seeks to characterize the primordial experience of self as other, it stands as an icon of that experience as re-constructed by one who is segregated from it. The segregation between intuition and deduction require that the writings about method (as intuition) appear as instances of that which is segregated from intuition (method).

The experience of the method as the action that is intuition is secured as the foundation for inference (for writing) which can never touch the experience itself. The experience of the method as an intuition must be hidden in all of the writing *about* method. The writing makes reference to that experience as foundation and ground and yet masks that experience by writing about it as an Other segregated from its founding intuition. This can be seen nicely in the *cogito*.

VII

Descartes showed how the *cogito* did not serve the purpose of *any* behaviour, but appeared as the essential icon. In other words, speaking about thinking is not speaking about any-thing, but about that which is essential to what is. To say that it is thinking that makes reference to Being is to say that it is through thinking that one makes reference to Being. In the language of Parmenides, any other predicate would not exist – would not have analytic status – for this is Descartes' method of showing his analytic conception of Being (of being human). The fact that the human performs a variety of actions other than thinking is irrelevant because the human exists (i.e., *is* analytically) a one who thinks. To say that the analytic character of the human resides in his status of a thinking thing is to say that the human surpasses by virtue of thinking, that the human *is* by virtue of thinking or *is* insofar as he is a thinking thing. Thus, he formulates man analytically as the one who thinks, and consequently he treats the absence of thinking as 'nothing.' Analytically, to think is to be: to be is to think like a thing.

There is a difference between the claim that to think is to be and that to think is to think Being. Whereas Descartes stipulates that one *is* insofar as he thinks (as he re-cognizes him-self as thinking) Parmenides' formulation asserted that to think (truly) was to think Being. For Descartes, thinking becomes *evidence* for Being, and Being and thinking are treated as two (even though the act of thinking which *essentially* makes reference to Being recommends their belonging-together). For Parmenides, what Descartes calls thinking is not (strictly speaking) thinking, because it is not an activity that makes reference to Being (it thinks of everything other than Being) and its belonging-together except in the most concrete sense: Descartes' conception of thinking as a capacity to speak which shows how it essentially belongs to Being accredits any speech as a showing and does not provide for the distinction between thinking Being and thinking any-thing else (i.e., between true and false speaking). In other words, one might say that where Parmenides conceives of the difference between true and false thinking as the difference between thinking Being and thinking nothing, Descartes's concern – the new interest – is to formulate the being of thinking. Just as Aristotle shattered the relationship between science and Being, Descartes re-forms the relationship between thinking and Being by no longer asking for how thinking belongs together with Being, but by directing his attention to the whatness – the being – of thinking.

Thus, if man is essentially a thinker and by thinking *is*, he is also one of the many things that belongs to Being, and thinking appears as one of the many ways in which Being is announced. Descartes' kind of thinking – as a competence or skill – is truly no different from 'walking' or 'swimming' (as Hobbes recognized) and is only granted its authority on the basis of a notion of the essentiality of thought. Yet, thinking is only essential insofar as it is a showing, and since all activities are showings, what is essential is not *that* which does the showing (the speaking that shows) but *that to which* the showing points. Descartes' formulation is then empty insofar as it treats thinking as an indicator, predicate, or performanative display not of what thinking thinks, but of what is most immediate and apparent to it, the common experience.

One speaks so as to show he thinks. If all speaking is a showing of thinking, then all speaking shows the speaker (thinker) as one who *is*. Yet we have shown that all speaking shows the dialectic between showing and hiding and thus, that all speaking is a thinking only in the most concrete sense: that to say speaking is a (showing of) thinking is not to address the kind of thinking speaking shows.

Furthermore, 'I think therefore I am' is really a different kind of saying and showing: if all thinking is a speaking, then 'I think' means 'I speak,' and since I only speak as an instance of the 'we,' I think becomes 'I think therefore we speak' or 'there is speech.' My thinking belongs together with our speaking – with speech – and 'I think' entails that 'we are one.' 'I think therefore we are one' suggests that thinking only elliptically points to a concrete experience as source, for this itself covers over the appearing of speech as a disclosure of Being. It is interesting then, that Descartes accepted his (thinking) speaking as a mandate for examining the state of the most concrete being – the source of speaking – as common experience: his option would have been to take up speaking (thinking) as an occasion to address discourse itself. I think therefore I am should be restated as – I speak therefore I am responsible (to something beyond 'what' I am).

Because Descartes' scepticism required him to doubt the possibility of discourse, concertedness, and Other, to take this latter tack would be to plunge with 'insipient haste' into an 'ill-founded impression.' Descartes' speaking did not announce Being as a disclosure, because he had willed as extraneous and faithful such a concern and the concerted history which it implies.

Descartes then appears as the paradigmatic exemplar of self-descriptivism: in trying to certify speech and to re-lay the grounds, he chooses to doubt everything but the primordial intuition that speech requires a speaker; yet, in such a radicalization of the problem he can only ignore what speech *is*. In electing to begin as he does, he chooses to disregard what speech says because he treats saying as an empirical problem which has to be re-experienced and re-encountered on the most concrete level.

He has to destroy the analytic character of speech as a saying because he sees the question of what speech says as a question of opinion rather than of knowledge. In locating the indubitable source of speech in the apparent, he re-defines speech so as to make it the concrete utterances of a concrete speaker and he re-defines thinking as conformity to a rule for concretely characterizing the apparent. It is only in this way that he can begin.

The primordial experience which grounds human discourse is the experience of the speaker as an other for himself. Speaking is rooted in the speaker's ability to intuit him-self as the source of speech, as a concrete other. Modern reflexivity is grounded in the requirement that the speaker control and guide his discourse by referring it back to this primordial occasion and thus, the speaker is compelled to describe himself (as the fundamental fact) and to re-constitute every experience as an instance of the experience of the self as other.

Yet, the very project of describing one-self and of characterizing one-self only occurs within a discoursing matrix; consequently, the project is gratuitous. Moreover, the unity of mind is shattered through its division into two – into mind and self – and this fragmentation covers over the unity which mind *is* and the experience of wrenching this unity from Being. That is, all self-characterization is in the grip of Being and all attempts to *describe* self as other imply the very resources which the project puts into doubt. In order to do self-characterization, Descartes has to divest thinking and speaking of its analytic character, while the conduct of such self-characterization can only occur intelligibly as a way of using as a resource the very conditions of discoursing which were withdrawn. Consequently, the characterization of self as other serves to reaffirm the authority of conditions that have been revoked and does not constitute a primordial description as much as a showing of the very authority which the description is designed to produce. To seek to enunciate the solidity and indubitability of self as other is to ignore the fact that the very conception of such an enterprise and the bringing of the enterprise to speech pre-supposes this solidity and indubitability as a pervasive human fact. That Descartes takes up for discussion what is self-evident and obvious in the most concrete sense is an honourable cliché; that ne attempts to *describe* what is self-evident and obvious is also a shop-worn charge.

Descartes thinks that to centre speech upon self is to centre speech upon its grounds, but self only becomes a metaphor for grounds when speech is so concretized as to lead to the identification of the speaker as its source (when speaker is withdrawn from speech as two independent things). In this world, the interior life of the speaker becomes external to speech only because he is identified as the casual agent. Yet, this world itself can only be intelligible because of the ability to imagine a speechless speaker (a brute) as a standard, i.e. by conceiving of some state of speechlessness as natural or 'pre-theoretic.' Self is a metaphor for grounds only when speechlessness can be imagined as first, but every such phantasy is itself a speech which denies what it imagines. Such impossible speech about the secondness of speech is nothing less than an explication of the idea that speech is first.

This is to say that Descartes' speech *about* him-self as an another conceals the experience (the *praxis*) in terms of which his oneness becomes sufficiently intelligible as grounds for the segregation: he writes from the perspective of the security (and limit) of the segregation (of self from mind); thus, the unity which the segregation shows is covered over. The covering over of this unity creates a difference as beginning, and sets for inquiry the task of reconciling this difference without reference to the resource of the primordial unity. The unity which his method is designed to re-produce will then be a concrete re-capitulation of the unity which his start covers over. 'I think therefore I am' only shows the aesthetic irreverence for the question of *what* I am. Authenticity and its record become the reason for speaking.

The method stipulates that speeches which at first appear complex be reduced to simple constituents, and then become re-experienced intuitively in order to lay the grounds for a decision as to their authenticity.[1] All the while, a record of the original speeches must be preserved, because given the re-experience of the simple the task becomes one of re-organizing them in order to re-produce the beginning (the complex) from which the beginning began. This is to say, that the action of the intuition not only grounds and authorizes the speaking (deduction) executed in its name, but serves as a standard to which that selfsame speaking aspires; the initial action of intuition is re-organized so as to re-constitute it. Since the goal of the project is to re-describe the original intuition or action, the project can never transcend convention because the original intuition occurred within a matrix of convention. Unlike Plato, the project does not want to *disturb* the basic intuition by making it transparent or by showing that which it hides; rather, the intent of the project is to strengthen and to

[1] *Ibid.*, p. 15 (rule VI).

make public and acceptable this intuition as the first experience. This project which begins in radical dis-trust can never trust its beginnings, yet the project accepts itself on faith, never choosing to submit this faithfulness to discourse.[1]

VIII

Adequate thought is thought which is conscious of itself, and such self-consciousness will be achieved when the thinker submits to the requirements of method. Only clear and precise thought will conform to such a nature (will confirm the character of thought as conscious of itself) and such an achievement depends upon thought's capacity to observe cannons of method. Method is incorporated into the nature of thought as that which is essential to its clarity and precision (to its rationality) and therefore, following the rule of method becomes an essential feature of the nature of rational thought.

Thought relates to itself only under the auspices of a rule which stipulates what this (nature of) thought really is. Thought relates to the 'concept' of thought which thought itself lays down for itself as its typified nature. Such a nature is typified in thought which maximizes the values of clarity, precision, and intelligibility, and the metaphor for such a typified achievement is a typical method.

What is then denied in this new formulation is that there is any ideal for thought beyond its requirement to pay heed to the method; the method grounds and limits any expression of the Rationality of thought because rationality is identified with conformity to the method. The method is then secure as a rule which is to say that the authority in which it is grounded is not to be taken up for discussion. The self-evident character of the method means that the method rules by virtue of the fact that a commitment to method is a decision to stop doubting, i.e., the decision to will as irrelevant that which the method covers over. Speech which shows an understanding of itself impersonates self-conscious thought. Speech must be forced to meet this requirement because it is only under this condition that thought's consciousness of itself will be maximized.

To use the method is to follow it as a rule of thought. It is only through this relationship of thinker to method-as-rule that the actual course of thinking will accomplish an achievement in conformity with its nature – Rational thought. The method permits the thinker to exclude extraneous, inessential, and irrelevant matters from con-

[1] In his '7th letter to the friends and companions of Dion,' *op. cit.*, Plato speaks of the generation of intuition as requiring long and intensive training, as an occurrence which occurs like a spark of light. Contrast this with the Cartesian programme.

sideration. In other words, the method permits the thinker to control will in the service of Reason. Since the method formulates the conditions of rational thought – the unity of thought with itself – the method provides a typification or idealization of true thought. Thought which conforms to the method – rule guided thought – is true thought, and consequently, to attain truth, thought must orient to its relationship to the method which it lays down for itself on every occasion of thinking.

If the natural world is organized mathematically – from the ground up – in a hierarchy ranging from the simple indubitable natures to the more complex wholes, then thinking must also follow this pattern; consequently, if ideas submit themselves to this method of thinking, they can automatically be accredited as authoritative, i.e., as ideas that re-present things that exist. Method unifies on the basis of a tacit assumption of the correspondence between thought and things, because method produces the order latent in both thought and things.

The method is selected because it is faithful to the structure of things and this is decided *by* method; on the other hand, thought as it is concretely done is disorderly. The task of theory is to create the same order for thought that is displayed in things, and this order is achieved only through method. Thinking must be ordered in exactly this way because *this* is the method that is faithful to the orderly character of the world; yet, this conception of things is itself an achievement of method.

Note the contrast between Plato and Descartes. Whereas for Plato the use of a method is grounded in the ideal of an order which transcends the instrumental context – that is, where the use of method is only intelligible in terms of a context of 'higher' purposes – in Descartes, method is that with which man begins. This is to say, that the *use* of method in Descartes is treated as that point of origin from which inquiry begins; method is a technique that is uprooted from the soul of the user even while it is grounded in a description of soul; yet it is a description of soul which still leaves soul untouched because it is a description. Rather than ground the use of method in the soul (as for example, Plato employs method as an icon of the creation of the *anamnesis* in which the soul essentially participates), Descartes' method is a determinant operation performed by an already clear and indubitable soul upon itself. The use of method is then not designed to transform the soul because the soul is the kind of indubitable nature that *uses* method to achieve a product (good sense, right judgement) but which is in itself unchanged through such an application and which shows nothing interesting about itself in such an application.

What is obtained is a mathematical conception of the soul in two possible ways: it is either beyond method, and uninteresting; or more usually, it is identified with method, i.e., soul becomes the indubitable nature of the 'one' who uses method (soul is a typical rational 'user'). In identifying soul with method, soul loses its analytic character as a medium for addressing Being, and is typified as the rational use of method (the loyal submission of self to *nomos*). Descartes then provides for the segregation of thinking from the soul, because if thinking occurs as a movement within the soul, to speak of it as an action *performed* by soul is both to concretize the notion of soul, and to divest the notion of method of its Good; it is to alienate soul from that which it essentially belongs, and it is to segregate method from a transcendental purpose.

Assuredly Descartes wants to surpass opinion and custom (just as Plato similarly aspired), but Descartes' version of surpassing is personified in the 'capacity' to decide (to act) among different opinions. Descartes' project of re-laying new foundations preserves the authority of that which he desires to re-lay. Scepticism is employed as the method of allocating authority to opinions in this way: to doubt is to withhold the assignment of authority to opinion on the grounds that it has not properly earned its authority, for to earn authority, an opinion has to be submitted to the court of method. The authoritativeness of an opinion resides in the determination of whether that to which the opinion refers (that about which it speaks) exists (merely exists). The procedure for resolving this problem is to show methodically that the opinion is one which scepticism cannot dissolve; such an opinion earns its authority as co-responding to things that exist because the concrete world is organized mathematically and the mathematical organization of method is loyal to this principle. The method guarantees the authoritative transformation of opinion into knowledge because it displays the opinion as free from doubt and thus, as an opinion which the speaker himself could not have authored. Such opinions are no longer opinions; they constitute knowledge. This is to say that the speaker's task is to discriminate between those opinions which *he* has authored (by entertaining them casually in his 'mind' or through his 'senses') from those *ideas* which exist independently of his work as icons of self-sufficient and indubitable 'things.' His task is to locate those indubitable natures which exist, and as he executes this task by putting their authority (the question of their author) into doubt, he is in the position of being able to decide if they are possible products of his method. The ideas which meet this task – which are produced out of nothing – can be accredited as Real because the method is itself Real (the method is the world).

If thinking *is* the human method, then the analytic character of the human (what the human *is*) resides in its methodicity; man is essentially a *user of method* (man is essentially an actor, one who intuits). Since the method is available in principle to all men, differentiation is a result of the differential use of the method, and the source of such differential use (of the difference between true and false speaking) can only be found in the passions and Will which deflect men from the proper exercise of mind. Since all men have equal access, thinking becomes a matter of personal responsibility, i.e., one is responsible for whether or not he seizes the opportunity to use the method. The essence of man as a user of method (as a thinker) is then a way of depicting man as essentially a loyal subject, i.e., if he is loyal to the truth, he will subject himself to the discipline of method. It is in the discipline of method that man shows himself as one with himself and consequently, Rational man is essentially one who submits to the law (*nomos*). Man is a 'nothing' outside of *nomos*, outside of law; man is some-thing only with reference to the way in which he displays his loyalty to *nomos*. Thus, the problem of inducing man to submit to method (for his own good) is bound up inextricably with the notion of how to create the right order. If the best order is the passionless science, man can only be made to submit to the rigours of such an order through their re-cognition of the need to control their passions. Yet, the re-cognition and desire for such control is itself an instance of the passions. Thus, the programme cannot provide for its own beginning without moving outside of itself to produce an external authority or force for submitting men to the demands of the programme.

The gap between the rationality of the programme and human nature cannot be resolved by returning to the study of human nature because such a study only re-produces the gap with which the programme begins. The Cartesian programme can only appear as yet another 'ideal' unless subsequent moderns find means for integrating the programme with human nature by showing human nature as that which essentially desires what the rationality of the programme recommends.

IX

The Cartesian *cogito* is an icon of the self-consciousness of man, as his consciousness of his independence and his freedom. Radical doubt is a resource for certifying such consciousness with confidence, with self-confidence; to be conscious of self is to be confident of self through such consciousness, and the problem is to ground self (confidence). The self can only become confident of it-self through the resource of scepticism which permits it to put it-self into question in the most radical way, through doubt.

If the subject of thinking is the common experience as the source of authentic speech, to doubt is to deny such authority in order to de-cide if what the speech recommends is authentic (is independent of its author, the speaker). Denial serves not only to establish the true author-ity of things (to which the assertion co-responds) but makes reference in its very occurrence to the authority of the speaker as one who issues *both* assertions and denials. Doubt serves to restore the speaker's confidence in self by re-inforcing the link between speaker and things as itself an assertable and decidable link. Yet, radical doubt (as distrust and fear)[1] testifies to more than the existence of the one who doubts (to the speaker as subject), for it makes reference to a climate in terms of which radical doubt becomes intelligible. One ought not doubt appearance but see it as a disclosure of Being.

If we follow Strauss' reading of Hobbes which formulates doubt as the covering over of the dialectic between vanity and the fear of violent death, we see that it is the subordination of vanity to the fear of violent death at the hands of others which grounds the intelligibility of radical doubt. The fear of violent death at the hands of others is a metaphor for the fear of nothingness, of silence, a fear of not being re-cognized by others. Vanity – as itself a metaphor for will – compels one into differentiating actions which threaten the grounds of human solidarity, and the effect of such differentiations is to arouse the anticipation that the gap between men will prevent other from cognizing One, because there will be no standard for re-cognition. Vanity will have differentiated men to the point where they lack resources for concerting, and such a lack can only promise that man's voice will not be heard. The differentiating forces of science (counselling men to start with their concrete experience of self) create the possibility that men will not be able to establish standards in terms of which agreement about these experiences can be generated.

The dialectic of science – as at once generating pressures towards solitude which are re-cognized as the danger of silence – is worked out in the establishment of a method. The communality of method provides for the certitude of conventional agreement required to re-incorporate the differentiated speeches of men within a matrix of communal rationality.[2] Science is then not segregated from this fear, but is *essentially* an organized resolution of this fear as re-stated in a rule of procedure. Yet it is science which creates the fear by conceiving of the immediately present as the authoritative. The authority of science is much like the authority of the sovereign that Hobbes produces. This is to say, that science appears and acquires its power as a method of resolving the dialectic between solitude and publicity by requiring every

[1] See L. Strauss, *The Political Philosophy of Hobbes, op. cit.*, p. 56, for a development of this interpretation.

[2] Perhaps more than any, Rousseau and Nietzsche re-cognized the disintegrative tendencies of science (indeed, of theorizing), but they accepted this as empirical fact, rather than as an instability to which science's re-constitution of itself is essentially oriented.

speech made in its name to respect this resolution as a condition of intelligibility. In this way, the anticipation of silence promotes discourse by providing men with the incentive to listen; self-consciousness as the re-cognition of the possibility of silence drives men to listen, and science re-constitutes itself out of this consciousness as a community of speakers and listeners. Thus, the modern reformulation of Reason marks a new attitude to the question of the possibility of theorizing in its conception of that possibility as arising from man's fear and distrust; theorizing grounded in self-consciousness which in its turn is promoted by the fear of silence is re-flected in the artificial concerting of men to protect themselves against nothingness. Contrast this with the conception of theorizing as emerging out of wonder and out of the Desire for Oneness, or for real unity that we find in the writings of the Greeks.

The moral sub-stratum of Cartesian doubt and distrust is then grounded in the fear of having no other listener and consequently, it requires men to desire to listen on the grounds that such desire provides the only support for trust. Man desires to make of himself a listener so that he will be listened to. Man's desire is rooted in the fear of not having his voice heard because concrete others are only empirically related to the voice to which he is essentially present. This concretization of hearing leads good speech to be identified 'communication.' Method as force is the only way to compel people to listen to one another in such a world.

The problem which the early moderns recognize was that the achievement of method (i.e., rationality) required the exercise of Will which the method was designed to suppress. Hobbes' formulation sought to make man's self-consciousness (and his reason) a natural development of the passions from out of the desire for reconciling silence and solitude. Theorizing does not arise out of wonder, but through fear and uncertainty, and it employs the very resources of fear and uncertainty, (of scepticism) to constitute itself. Thus, the order of man's world as reflected in the rationality of man's scientific and theoretic projects does not rest upon standards that transcend the concrete characterization of the human, but derive from human will. There are no theoretic grounds for this order and man justifies the order only by virtue of his activity of ordering.[1]

Nature as the state of nature is no longer formulated as the firstness that is Being, but as the isolation and dis-association of men engendered by nature's concrete brutishness; nature disperses and fragments and the Real unity that is society can only occur through a radical operation performed upon nature. The radical character of this alteration is presupposed by the fact that Being has been withdrawn: because there is

[1] See L. Strauss, *The Political Philosophy of Hobbes, op. cit.*

nothing higher than man, concerting is only possible through an external force, or through the concrete and fortuitous development of man's nature (re-interpreted as necessary through the idea of history).

It is precisely the fortuitousness of this transition as a development within nature that revokes any grounds for gratitude from man, for since there is nothing higher than man, his works – both good and bad – are results of fortune.[1] While as Strauss points out, good fortune leads to self-love and blindness, only misfortune creates the opportunity for reflexivity. Since there is nothing higher than the source of speech – the human subject – good fortune increases narcissism while misfortune creates the opportunity for fear and distrust upon which self-consciousness grows.

The consciousness of self exemplified in Plato – the consciousness of what belongs to one as that *to* which one belongs in an essential way – makes necessary reference to that which lies beyond man, to an order beyond human passion. In the modern re-interpretation of self-consciousness, thinking has nothing to thank; consciousness of oneself becomes consciousness of one's interpersonal situation, i.e., of what one is in comparison with others like himself. Self-consciousness is then constituted through comparison with other men, rather than by addressing an order in which both one and other participate and to which they belong as something which is beyond them.

Note the difference between the Socratic notion of death in the *Phaedo* and the Hobbesian-Cartesian notion of death: in one case, death is release from the body – the theoretic state – and in the other case, death is being unconvincing or inarticulate. For Socrates, death is being able to execute perfect *anamnesis* because of the soul's liberation, and the kind of selflessness personified by death is the integration of the soul with *Logos* (with what owns it). For Hobbes, death is the loss of self through the lack of *contact* with a concrete other. The two forms of death parallel the two kinds of relationship in which thought can enter (see Chapter 2).

In the relationship of thought to Being (to its true subject), to die is to free this relationship from what covers-it-over in the passage through life. Philosophy as a rehearsal for death means that while philosophy addresses and seeks a glimpse of the One, only in death does the soul become re-integrated.

In contrast, Hobbesian death starts with the relationship of the thought of one being to the thought of an other being, where that relationship is secured by having a subject in common. The subject as the fear of silence in the positive sense is the desire to listen and to be

[1] See Strauss' mention in *Ibid.*; Heidegger's notion of how thinking thinks in *What Is Called Thinking, op. cit.*, is most relevant.

listened to (or the desire to listen because of the primordial desire to be listened to), which in its turn produces the idea of a topic (see Chapter 2). Without a common project, thoughts do not intersect and death comes to mean the isolation of living incorrigibly within one's own voice. Courage for the aesthete then means the will to relax one's grip on what is present to one (as property) in order to distribute it; although sharing requires 'courage' it is undertaken for egocentric reasons. This kind of 'courage' is only required because the idea of what is present as authentic (and as one's own) is itself egocentric.

Hobbes demands that the norm of rational science be developed in accord with the passions even though this Rational idea is a passionless science. Only if the science is constructed so as to co-respond to what men concretely do and to that for which they have no option will the science be recognizable. Hobbes then recognized that the modern science requires a kind of courage and thus, must answer-to the passions. Because self-centred men will not naturally relinquish their property, they must be made to. Theorizing should try to formulate a method for inducing sharing – communication – by exemplifying in its occurrence such a method to make one's voice heard.

Descartes realizes this demand in his conception of the rational science as a science of Rational action – the capacity to make sound and correct judgement – because this Rationality is designed to concur with the essential character of the human agent as one who intuits (acts). Thus, Descartes accepts the classical ideal of infallible knowledge but he re-interprets 'infallibility' so as to make it answer to man's 'capacities,' i.e., that which he is capable of experiencing. Such capacities are rooted in man's character as an actor, as a decision-maker. This re-conception is necessary in order to provide for the realization of the ideal.

Method then becomes transparent as a kind of un-natural or external 'forcing' which re-groups or re-organizes the essential elements, but always as a force that is not itself one of these elements. Aesthetics formulated method as a project for inducing courage as the willingness to submit to the standard of the commonness of experience as the only authentic standard. Since the science of speech requires of itself that it answer-to the authentic common experience it justifies itself in its very creation by *appearing* it-self as such an authentic experience. The difference between the theorist and all others is that he creates and administers a record of creativity itself as another authentic common experience for all men. In studying common action theorizing affirms it-self as a monument to action by constituting itself as the same kind of 'thing' which it studies. The record (data) then becomes the authentic common experience insofar as it simultaneously preserves the experience and affirms itself as the kind of experience which it preserves.

Thus, the record achieves its ideal by imitating what it records; speaking imitates nature by becoming natural; speaking imitates what is present to all by becoming the kind of 'thing' that is present to all. In the first wave of modernity symbolized by Descartes and the British empiricists, the right order of speaking was identified as that order which imitated nature by speaking naturally, where nature was re-conceived as that which is most apparent to the speaker. Speech makes itself into that which is apparent by imitating that which is apparent, and the success of the imitation resides in whether the speech so constituted is as apparent as that which it imitates. Though natural speech records 'nature,' as a record it re-affirms the authenticity of speech that is natural.

To celebrate such speech is to demand of theorizing that it affirm the ordinariness of its achievement by denying its origin in (genius) that which is not apparent and present to all. It remained for later moderns like Rousseau, Kant, and Hegel to point out how the aesthetic denial of genius as a passionate confirmation of genius it-self was now masked by the empirical fantasy of natural speech. The aestheticization of grammar was now rooted as an authoritative conception of authentic speaking (in a grammar) despite its re-distribution in metaphors like 'method' and 'description.' Consequently, the claim of aesthetics to destroy genius in a record created an irreconcilable tension: if the record truly destroyed genius then the apparency of what it created – which was its only justification for the destruction – was too clear to require saying. So it would have to re-cognize that it was speaking silently, redundantly, without any Reason to talk. Because aesthetics attempted to justify itself by becoming what it spoke about, it could only justify itself as a ritual demonstration of the apparent, as an artful celebration of its own artfulness (empiricism as art-for-art's sake). It remained for Rousseau, Kant and Hegel to revive the Socratic argument of the *Charmides* against aestheticism; that in asserting the first-ness of itself as the only nature to which men ought orient it denied its responsibility for speaking and showed how even this denial enunciated the centrality of that which the denial denied. In having to conceive of it-self as an appearance which is mere presence, asthetics could not face itself as a disclosure of the authority of which the present is an appearance. Yet, to deny that the present is an appearance of the underlying is for aesthetics to claim that it is apparent and present to all. To make this claim is to raise the problem of why aesthetics thinks that what it speaks is worth speaking. Aesthetics then has no Reason to speak except to celebrate it-self (its own artfulness). Because aesthetics cannot prepare such a Rational denial, it has to accredit the extra-ordinary character of (it-self) its own achievement and thus, that its claim is denied by its very possibility, that the authenticity of its achievement is grounded in an extra-ordinary conception of discourse that does not answer to its own standard of authenticity – a standard that is neither apparent nor immediate. In pointing to the grammatical source of asthetics, later moderns showed how the aesthetic claim denies it-self (makes it-self impossible) by re-asserting the inexplicable authority of genius as its source.

X

The syllogism was Aristotle's method for preserving the tension of theorizing as a course of action. He treated the failure of his predecessors as their failure to grasp the implications of their speech, of discoursing, i.e., as a failure to grasp the analytic character of an assertive language. Aristotle's notion of such a failure meant that they did not grasp the way in which language mirrored the structure of things; but such a grasp is difficult because the structure of things only becomes discernible through method, and method itself can only be used with a conception of the structure of the things in hand. In Plato, the task of discovering the structure of things was an achievement of a communal search because out of the interchange of opinion emerges truth. Truth does not require a system but the lived experience of wresting unconcealment from its hiddenness under the pressure and impetus of otherness. Otherness grounds and provides incentive for theorizing because theorizing only emerges through such an encounter as the Desire to address the Oneness which all such encounters cover over. Theorizing then occurs under the impulse to speak about the essential collectedness, the Good. However, since this collectedness is hidden and concealed, to speak about the Good requires work, the work of bringing this concealedness to speech. Dialogue functions as man's paradigmatic medium for addressing such Oneness.

Descartes attempts to restore the dimension forgotten by Aristotle, the feature of confronting otherness, of conflict and experience, and he does so by treating otherness as other persons empirically connected to one's voice and as displays of the source of this differentness, a source which resides in the distance separating me from my voice and others from my voice. Descartes does nothing less than create the foundation for the concrete distinction between individual and society, self and other, later to be articulated as political theory.

Thus, even the syllogism glosses the tension, negativity, and violence of theorizing because as a method everything it pre-supposes is treated as a secure achievement rather than as the work of bringing concealment to presence. So, the question is posed: how can the method be grounded and wrested from nothingness?

To bring the method to unconcealment requires beginning a-new and results in so transforming the character of the method as to give it a new look. The weakness of classical thought was that it did not reflect upon thinking, it did not reflect upon its beginnings. Its beginnings in convention, opinion (and consequently, its conclusions as achievements of opinion) are not firm. The beginnings must be solidified and certified. He thus overlooks the crucial classical principle that the false beginning, the beginning in negativity, is essential to theorizing. He wants to begin correctly, and consequently the tension and *aporia* of the beginning and the way it is surpassed can only be written about as autobiography. He writes *about* the tension rather than showing it. Descartes' beginning is not to be surpassed but it is to be adapted to; to know is then not essentially to expose the beginning as a temporalization, but to criticize self for mistaking inauthentic for authentic beginnings, i.e. for not universalizing the first temporalization. Negativity for Descartes then becomes a matter of mistaking true and false beginnings and true and false derivations. However, since true and false derivations are themselves grounded in the mistake of failing to discriminate true from false beginnings, everything reduces to the search for a complete speech. This negativity is only a product of will overtaking rationality; to describe the achievement of true beginnings is then to do a re-description of the same beginnings from the perspective of one who seeks to re-lay their ground.

Descartes' *Rule for the Direction of Mind* then suggests: how to create a foundation for thought which will guarantee the reliability of what it thinks. But since all thought begins and terminates in the conventions of public speech, and since the dialectic between this beginning and end is an essential feature of thought, the notions of certain beginnings and determinant ends merely masks the tension and dialectic of thinking. Reliable thought as agreement between (speakers) is an appearing of the dialectic between thought and its origins which his method does not address. This is to say that the travail of his solitary achievement and the objections of his critics are not even incorporated into his conception as Otherness which is essential and surpassed, but are instead, treated externally. His method itself fails in its own terms because it generates objections and the objections are addressed to the grounds of the method which were not addressed by the method itself.

These problems have their source in the public which Descartes reformulates privately instead of including as essential features of his beginning. The problem of the grounds of his method is the problem of the essential critique of the conventional which the achievement of his method shows. For example, in denying existence (in bracketing) he segregates thought from the public. His problem is to re-think the possibility of what exists not by bracketing and then affirming it a-new, but by addressing what is concealed by 'what exists.' He treats *existence* as in need of solid confirmation rather than of perfectability and rationalization, (he treats the question of mere existence as a decisive problem). To rationalize what exists is to restore its Rational, perfected character by displaying it as a concrete moment in the career of the analytic (of the absolute). Instead, Descartes treats 'mere' existence as a descriptive problem, and in an important way he accepts the Aristotelian ontology by operating within the ontology to re-ground it and to solidify its beginning.

Both Plato and Aristotle accepted the notion that the mind and its objects are linked by an essential kinship. That is, the very meaning of Rational thought is to grasp 'what is.' This unity is given. Thus, knowledge is formulated essentially as that which thinks what is, where what *is* is not what exists but that which ought to be spoken. Consequently, though discrepancies are empirically possible or probable, this is beside the point for the Greeks. Since objects only take on life as they are situated within speech, it is speech which mediates this connection. On the other hand to take the unity of the given as a topic for description is to do sophistry.

The problem is rather, to grasp the sense in which thought (or its icons in speech) thinks (or says) what 'is' where the emphasis is on 'is.' This means not: does speech touch objects or no-thing? But, does speech speak about what is essential or peripheral? Plato and Aristotle then agree on this, while differing on the 'essential' and on how to achieve it. Descartes adapts 'what is essential' to 'what the human is capable of de-ciding' and consequently changes the classical problem by modernizing and transforming it. True speaking as speech that shows that thought is thinking of Being (i.e., of what is, rather than of what is other-than-what-is), is not re-flected in Descartes' programme. True thinking is a re-collecting of the unity of thought with itself which had become dispersed through the otherness of opinion, convention, and social speech.

Although the segregation of subject from object pre-supposed such a unity, it obscured the process of re-collection or *anamnesis* in terms of which this unity was re-collected, and it treated the achievement of this unity not as re-collection and critique, but as empirical, causal, and descriptive. Whereas the classicists asked – given this unity, how can it be restored and re-collected to point beyond itself? the moderns asked – how is this unity possible not as a re-collection, but as an empirical achievement? Thus, the moderns attempted to bracket out or to ignore precisely the given unity which grounded the enterprise (they tried to think away the given) and in so doing, they transformed theorizing as *anamnesis* into theorizing as epistemology, i.e., as discovering.

To accept the modern enterprise is to begin to transform theorizing by wrenching it from its origin in the given. It is to depict theorizing as having a quiet beginning. Thus, it transforms the classical problem of the way thought is controlled by the givenness of the analytic (i.e., that thought must Rationalize this givenness and bring it to speech), by trying either to eliminate the givenness, by treating it as a concrete origin which is added to, or by segregating it from objects by calling it 'mind.'

The classicists treated the beginning (the given) as concealing what it essentially contains within. To make it a topic is to wrest from concealment an experience, an encounter. In other words the Greeks desired to *face* the beginning. The moderns also treated the given as confusion, error, and otherness and they desired to think in spite of or without the given, i.e., to make it a topic by putting it in its place.

XI

Aristotle grounded his achievement in terms of whether or not what it formulates coheres with standards of consistency and rational communication. The formulation justifies itself by creating a lawfully regulated relationship, a relationship that exemplifies a society organized by the law.

The aesthetic attempt to democratize privilege appeared as a relationship of the many to one experience and justified it-self as a formulation in terms of whether it was an appearance of what it recorded, i.e., whether the description was the same kind of experience as that which it imitated. Aesthetics succeeds when it becomes what it imitates whereas ethics succeeds when it becomes a method for idealizing – in images – the law which it imitates. Whereas the concrete success of ethics resides in whether the theory (as a method) can make the law *appear*, the concrete success of aesthetics resides in whether the theory (as description) *looks the same as* that which it describes. Whereas grammar is a method in the service of its law, description is a product of that which it describes. Ethics requires of a reader that he face the question of whether the method serves the law by making it apparent and urges a disregard for the question of the source of lawfulness itself; aesthetics requires of a reader that he decide whether the description exemplifies what it describes and that he disregard the question of the Rationality of such exemplifying and preserving.

Aesthetics seeks to preserve a common experience by making

preservation it-self such an experience. Aesthetics conserves and memorializes the actual society by showing conservation itself to be artful. For aesthetics, the nature of the art of theorizing lies in its ability to produce that which creates it as it-self an object. The nature of theorizing lies in the one-ness of speech and nature, in how speech constitutes it-self as an instance of that which it speaks about, how speech imitates by becoming an item in the environment of that which it imitates. Aesthetic speaking about nature is speech which seeks to become natural.

Ethics seeks to create a possible society exemplified as a community of rational co-speakers which idealizes its law. For ethics, the nature of the art of theorizing lies in the unity of speech with it-self and in the way in which speech exemplifies mathematical principles of organization and relatedness in the products it makes. Ethical theorizing seeks to concretize and re-produce its law whereas aesthetic theorizing seeks to concretize and produce it-self.

In both ethics and aesthetics theory becomes good speech represented as a concrete object which is another thing. The grammar is a concretization of lawful, mathematical principles of relatedness; the description is a concretization of the artfulness of experience as a work of art. Both ethics and aesthetics are grounded in a vision of rational communication: on the one hand, as a system of intelligible co-speakers; on the other hand, as an organization which is in the same position with respect to what is present to them. The rationality of ethical discourse is rooted in a conception of laws and principles for reconciling difference where difference is understood as the perspectiviality of being able to see only one part of what is. The rationality of aesthetic discourse is rooted in a conception of rules and procedures for reconciling difference where difference is understood as the perspectiviality of being in a privileged position in relation to what one speaks. Although ethics and aesthetics differ only in degree, the concrete distinctions between them point to different theoretic moods, to different manifestations of the modern – post-Platonic – interpretation of theorizing.

6
Rhetoric

I

Although both ethics and aesthetics are grounded in ethical ideals of adequate discourse, such ideals are themselves organized around images of 'coming to know' that are aesthetic. Ethics and aesthetics seek confirmation by making their products – grammar or description – apparent and immediate to an other. Regardless of whether truth is re-flected in the certainty that is grasp of principles, or in immediate apprehension, what the grammar proposes and what the description records as formulative products must be made experience-able as a product that is immediate and present to an other.

The rhetorical character of theorizing made reference to the theoretic attempt to speak in order to command assent and the organization of the theoretic enterprise was a response to a common aesthetic conception of convincing speech – of speech that ought convince in its very accomplishment. Knowledge and rhetoric were connected inasmuch as modern traditions of theorizing rested upon standards of knowledge that personified an aesthetic relation of man to speech (the aesthetic notion of presence and immediacy). The idea of rhetoric expresses the aesthetic character of modern theorizing (even in what we have called ethics).

To say that the modern tradition of theorizing is fundamentally aesthetic is not to discredit its ethical character. It is an ethics ultimately grounded in an aesthetic image of the relationship that is knowing, an image that seeks to re-produce the sense of being present to one-self as an authoritative (ethical) standard. The concrete differences surveyed here are ways of pointing to what is essentially the same – that man's relationship to his speaking is authorized by a standard derived from the aesthetic conception of man being present to his speech as an experience. The dilemma of aestheticism – on the one hand, that it must hide the experience of theorizing behind the privileged immunity of inexplicability, or on the other hand, that it must liquidate it-self by showing that it has no Reason to speak – is reflected nicely in the asthetic notion of rhetoric.

Whereas modern theorists treated rhetoric as the concrete kind of convincing – the artful, forensic style of persuading – which ought be external to theory, every theoretical formulation was developed on the grounds of an aesthetic conception of knowledge that was essentially rhetorical. This is because convincingness was seen as making something apparent and was modelled after the idea of the speaker's immediacy to that which was present to him as an apparent experience. The rhetorical character of good speaking was seen in its efforts to constitute itself as speech that is commonly experience-able as a presence to others in the same way that it is present to self.

The very attempt of theorizing to speak rationally was the speaker's attempt to speak convincingly to himself under the auspices of a standard of convincingness which he anticipated as a common experience. Speech included in its very accomplishment the anticipation of its convincing character on the grounds that what is convincing to one ought be convincing to all (or else it is mere 'faith,' caprice, idiosyncrasy).

Although all theorizing accomplishes it-self as a rational and intelligible 'convinced' surpassing of possible objections – and therein lies its Rational character – such rationality does not necessarily consist in being able to convince one-self as one would an other (or being able to convince an other as one would one-self). The idea of *showing* one's conviction is different from the idea of convincing. To show one's conviction was to speak in a way that shows commitment to a standard of rationality where such showing takes the form of affirming one's faithfulness through speech that displays the rational re-creation of this faith on every occasion.

Such committed speaking differs from the idea of speaking convincingly because convincing is a giving of reasons which is – strictly speaking – external to commitment as the rationalization of a commitment already secured. Since one can only speak about a commitment in a committed way, one organizes his speaking as a showing of the Reason for which it speaks.

Committed speaking as speech which shows its faithfulness to Reason (and not to the standard of 'giving reasons') is not persuasive speech. Persuasive speech identifies the goal of speaking with political purpose; committed speaking persuades only in the sense that it shows the speaker as one engaged in persuading him-self on every occasion of speech that his Reason for speaking is worth speaking.

The committed speaker does not speak about what is apparent because what is apparent is not worth speaking for – it is apparent. The committed speaker *uses* what is apparent to speak about that which it covers-over. Given the modern notion of persuasion as convincing an other (as creating an aesthetic relationship), the moderns re-cognized that the convincingness of speech diminishes as it turns away from the apparent. Given the authoritative character of the standard of aesthetic conviction as knowledge, the moderns elected to speak apparently (to say no-thing) in order to speak convincingly. Aesthetics requires the concretization of speech.

II

For Plato, the task of theorizing was to make men better; to arouse in men a Desire to re-assess their place in the order, and through the action of such a re-assessment to become beings better fitted to participate in that order. Theorizing was a continual effort to re-convince one-self of the Rationality of one's fate-ful participation in this order. For the moderns, such a version of theorizing could not lead to success because success was understood as the convincing that is communicating and persuading an other. The moderns saw the principle task of theorizing as one of communicating, of producing agreement among speakers. Theorizing became re-defined as a method for producing agreement, i.e., for silencing rhetoric, because rhetoric was used as a metaphor for difference.

In dialectic, thinking is more like a re-producing than a producing, because the thinker seeks to re-enact in thought the history of a notion already produced and secured. Thinking is action only in the sense that the thinker is one who re-enacts and imitates – who answers to – the togetherness of language and Being. Thinking is acting only in the sense that thinking is an answering-to Being and in such an answering is a re-enacting or re-producing. Therefore, successful theorizing is speaking which succeeds in showing the thoughtful achievement of a notion already secured in discussion. Success is not a concrete performance, but a speaking which shows the re-opening and re-centring of a discussion long since repressed and covered-over by routine usage. Thinking *is* action, but it is the Action symbolized by the idea of a movement within the soul; it is Real action and not inter-action.

The success of theorizing for Plato resided in its capacity to symbolize Desire. The success of theorizing consisted in the fact that in being done it re-created occasions of critical speech. Such a re-creation is concretized in the way in which the speaking shows in what it says its contest with the unthought as a Rational movement. Theorizing is speaking that shows the Reason of critical speaking to lie in the imperative need to re-assert itself as an instance of faithfulness to Reason itself. The success of theorizing in the deepest sense lies in the fact that it re-directs attention to the grounds of speaking by speaking so as to evoke in its very speech the ideal of addressing grounds as the

Good. In this way, dialectic recognizes the essential liaison between theorizing and rhetoric that is captured by the idea of displaying; theorizing is a speaking that acknowledges in its very activity the commitment and authorization which makes it possible, and which shows such an acknowledgement by making this commitment the topic of the speaking. From a dialectical perspective, theorizing is the speaking which understands itself as inescapably rhetorical, and which acts upon such an understanding by preparing its very speech as an argument for the Rationality of that commitment. Theorizing then achieves its purest character when it conceives of itself as the speaking that is displaying and arguing rather than the speaking which seeks to create a unity among different arguments and different displays. Whereas moderns regarded successful inquiry as that which silenced discussion by producing speech to which one must assent, dialectic treats inquiry as the re-opening of a discussion that routine usage has long covered-over. Yet the arguing which theory is is not the giving of reasons, but a showing of the achievement of its authorization as a way of affirming the Rationality of that author.

The fact that men disagree was taken by Plato's successors not as the appearance of an origin to be made transparent, but as a concrete origin itself – a social problem – which it was the task of theorizing to resolve. Given the fact of the primordial distinction between theorist (as speaker) and hearer – if there was no difference the speaker would have no moral mandate to speak since he was only repeating what is apparent to both – the very speaking situation raised for the speaker his responsibility to ground his claim to have some-thing to say. The rhetorical possibilities of speaking are disclosed in the act itself as a claim to knowledgeability. Yet it was just this claim and the differentiation which it tacitly created that the moderns had to repress under the force of a stipulation which promised to suppress the differentiation that the very speaking had created. Since such repressions work against the essential impulse of theorizing to address its origin, the persuasive silencing of rhetoric could only be grounded on the promise that the repressed difference would be re-experienced as a moment in the course of talk to follow (but not as a course of action to be described like one's 'assumptions' etc. for that would still preserve the repression of the difference). Because the fulfilment of such a promise meant that theorizing would forever circle about its origins without progressing to a conclusion, no theorist after Plato could mobilize the nerve to resist the impulse to progress; consequently every theorist after Plato abandoned this promise by silencing rhetoric through a persuasive repression and by moving forward on the basis of such a repression now secured and protected from scrutiny.

Whereas the moderns regarded theorizing as the overcoming of rhetoric, this desire was grounded in a concrete notion of rhetoric as dispute and disagreement (as a communication problem, a 'social' problem): in contrast, given the understanding of rhetoric as a speaking which *says* – as the speaking which seeks to make reference to its self-same authorization, and which in so doing affirms the authority of the authorization – theorizing was essentially rhetorical and could no more overcome rhetoric than it could speak about itself without speaking.

III

The ability of theory to communicate – to overcome rhetorical differences – is impaired unless communication is guaranteed at the start through a willful stipulation which imposes unity upon a circle of speakers and hearers. Thus, the ability of theory to overcome rhetoric depends upon its rhetorical character. Aristotle and Descartes tried in different ways to argue that their programmes eliminated rhetoric, that their respective creations of unity – of secure starting points – were respectively rational (legal), and apparent (natural).

Aristotle adopted the perspective of a rational user of ordinary language – of one who knows the rules of usage – and he argued for the binding and cohesive character of such rules as a method for enforcing unity. Such rules could only acquire their character as binding and intelligible if members had available the entire apparatus of Aristotelian ontology and language from which the intelligibility derived. Consequently the member of the Aristotelian system had to begin by an act of wilful belief in the system itself whereas the subsequent programme developed by Aristotle made no attempt to expose the achievement of the system to the member as an on-going commitment secured and wrested from concealment. The elimination of rhetoric proceeded by legislating a rational form of language claimed to re-construct ordinary discourse in order to meet mathematical conditions of intelligibility as formal rules of procedure that co-responded to some unanalyzed version of the rational use of language to assert, deny, relate and conclude. Aristotle's problem – fully recognized by Descartes – was that such a creation masked the experience on which it was grounded by legislating as extraneous any concern with the achievement of the experience. Although the authority of this language was licensed by the Aristotelian claim that it answered to a rational transformation of ordinary usage, the very achievement of this transformation as an instance of theorizing was suppressed and its result was rhetorically acclaimed as a secure point of departure for subsequent speech.

The experience of authorizing the programme was not itself a topic for the programme, the experience of authorizing the programme was a suppressed feature of the programme. The authority of the construction remained to be experienced, for if not, it was merely legislation. Descartes argued that the experience of the construction required that it answer to the first and basic conception which the human developed of the world. The conception around which Descartes wanted to organize the programme was the person's conception of him-self as an object for himself as this conception was articulated in the notion of the experience of anyman. Descartes argued that the essentially rhetorical character of rudimentary experience – its capacity to symbolize what was present to anyman – must ground any programme or method. That is, an adequate method would silence rhetoric in its very production because to produce the authority as an answering-to the experience of anyman is to guarantee the persuasive, i.e., standard and universal character of the authority (of the method).

Both Aristotle and Descartes sought to develop programmes whose very production would maximize communication and agreement. They sought to make the decision to accept the programme irrelevant on the grounds that its very production would guarantee its acceptability, that its very production would silence the rhetorical propensity. Aristotle could only supply such a guarantee through the stipulation that his programme was self-evident to a rational member where the achievement of such self-evidence was protected from scrutiny; Aristotle's entire programme was based upon a conception of the rationality of an ordinary member which grounded his programme as an authoritative version of rationality. Aristotle tried to argue that the 'results' or works which the programme accomplished would testify to the solidity and persuasiveness of his beginning, but this could only be an effective demonstration for one who had already accepted the authority of his beginning. Aristotle could then only silence rhetoric rhetorically by inducing men to accept on faith the idealization which his programme recommended. The idealization itself as an achievement and topic of theorizing was never re-entered into the programme and Aristotle never sought to show the achievement of the idealization as a movement within his very writing itself. Thus, the first great effort to silence rhetoric only succeeded through the creation of a circle of believers, of men who refused to theorize or who were prevented from theorizing by being protected from exposure to the achievement of the authority of the programme.

Descartes realized that the acceptance of the programme had to be a topic of the programme itself, i.e., that the authorization of the programme had to become a feature of the selfsame programme. In order to secure the programme on a ground of knowledge rather than belief, the idealization which it recommended had to answer to the experience of anyman. Descartes' democratization led to a new version of theorizing as that kind of speaking which is essentially persuasive because it makes it-self into the kind of appearance (fact) from which no one can dissent. Descartes tried to re-lay the grounds of speech by concretizing speech so totally that it could only speak what is apparent and if what it speaks is apparent, what it speaks about cannot be doubted. Yet if what it speaks cannot be doubted on *those* grounds then what it speaks is banal (it says nothing) is silence. However, because Descartes' concretization of speech could still be seen by those who followed him to preserve an unanalyzed authority as its ground (in the Cartesian ideal of rationality), it remained for later empiricists to create the most concrete speech – the perfect record – as the speech which says no-thing, the description.

The starting points or beginnings of each programme treated themselves as secure beginnings; regardless of whether the start was from the rationality of a conventional member, or from the security of an apparent presence, both notions were achieved in terms of the unity of understandings which provided for their possibility. Consequently both programmes accepted their starting points as real starting points and moved on to other matters without making the very achievement of their beginnings topics of their speaking. In both programmes, rhetoric was silenced through the use of rhetoric; through the forceful and extraneous creation of an authoritative form of sociality, of discourse whose character was not to be re-explored. Each programme claimed that the authority in which it is grounded – the untouched, secure and protected authority of the programme – is to be *tested* in this way: that whatever the programme achieves will be counted as evidence for its authoritativeness, where 'test' means that users of the programme agree and concert in treating the 'result' as adequate evidence. Consequently, the security of the programme as starting point is strengthened on the grounds that results are contingently connected evidential demonstrations of this authority. Yet, since every demonstration presupposes the acceptance of the authority being demonstrated, the programme produces evidence for itself only if its authority is already accepted; the authority for the programme cannot be subjected to tests independently of its exercise.

That both Aristotelian and Cartesian programmes silence rhetoric rhetorically by treating extensions of their authority as independent tests is seen in the fact that the persuasiveness of the programmes terminate at the point at which their authority is rejected, thus creating the very dispute and contentiousness which the respective programmes were designed to eliminate. In this sense, the achievements of programmes never silence rhetoric because such achievements never stand as descriptions independent of the authority which licences them; rhetoric can only be silenced if men are already of one voice, and to talk about the silencing as a 'test' is to misconstrue the nature of speaking, and is to strengthen the authority through surreptitious means. The analytic character of the programme consists less in what it concretely achieves than in how it shows the necessity of speaking in the way it recommends as a Rational and moral necessity.

In this sense, the political philosophies of Machiavelli and Hobbes intended to show that the only option for theorizing lies in its demonstration of the necessity for speaking in one voice as the only concrete solution to the problem of order. Programmes of theorizing only tangentially demonstrate the adequacy of their authority through 'works,' but must be essentially construed as arguments for the requiredness of the acceptance of their authority on the grounds that such acceptance is a necessary condition of failure for order, that in its absence there will be rhetoric, i.e., conflict, isolation, coercion, force. The demonstration proceeded by normalizing the discontinuity between the achievement of speech and its source by forcing speech to answer-to that which it speaks about when that subject is the ordinary ways in which men speak. To show how possessive speech is superseded by speech which displays sharing is to produce a speech which exemplifies sharing. The justification of such a speech is that it recapitulates what it records, it becomes what it describes. The grand political theories which recorded the growth of order (of 'society' from 'nature') were – as speeches – instances of society. In this way, writing justified its claim to write – its Reason – by exemplifying the history which it was recording. Political theory further aestheticized the Cartesian programme by adding to the desire to become – what was being spoken about, the ideological claim that such writing exemplified the Rational state as the Good, as the ideal communicative possibility. In this way, the Cartesian ideal of rationality as a typification of pure mind was revised on the grounds that its authoritative grammatical roots were still extraordinary: to force theorizing to answer-to the ordinary was to convert the authority on which it was grounded into the most apparent *image* of commonality, the ideal of a political society. The Cartesian conception of the fundamental apparency of the common experience was seen as unjustifiable because it failed to respect the iconic character of this intuition as an image of the most apparent and immediate (common) desire for communality and order.

IV

Theorizing – like society – is a method designed to overcome dispute and difference, to silence rhetoric in order to establish the unity of one tongue. Aristotle attempted to create this unity through his excavation of ordinary language which was grounded in his vision of the rationality of ordinary language. Yet such a vision was an instance of belief rather than knowledge as long as its foundation remained unexplored.

The moderns saw this well. Descartes and Bacon before him, recognized that the very rhetorical character of Aristotle's start merely served to preserve rhetoricizing in his new speech. As Bacon put it, Aristotle did not take his bearings from nature. Speech had to take its bearings from nature, i.e., from the logos of the natural, where natural became re-defined as that which is most apparent to anyman.

The empiricists argued that that which is most apparent – nature – is not one-self because to even re-cognize this presence as apparent requires a language and limits of grammaticality. The most apparent 'fact' intuited by men is that without language there is silence and what is first present to man is the necessary condition of failure for language – that condition without which speaking would make no sense. To the empiricists, speech was possible only on the condition that it was heard and to hear speech was to assume a common understanding. Such common understanding makes reference to the most apparent common need to communicate – the need for order – and thus, the common and first appearance which is present to man is a need, his (common) need for order. This ought be the most apparent fact.

Theorizing ought then take its bearings from nature which meant: not from the experience (of the speaker) which is most apparent, but from an understanding of the need which is most apparent (the need for order). The apparency of such an understanding is achieved when man reflects upon what is most immediate – his language – not through grammatical analysis – but by *describing* why men speak (in the most concrete sense) as their method of achieving satisfaction – of satisfying needs – of attaining pleasure. What is apparent about such an inspection is that men are seen to speak in order to communicate and to communicate as a way of satisfying their need for order – for the pleasure of order. Man's basic need to become convinced is a need for order, and since he is only convinced by what is apparent, speech which takes its bearings from nature will make it-self apparent.

To study nature – the apparent human need for pleasure – represented in the icon of the political state, by becoming an instance of that pleasure. As a product theory is no longer merely commemorative, for it serves to exemplify the symbolic satisfaction of the most basic human need. Theory becomes totally aestheticized.

The ideal of imitating nature is preserved but in a new form. Aristotle saw the nature of an art as speaking which artfully coheres with various authoritative standards of grammaticality. The nature of art like theorizing lay in its faithfulness to it-self, in its one-ness with itself. For example, the classical Aristotelian notion of unities meant that good speaking ought preserve the authority of grammatical standards based upon some conception of the rationality of the grammar.

In a way, the moderns accepted the Socratic challenge of the *Charmides* that the nature of an art cannot be internal to it – it cannot be a standard of artfulness – because this produces the insular formalism of grammar as a mathematical system. The moderns sought to divorce nature from the art on the grounds that intelligible justification of the art could only occur within the context of such a relationship.

If the good art imitated nature and if this was to mean more than narcissistic self-celebration (which the moderns associated with classicism) then it must imitate some-thing external. This is because imitation presupposes a relationship and since what is internal is not other, to speak of 'imitating' what is the same is gratuitous. They reasoned that to imitate nature is to imitate that which is external to the art.

Since the art of theorizing was essentially speaking, theorizing must imitate what is external to speech. Yet, instead of seeing this 'external' condition as no 'condition' at all (as no-thing, silence, the void), they formulated it as that which was most apparent and immediate to the speaker. Whereas Descartes identified such an apparency with the experience of one self, empiricists re-cognized it in the common need. The firstness of nature lay in the fact that it was the most apparent experience or need re-cognized by the speaker.

The problem of empiricism lay in this re-cognition, for the apparency of the common need for order was covered-over by the appearance of self-interest, disorder, war – all of the icons of rhetoric. Consequently empiricism had to admit that its common re-cognition was more than apparent – that *it* was speaking extraordinarily – and that consequently, its claim to make the origin of theorizing ordinary was denied by its very speaking. Empiricism like Descartes had to affirm its conviction as an extraordinary achievement. The attempt to make theory ordinary by forcing it to answer-to the apparently common is an attempt which re-asserts its own extraordinariness.

The idea that theory could be normalized by answering-to an external nature meant that speaking could only speak what was most apparent. To speak about what is most apparent is to have no reason to speak and produces the nihilistic character of empiricism. Yet the very idea of what is most apparent is not an apparent and common idea but a particular (extraordinary) achievement: consequently, empiricism denies in its very occurrence the claim it makes for itself against classicism because empiricism still (whether Cartesian or later) protects its achievement under the immunity of genius.

V

With the rise of modern traditions Being no longer refers to the Good, but rather, comes to stand for the re-cognition of the commonness of interests, of the common need, the common experience. Because of this re-cognition theorizing ought to be responsible to the source of commonness where such a source can only be a grammatical rule. Given the irrelevance of Dialectic to the moderns, the failure of aesthetics could only re-assert the imperativeness of a grammatical solution, a law. The post-Kantian need was to develop a new icon for law, yet a metaphor which was responsive to the aesthetic requirement of presence and apparency. What is needed is a law that can be mathematically re-created both as a product of the possibilities of presence and as a resource for generating speech which is immediate and apparent – which is present – to all. To be rational is not to understand the coherence of things, but is to grasp how self and other *need* one another: since self and other need one another, and since they are two different things, this need can only be actualized when they re-cognize its commonness – that this need is what they have in common – and it is symbolized in their understanding that a third (standard) is required to mediate claims arising from their status as two different or unlike things. This standard is exemplified by external authority or law. The recognition of the requiredness of law then exemplifies the modern theoretical paradigm.

In scientific programmes, the very same problem occurs. Science is the re-cognition of the requiredness of law to mediate the different speaking practices of different speakers, or the observations generated by different observers. Science arises when man re-cognizes the need for law as embodied in programmes of method. Science is possible in the same way that society is possible and the actualization of association testifies to the rationality of science. Science and society become mutually exchangeable metaphors for man's willful decision to submit to law under the auspices of his recognition that such submission is the efficient method for preserving self-interest in a peaceable way.

The moderns then use some conception of the social relationship as a metaphor for the development of theorizing and in such a formulation modelled theorizing after the rationality of a particular kind of association. Either the political state or the democratic social relation became the metaphor for theorizing; consequently the moderns re-interpreted the notion of relationship. Underlying the modern re-formulation of theorizing was a deep re-assessment of the notion of a social relationship against which theorizing was modelled. The moderns re-defined theorizing because the relationship – the typical metaphor in terms of which theorizing was formulated – was simultaneously re-formulated through changes in notions like unity, difference, social, and togetherness. Through this shift, the moderns made theorizing equivalent to the organization of rational association; through this shift, the moderns transformed theorizing into a method for the production of communal agreement. Theorizing becomes re-formulated as a method for producing a democratic state. Sociology as the first science then acquires its character through its promise to preserve and affirm the ideal of science as the ground for all genuine community building. Science and democracy become theoretic and lay metaphors for the goal which theorizing is intending to produce.

The modern version of relationship as the problem of the social then appears in this form: given man's alienable, incorrigible, and indubitable right as the discoursing subject – a right which is not interrogated – how is a common order created? The common order is understood as arising from the desire of each to sustain and protect his right as a discoursing subject and from the re-cognition that only through such an external standard will this inalienable right be preserved. The standard must answer to what men have in common despite their differences as possessors of this right. What men have in common is *that* they possess the right to speak and *that* they recognize the need to preserve this right. This modern version of the idea of relationship addresses man's recognition of his right to speak – man answers to this right by accepting the constraint of the standard which will preserve it. The common order arises out of self-interest because the logos of relationship now addresses man's capacity to act upon his right and to make his behaviour correspond to this right and to answer to it.

The modern notion of relationship then makes reference to this feature of the togetherness of men: that their concerting appears as a method of symbolizing their desire to preserve and protect their free and inalienable right(s) as discoursing subjects. To relate or to belong together is to be (similar) in the same position with respect to this desire. Men relate as a showing of common interests (of having desire, impulse, position, in common). Being appears through 'relationship' as the rational character of the common. The modern version of relationship takes as its problem the bringing together of analytically differentiated 'things' and thus, begins in willful violation of the notion that all-is-one.

If speaking can be seen as a right, its rightness is secured. The approach of sociology to the logos of relationship covers over the resonances of belonging-together as a duty: if discoursing is a duty it is that which re-cognizes its responsibility to that which owns it and to which it *essentially* (and not contingently) belongs. The duty of discourse is to address itself as a relationship (as a belonging-together with that which rules it). 'Relationship' ought address the dutifulness of discourse to that with which it belongs together and it is *this* notion of togetherness as relationship that sociology obscures by beginning with the security of discourse as a right rather than as a duty.

The modern version of a relationship is based upon the conception of speech as free speech: speech is free to speak any-thing other than nothing and the essence of man – as a speaker – is this freedom. This freedom which sees man as all right and no duty then creates as the problem of theorizing: how to preserve this freedom while introducing a duty (rationality) which is designed to correct the very nihilism which the idea of the basic 'freedom' created. Because man is not conceived essentially as a responsible speaker – because there is nothing beyond his relation to his voice – what man *is* is the preserver and publicizer of this relation. Theorizing is concerned with communicating a standard for helping men to speak dutifully where the duty is re-cognized (ego-centrically, self-centredly) for reasons which deny the thoughtful resonances of dutifulness as man's relation to Being. The problem which theorizing sets for it-self is a modern problem: it is only intelligible as a result of the destruction of the ideas of dutiful speech through the esocentric stipulation that Being is equivalent to the temporalization that life is equivalent to the voice as an immediate presence.

The idea of relationship as belonging-together is essential to dialectic and in its new approach to the idea of relationship sociology shows a radically new attitude to the problem. Sociology as a metaphor for modernity impersonates the modern re-thinking of Being and to address sociology is to confront the modern situation as a new context of thinking, and Desire.

VI

If the moderns conceived of theorizing as a method for overcoming rhetoric, this was only because they had a concrete understanding of rhetoric as those differences between speakers and hearers which require convincing re-unification. One might say that true theorizing appears as the recognition of the analytic character of rhetoric, for with this recognition comes a rational orientation towards speech.

The moderns then began by recognizing the analytic centrality of difference as the problem to be overcome because they accepted the indubitable necessity of interiority as the first relation. Theorizing had to be a method for creating unity because unity was the essential problem formulated by the aesthetic paradigm. Yet the unity created could only be grounded in the commonalities underlying the taken-for-granted differentiation. Where the problem for theorizing lay in the differences to which theorizing was a response, the standard for resolving the problem was anchored in an ideal of commonality re-formulated as the necessary conditions of failure for unity. To theorize was conceived as a method of speaking under the auspices of such a standard with the concrete expectation that such speaking would silence difference, i.e., would quiet rhetoric.

Plato reasoned otherwise: what the moderns took as difference – as the concrete, empirical starting point or problem to be resolved – is actually a display of community, the community in which speaking unfolds and which is affirmed in the very act of speaking. The task of inquiry is not to create concrete community but is to re-assess the analytic character of the community which becomes available and hearable through speaking itself. The task of theorizing is not to over-come difference but to see *this* difference – as itself the disclosure of a unity. The problem of theorizing for Plato is the difference between a collective and a community and the problem of theorizing is resolved when men come to treat their speech as the display of such a difference and when they come to orient to this display as the central topic of their speech.

Thus, to start with difference as the problem – to begin with a con-ception of the external relation between theory and rhetoric – is to see theory as the third thing, i.e., as that which is common to two different things. Theory appears just as Aristotle's idea of science stands to the special sciences; yet, an analytic notion of theory must be grounded in something beyond the commonality underlying difference because such a commonality is itself differentiated from a unity which makes it possible.

The modern view isolates the theorist from that about which he speaks because the unity and difference about which *he* speaks is itself the production of a unity of understandings of which it is an appearance. This isolation is necessary given Rousseau's attempt to induce the speaker to treat language as a natural thing. In contrast, theorizing and rhetoric interrelate in the sense that all speaking is a display of this commitment; theory then unifies differences only within a context that stipulates and pre-figures that unification. The view of theory as a solution to rhetoric then leaves out the organized conditions which provide for the intelligibility of the view itself.

True theory is then a way of making reference to the difference between real and natural community or between rational and conventional community: but it is a way of making reference that treats its very own speaking as a display of that difference, a display that is committed to the version of community that provides for the intelligibility of the self-same difference. True theorizing is speaking that understands itself as a display of the rational community that lies covered-over by conventional and routine concerting and speaking.

For theory to seek to overcome difference is to overlook the crucial identity of theorizing and rhetoric: that theorizing is a display of the theorist's commitment to some conception of the difference between his speech and that about which it speaks. Theorizing is then an argument for the rationality of the authority under whose auspices it speaks. As an exposure of its own commitment, theorizing displays its Reason for speaking in its very speaking. Theorizing which seeks to overcome difference takes this Reason for granted, and silences its possible topicality. The modern attitude towards theory then sees it as the method for creating a new thing out of two, instead of as a way of making the unity underlying all things transparent and Reasonable.

Genuine theorizing can never overcome difference because each such effort displays a commitment which is itself a difference: every such 'solution' testifies to the impossibility of a solution because each solution is possible only in terms of a commitment to difference. The idea that theory overcomes difference is based upon the ideal of normalizing theory – of suppressing its ordinary origin – because difference enunciates the discontinuity between what the theory speaks and the claim which its very act of speaking makes. The idea of unifying difference *through speech* is still a speech which in its very speaking claims itself as a difference. This indifference is expressed in the very act of speaking because if it was not claimed the speaker would be speaking irresponsibly. Inasmuch as theorizing is responsible saying, its occurrence is extraordinary on the grounds that what it says cannot be apparent. Theorizing is the speaking which shows the difference between what it speaks and its grounds as a difference worth preserving, as a difference worth exposing. To forget that difference is to forget why we speak.

The mathematical structure of grammaticality is symbolized in the formulation of rules which are designed to re-conciliate as an ethical imperative (idealized as grammar) the differences elicited by a notion of free speaking (by the idea that man is essentially a free speaker because he is free to make any noises). This concrete, aesthetic conception of man produces the problem for theory of reconciling difference and its grammatical formulation of a solution in the idea of rule. With this problem occurs the forgetting of difference – as difference – and of Real unity, the unity of Being.

Rule becomes that which is common to two unlike things, that third thing or standard which provides for their related character. Rule is the common speech within which speaking differences are produced. What rule rules is then difference, i.e., rule rules by commanding the unity of different things and consequently, rule acquires its analytic power as the source of communality, as the grounds of similarity. Rule among the moderns, and particularly for sociology, acquires its force as a political power, i.e., the analytic character of rule is established by considering how rule rules.

Speech rules man but what rules speech? What is speech ruled by? Speech is ruled by that which allows it to speak; as a speaking and hearing, speech is ruled by what it hears its speaking as saying; speech speaks only by hearing and heeding what it says. Speech is ruled by logos which it follows in its speaking; as a way of making reference to logos, speech speaks under the rule of what it hears.

The modern version of rule treats the essence of language as ruling rather than as being ruled, of establishing value and 'meaning' through its unifying, political power; the modern version of rule leaves untouched the question of how language is ruled. Language as the repository of common value acquires its value through its commonness: yet the commonness of language is just a covering-over of that which rules language.

The modern concern with the rule of language was then directed to establishing rule through the use of language; it was an essentially political rather than theoretic concern. In this sense, the establishment of rule meant the silencing of rhetoric through forceful and authoritative speaking the success of which was seen in its capacity to rule. In terms of a political interest a modern could never allow the grounds and authorizations of rule to go exposed and challenged, but had to secure and to fasten tightly this authority as the starting point of subsequent speech, i.e., of subsequent exploitation. In contrast, the dialectical conception of language conceived of it as a speaking which addressed that which ruled it; in this view, speech addresses the rule which authorizes it – which it hears in its speaking – rather than attempting to establish *its* rule through speaking. The moderns misunderstood the character of language because they politicize speaking through the notion of rule.

The version of theory as the silencing of rhetoric through the creation of unity overlooks the question of the unity in which the very speaking that is theorizing is grounded: theory displays a unity already achieved. The dialectical view of theory then divests the activity of the central feature which moderns had assigned to it, for any creation of community is an extension of a communal commitment already secured. Theory is known not through its works or productions but in its re-production, because the theorist re-produces the achievement of authority which gives his speech life, and he organizes such a re-producing so as to invite others to participate in its re-experience. Theorizing seeks to display its commitment as a Rational commitment by intending its speech as an exemplification of the *analytic* community which authorizes it. In this sense, theorizing actually preserves rhetoric as the intelligible display of a differentiated commitment to analytic authority and does not seek to silence rhetoric whether in the name of the firstness of commonness, self, or nature.

Theorizing does not create community, but affirms it; theorizing is not guided by the desire to establish a community of speakers and hearers, but by the Desire to expose its self same commitment to a conception of that which makes speaking and hearing intelligible as the speaking that *is* hearing. Theorizing does not bring speakers and hearers together but affirms their togetherness in its very act of speaking. Theorizing does not seek to bring speaker and hearer together because theorizing *is* a speaking that is a hearing. Consequently theorizing does not build communities, nor accumulate power and riches, it does not force men to hear in one way so as to treat such induction as signs of success or failure. Rather theorizing affirms the community in which it is steeped as a difference wrenched from that which unifies all speech. Successful theorizing in this sense is speaking which invites Other to participate in the re-experience of this achievement. The metaphor for theorizing can never be the social relationship or the political society as it is understood by moderns because both of these images are grounded in conceptions of relationships that are antithetical to the very notion of theorizing, conceptions that deny the analytic notion of togetherness.

The idea of relationship in which dialectical theorizing is grounded is the idea of the relationship of speech to that which rules it. In contrast, the notion of a relationship in which modern thought is grounded – the metaphors of the political state and of the democratic social relationship – are grounded in conceptions of the relatedness of different individuals, i.e., of the relatedness between speakers and hearers in a community of concrete selves.

The modern idea of theorizing is then exemplified through the metaphor of democracy; democracy is a typification of the ideal of relationship or state which theorizing intends to accomplish in its speaking. Democracy is a typification of the unity which theorizing intends to accomplish in its overcoming of rhetoric. The virtue of democracy is that it is a unity whose assembly is guided and controlled by each of its participants. The method for the achievement of democracy is paradigmatically science, i.e., science has developed historically as the most efficient method for the achievement of the unity that is democratic community. Thus science and democracy run hand in glove, as mutually exchangeable method and product entering into the production of ideal modern community. Theorizing as the handmaiden in such an operation is the kind of speaking which intends to accomplish the production of such communality, and sociology then emerges as the first science on altogether different grounds. The firstness of sociology lies in the fact that it is the only art which recognizes the authority of the democratic social relationship as a moral mandate for speaking. Thus sociology establishes its priority on the grounds of seeking to affirm in its speaking the ideal of conventional democracy re-flected in the image of the scientific rationality.

Science is the happy blend of freedom and efficiency. Sociology does not intend to eliminate rhetoric but to eliminate rhetoric in the name of a law that is altogether superior to any other form of ethics because it exemplifies the highest synthesis of man's free speaking and peace-ableness. Thus the law of science is exalted by the science of sociology as an exemplar for ordinary men. The law of science promotes values of freedom by allowing every man to speak, but by constraining him to speak about what is present and apparent through the provision of an inventory for such speaking possibilities. The society that speaks under the auspices of such a law – the possible society – will be a rational and ethical society. This will be a truly 'open' society though as Rosen says, it will not be open to Being. This society will be 'open' to what is apparent and present and to the legality of its method of speaking. The new science will be sociology – that science which will seek to produce images of the 'open society' in its speech. This new science will be beyond rhetoric because its ideal of democratic conversation is apparent and present to all (is apprehended as an instance of democracy) because it is grounded in the basic human need (for order) to be convinced.

The Good of sociology is then this: its very accomplishment shows that rhetoric can be overcome and that rhetoric can be overcome in a way that serves to re-produce the ideal of community exemplified in the image of the 'open society.' Sociology is the active promoting of science as the ideal society. Sociology becomes a method for over-coming rhetoric that in its overcoming idealizes the character of science as the grounds for ideal community. Sociology then bases its claim to firstness on the grounds that of all the sciences, it is the only science which understands the community building power of science itself, that sociology will be the science that will guard, preserve and affirm the moral character of science itself as the grounds of communality. The firstness of sociology consists not in its lawfulness – its willingness to follow the law – for all 'sciences' do that, but in the fact that it will seek to create aesthetic images of that law in its various possible societies which it will generate as grammatical consequences of the law itself.

The aesthetic conception of the human produces the imperative need for a grammatical solution that fulfills aesthetic criteria. The law of science is re-organized as a possible society which displays men as aesthetic objects for one another, as objects who are apparent and present to one another. Such criteria must be 'generative,' i.e., they must be re-produceable by an inventory of possible ways of speaking about such an aesthetic organization. The notions of culture and social structures, of norms and values, roles and statuses, classes and power, racial and ethnic groups, are methods for controlling and anticipating speech about the aesthetic inter-actions among men. Yet despite its ingenuity every such grammar – regardless of its consistency and of the apparency of what it speaks – will not itself be an aesthetic object (or, if it seeks to aestheticize itself totally it will become speechless, banal) but can only be seen as an extraordinary achievement. As a necessary condition for reading any grammar aesthetically, for his very notion of ordinary is extra-ordinary the refusal of grammarians and describers to face the extraordinariness of their achievements re-invokes the immunity of genius.

Rational speech is identified with Rhetoric because the aesthetic paradigm identifies externality (what is Other to speech) with the speaker assuming that what is essential to this speaker as a speechless 'thing' is that he (unlike other things) has an interior life. Externality is identified with the interiority of the speaker's perspective, thus creating the incorrigible isolation of the speaker's relation to his voice as first. If speech is essentially perspectivial (if this is its empirical character), good speech can only be speech which overcomes this isolation, which unifies and establishes concrete contact between speakers. The rational speaker is one who understands the requiredness of organizing his speech as a concrete and immediate presence for other persons. Sociality becomes a metaphor for the contingent attachment of others to my world (where that world as 'me' is symbolized by my primordial relation to my speech, I 'am' that relation) and consequently, Other is transformed from that which (as first, unconditioned and ineffable) is other than speech (*because* of its firstness, unconditionality, ineffability) into that concrete collection of alters (other persons) who stand at varying distances from my self (my relation to my speech). Because self is conceived as this primordial relation (between speaker and his voice), other is formulated as other persons who are external to this relationship (to what is now, self). The line between self and other is concretized and drawn between bodies because speech has already been reformulated as a body.

7

Commonality and Communality

We are so little accustomed to treat social phenomena scientifically that certain of the propositions contained in this book may well surprise the reader. However, if there is to be a social science, we shall expect it not merely to paraphrase the traditional prejudices of the common man but to give us a new and different view of them; for the aim of all science is to make discoveries and every discovery more or less disturbs accepted ideas.[1]

Durkheim, *The Rules of Sociological Method*

I

To make 'social phenomena' present and apparent to the reader will be 'surprising' because – after all, they are not present and apparent. The surprise shows Durkheim's response to the claim his very act of writing makes: this claim denies his aspiration to make his speech apparent because the reader has to see beyond what is apparent in order to accept this apparency.

We see the idea of the critical character of the science and the question we want to raise is: in what does the power of the critique lie? *It disturbs accepted ideas.* Thus Durkheim warns the reader that

The reader must bear in mind that the ways of thinking to which he is most inclined are adverse, rather than favourable, to the scientific study of social phenomena.[2]

Evidently, science will go beyond the apparent. In the preface, Durkheim constructs a relationship with the reader; if preface means that which is prior to being faced, Durkheim is seeking to instruct the reader into a way of comprehending the speech he will face as an experience. The reader shall face the idea of a science and of sociology and Durkheim is doing instruction and preparation, i.e., Durkheim is counselling the reader in the proper way of attending to this idea.

[1] E. Durkheim, *The Rules of Sociological Method*, Glencoe: Free Press, 1964, XXXVII.
[2] *Ibid.*, XXXVII.

He must consequently be on his guard against his first impressions. If he indulges in such loose habits of thought, he is likely to judge this book without having understood it.[1]

The reader must guard against (the high-sounding) what *seems* apparent in order to see what *is* apparent. What is real because it is really apparent is what is authentic. To understand his speech the reader must learn to hear it as an authentic record. What could lead the reader astray and induce him to value Durkheim's speech differently than Durkheim intends? Why does Durkheim anticipate that his speech will be misunderstood? Why is the founder of a science so concerned with the rhetorical character of the speaking situation?

Durkheim and the reader participate in a unity sufficient to allow them to speak together. That is, Durkheim speaks under the auspices of his expectation that the context of intelligibility will be provided. Yet, such a unity is not enough for Durkheim, for his very act of speaking testifies to his differential claim to know and he anticipates that this original difference will be re-produced in the reader's resistance to what he speaks. The 'common sense' which Durkheim imputes to the reader in anticipation of his reaction is the very notion of 'accepted ideas' that Durkheim seeks to disturb with his science. Durkheim is speaking to those who his very speech is designed to disturb. Durkheim proclaims his task as one of disturbing accepted ideas at the very outset, and in his preface argues with the reader, urging him to suspend his accepted ideas in order to allow himself to be disturbed. Durkheim is then putting the reader in a strange position.[2] This 'common sense' is not the sense of what is authentic (and common), but symbolizes a refusal to experience the authentic. Common sense is to resist the aesthetic demand by accepting as authentic and real what one has not experienced; to speak in such a way so as to show (to the aesthetic) one's alienation from the experience which ought authenticate the speech.

The reader is lazy and inclined to first impressions: he accepts the most accessible understandings. The first impression as the impression one first has must be distinguished from the intuition of what is first (authentic). True understanding requires the courage of patience and a willingness to reach beyond first impressions. To describe the omnipresence of crime is not to condone it says Durkheim, and he seeks to prepare the reader to understand a description and to evaluate the authenticity of speech. A description is independent of the interests and inclinations of either those who produce it or receive it; a description has to be treated as something external to these interests. Authentic speech is speech that is so fundamental and authentic, that the question

[1] *Ibid.*, XXXVIII.

[2] This is much the same situation that Freud spoke from in his introductory lectures at Clark University.

of its source is irrelevant; its authenticity consists in its incorrigible and indubitable apparency to all. In the preface, Durkheim tells the reader that the condition for treating social facts as things is to treat descriptions as things. There is a correct attitude for reacting to speech, for opening one-self to what the speech speaks. This attitude requires evaluating speech in terms of whether it records the authentically apparent against the possibility that its apparency is private. The reader must be willing to enter into the same relationship with the author that he (the author) created with his environment. Both must *sacrifice* what is their own for what can be shared.

To treat descriptions as things is to develop a radically new attitude to language and self. It is to will the segregation of the description from its source and to ignore the understanding which gives the description life; it wills as extraneous and irrelevant such a source. Durkheim seeks to create a new form of life in which history as the resonances and resources of speaking will become obsolete and will be replaced by a conception of history as the imitation of nature. He seeks to eliminate history from speaking, but only under the condition that history is re-interpreted now as the possessiveness of what is immediate (as privacy, interest, difference, and rhetoric), as any influence which diverts the reader from attending to the commonality of speaking.

To treat descriptions as things is then to turn away from the Real origin of speaking to the origin which is common human experience, to turn from Being to 'human nature,' from *arché* to experience. To turn towards the origins in human nature is to turn away from the resonances of speaking as an appearing of Real firstness by re-conceiving of firstness as common experience, as what is most immediate; it is to face the description as if it has no history. This is a history to which author and reader have access as the source of intelligibility for producing the description. It is the history which will be ignored or disregarded. To treat the description as if it has no antecedent in the communal relation of the participants to the language they speak is to urge both author and reader to join together to re-create this union freshly in terms of how it originates as an imitation of nature. To treat descriptions as things is to attempt to assess the status of a description when its support in the commonality of the relation of language to Being is removed, in order to re-discover this support as 'an empirical achievement' or fact. To justify the authenticity of the speech is to see it as a successful imitation of nature. This success is shown in the speech which becomes part of nature; to imitate nature in speech is to make a natural speech. Since nature is conceived as the *matter* which is external and thing-like, successful speech is that which constitutes it-self as an other external thing. The exercise is designed to authenticate the foundation and to secure it more solidly. Durkheim wants to jointly participate in a solidification with the reader which depends upon what he and the reader share and know. But in order to accomplish this solidification he has to urge the reader to join with him in disregarding what they know in order to accomplish the solidification authentically. Durkheim wants to justify the authenticity of the common life as a 'matter' of fact rather than fancy, as a matter which is experienced rather than stipulated. The bind into which Durkheim puts both reader and self is the bind of disregarding what must be used to do the disregarding. The collaborative sacrifice required in orienting to the natural speech can only be accomplished un-naturally (as one who is other than matter). The authentic foundation which grounds man's speaking is to be converted into a topic for the speaking itself, but the conversion is designed to produce speechless speech because to imitate nature through speech is to speak silently, i.e., to become some-thing is to say nothing.

Therefore, the problem to which Durkheim addresses the preface – the problem of the reader's 'understanding' what Durkheim says – is itself created by the fact that Durkheim has segregated himself from reader by destroying or by willing as irrelevant the tissue of understandings which bind them together. By making *this* relationship problematic Durkheim creates a problem of their very togetherness. This togetherness is the achievement of a history over which they have no control, for it is this which provides 'common sense' with its character; common sense never takes itself as a thing. Durkheim wants to re-experience the experience which men ought address by joining reader and self together in the experience of authenticizing it. Because Durkheim formulates himself as nature, the reader is required to become a thing which is it-self natural; the problem of theorizing is to re-late these two things – author and reader – which is misleading because to relate them requires them to be more than things. Consequently, Durkheim must accept their differences as un-natural and he must recommend procedures for naturalization which deny the programme itself. The programme for imitating nature is only possible because of its extraordinary-un-natural-character. Since the programme is only possible if it denies what it speaks, the programme is impossible, and it says nothing.

Durkheim wants to re-experience history not through the concerted use of such a resource but by describing it; he wants to describe what has been taken as a resource. Yet, since it is this resource which provides for the intelligibility of Durkheim's encounter with the reader in the first place, his effort to convert history into a topic simultaneously serves to segregate him-self from reader. It is this segregation which he seeks to address in the preface and which he attempts to prepare the reader to resolve in concert with him. In order to create unity Durkheim has to destroy the very grounds which make unity possible.

Durkheim wants the reader to understand while exorcising the very condition which makes understanding possible. He wants the reader to join with him in the ceremonial expurgation of pre-supposition but the very enterprise is controlled by the pre-supposition which is being expurgated. In this way, Durkheim creates a reader who is no longer one with him, a reader so radically 'other' that the very restoration of their unity has nothing communal to draw upon and can only be achieved through their concerting around some coercive force that is external. The focus of their re-organization will be some subject-ed matter. Durkheim seeks to make belief a topic for a hypothetical non-believer. The curiousness of this enterprise, however, resides in the fact that the non-believer's possibility of formulating belief as a topic itself draws upon a corpus of beliefs. The strange feature of science then lies in the fact that it makes a claim to exorcise pre-supposition, authority, and commitment as a claim which affirms the very matters being exorcised. To so individuate self and reader is to will the externality of all they share and consequently is to construct impersonations of self and reader in 'individuals' who can only restore their shattered unity by concerting mechanically. Author and reader share a common exposure to the single stimulus of the description; in treating the description as a thing they are induced to regard as extraneous any other communal grounds, they are invited to differentiate themselves in order to prepare for a re-collecting around the only authentic grounds of commonality. What they share as common actors is to be disregarded, but what they share as the concerted effects of a common exposure is to be incorporated.

The individuation of author and reader guarantees the restoration of an authentic unity, their unity as a single recipient for the forces which emanate from that which the description is *about*. To prepare this individuation is to purge as irrelevant the very unity which makes their re-integration possible. This is a plan for constructing the ideal member of the scientific community now typified by the non-believer; the non-believer as one whose only commitment is to non-belief, and yet, it is a commitment to a *belief* in non-belief. The question of science does not then turn on whether or not science is ruled by belief, but rather, on what a belief in non-belief – as a Rational ideal – is worth. The ideal rational inquirer is one who is committed to disbelief, is one who hides from himself the re-cognition that his commitment to disbelief is a moral affirmation (is a belief) of the Good of disbelief. The rational inquirer is a deceiver, one who treats his commitment *as if* it was no commitment.

The unity of author and reader is transformed into the empirical problem of their re-integration in terms of a common speech, to come together as a One around the speech. This requires the many to hear what the speech says as a one, which in turn means that the speech must say one thing and that its multiple resonances be controlled. The oneness of the speech consists in the fact that in asserting something about something it speaks of a common subject. Re-unification requires attending to the subject which the speech speaks and excluding anything which the speech leaves unsaid. To treat description as a thing is to begin by locating its subject as that point from which they each decide to begin.

To begin with the subject – with the underlying matter – is the way to begin because only from such a start can men control inquiry as a joint and communal product. The problem of previous inquiries is that they each fail to free their speeches from the interests out of which the speeches grew; to create such freedom as the liberation of individuals from interest is to convert such interests into topics – to making them things – where the very liberation divests individuals of the knowledge necessary to comprehend the selfsame interests as topics.

Durkheim's individuals can re-create unity in the only way in which organisms can concert, mechanically, around some concrete external force. Yet, since this re-unification is only possible though the use of the suppressed resources, the organismic contact between author and reader only serves to re-establish their beginning under the control of the very common culture which they had suppressed. The individuation which Durkheim's programme creates ultimately has to be resolved through the use of the very unity which the individuation sought to destroy.

Man is essentially a free speaker, he can speak about anything. Because man possesses (as his) what is immediate and present to *him*, he tends to speak about such possessions as true. Man has a selfish interest in authenticating his possessions as common possessions and he protects this interest not by inspecting what is present to all but by legislating and assuming that which is present to him is present at all. Common sense symbolizes the interest that animates man's refusal to sacrifice his possession for the common good. It is this man whom Durkheim must 'socialize.'

The unity which Durkheim's preface addresses is a re-affirmation of the unity which his programme was designed to disregard. Durkheim's polemic against common sense is then a peculiar impulse, for it actually amounts to a re-assertion of the authority of common sense; it is an attempt to ground and to lay the foundations for common sense in a radically new way. It is a project for re-laying the grounds of common sense by making common sense a topic, an object of reflection that is a thing because it is only external things which are apparent to all (authentically present). The programme personifies the reflective use of common sense to understand itself.

II

To ground common sense reflexively is to re-construct its development as a rational programme.

As a matter of fact, our principle objective is to extend scientific rationalism to human behaviour.[1]

Durkheim does not mean that our principle objective is to theorize about human behaviour scientifically, for the notion of 'extending scientific rationalism to human behaviour' refers to the sociological impulse to introduce scientific rationalism into the world as a moral, ideal typification of the Good society. To rationalize common sense is then to show that behaviour

When analyzed, can be reduced to relationships of cause and effect.[2]

This means more than to demonstrate the possibility of descriptions, but that in such demonstrations ideals are being offered for ordinary members as courses of action for exemplifying community participation. Descriptions are aesthetic (authentically apparent to all) images of social relations as external contacts between things; a description records the ideality of such a contact as the Rational method for achieving community.

The project is designed to re-describe what common sense has already spoken of, but in an altogether new speech, a speech of 'cause and effect.' To re-lay the foundations is to re-speak the opinions, fancies, truths and superstitions of common sense in a language of assertion – of speeches which are either true or false. It is to translate the language of common sense into a language of subject-predicate relationships. Yet to prepare this programme is to first train men to divest themselves of other ways of speaking and to rivet their attention upon the focal dimension of this new language.

Why re-lay the ground of common sense? What is the problem with common sense? Common sense is lazy, passive, and acquiescent in the face of the irrelevant, the extraneous, and the authoritative; common sense consists of opinions which go this way and that, a dispersed collection of impressions and understandings that lack solidity. Common sense lacks discipline, it can always be otherwise, it lacks consistency and security, it is inseparably intertwined with the pleasures of those who speak it. Common sense is a metaphor for the undisciplined and dispersed mouthings of unreflective men. Common sense is a notion that describes the possible consequences of free speaking, for without a

[1] Durkheim, XXXIX.
[2] *Ibid.*, XXXIX–XI.

standard, speech disperses (into anarchy) and speaks what is apparent rather than authentic; yet all of the grammatical standards for producing authentic speech are themselves grounded in-authentically. The grammar must be totally aestheticized to become what it speaks about: the grammar can only *describe* common sense by becoming another item in the environment called common sense. In such an act the grammar then frees itself from common sense because it makes no claim to *be* more than what it speaks about. The grammar becomes common matter and 'succeeds' in this very accomplishment. In becoming a thing the grammar becomes an image of what all men are and its apparency is immediate and present (authentic) to all because all men can see how they are things. To see one-self as a thing is the easiest way to see.

Durkheim's programme is designed to induce common sense to question what it accepts, to distrust what it trusts. How is this questioning to be done? Recall in Plato and Aristotle how questioning was often described as dialectical, as creating through the exchange of inquirer and Other an impulse towards hearing that which is unsaid, an attempt to hear the unthought resonances which the speech conceals as a circulating, evolving contest between truth and falsity. To question was to listen to what the question asks within the context of an answer already re-covered. To question common sense was to engage it out of respect for the very language which gives life to both the question and that which it questions; to face both question and that which it questions as organically connected moments in the re-construction of the language as a language worth speaking, but only in a truly listening way.

Durkheim proposes an absolutely new kind of questioning. Rather than enter into an exchange with common sense, he chooses to disregard it, and he accomplishes this by so radically treating common sense as 'other' that any effort to enter into it is defeated at the outset because its otherness makes it unintelligible. Yet Durkheim's programme for disregarding common sense is grounded in the most thorough and practical sort of respect and regard for common sense and in this resides the duplicity of the claim of the programme to greater critical power. Durkheim questions common sense by forcing its withdrawal as a support for the reflective attitude of questioning and in so doing renders the questioning impossible. Consequently Durkheim continually has to draw upon the resources which he has already claimed to withdraw. The new science then manifests itself not through its critical power but through its complete and radical misunderstanding of the character of the speaking in which it is engaged; in this sense the new programme can be seen as lacking the moral vigour of what it calls common sense because this common sense does not make the claims that the science of society does.

The programme originates in the impulse to abandon common sense by withdrawing it and in this action segregates questioning from the communal support in which it is secured. The interdependence between thought and convention is destroyed by radically converting convention into what is other than thought and this creates a kind of thought that is impotent to think.

The Durkheimian project begins with the recognition of the unity in which men are rooted as the common and mechanical unity of convention and custom. He equates the unity of the social with 'common sense' and he trivializes this unity by characterizing it as the most common and mundane kind of belonging-together, the belonging-together which sociologists have traditionally called culture. In brief, he transforms the unity which men share as men vis-à-vis their desire to bring this unity to speech – he transforms the Oneness of men trying to speak about this oneness – into common culture as the repository of common opinions, fancies, and customs. Custom then reinforces rhetoric because men trust custom and fail to exercise will to overcome rhetoric. Durkheim's programme argues that custom must be made an object of study so that its trustworthy character can be re-assessed and firmly validated as an object of communal control, i.e., as a topic for a democracy. Custom must be rationalized through its conversion into an authentic thing.

To withdraw custom by forcing men to speak without it is impossible. Men who treat custom as such a thing under the illusion that they are providing for an independent assessment of custom are actually using the resources of custom to speak about it. Since custom is what provides men with their unity – as common men – to speak without custom is to speak silently. The very idea of 'withdrawing' custom is an aesthetic fantasy (think of the idea of 'bracketing,' of 'becoming a stranger' of the epoch), because every such withdrawal only affirms that which it withdraws. The idea of 'withdrawing' is animated by the aesthetic search for the most immediate presence as an 'experience' which is certain.

When men are divested of custom, what remains are the differences between men, or the conditions which provide for their differentiation. That which provides for the differences among men are the concrete differences which mark off one man as a thing from any and every other. Since men can be said to differ from one another in terms of their most concrete capacities, it is only by re-constructing the speeches of men from out of this common beginning in their differentness that the custom with which men routinely and unreflectively begin will be seen as a controlled product. Custom is treated as a thing by first maximizing the concrete differences among men so as to guarantee the fidelity of the consequences of derivations from these differences. The attempt to lay a foundation is the attempt to secure custom by formulating it as an inevitable and controlled product of the most concrete, differentiated features of individual men because it is only custom so grounded that can be trusted as authentic.

Custom is questioned by inducing men to re-describe their environments without using custom. In order to determine if what these many descriptions recommend corresponds to what the unreflexive conception of custom recommends these many descriptions must be transformed into a one description. Because custom itself is seen as the plurality of possible speeches that is free speaking, the power of Durkheim's programme consists in its organizing potential, i.e., that it – unlike free speaking – can create one speech from the manyness of free speaking possibilities.

The manyness of custom is then questioned by reducing it to the one speech, the one description. Yet, for Durkheim, the product of such a programme is not the re-construction of custom but the production of 'facts.' *Facts* are speeches which ought be accredited as authentic customs in Durkheim's programmes; facts are speeches about customs which ought become customs themselves because they are assembled as the concerted product of the many (as speech which imitates nature), and the power of fact over custom lies in its character as the speech of the one rather than of the many. Whereas custom is the many apparent speeches about nature, fact is the one authentic speech.

Durkheim's project 'disturbs accepted beliefs' because it refuses to allow custom, belief, and opinion to reverberate with their many resonances; it imposes a plan for assessing the truth by differentiating these beliefs which can be reduced to one speech (facts) from those which cannot. The programme for surpassing custom by exorcising it is at its deepest level a project for re-describing custom under the auspices of a drive to unify all speeches under one speech which cannot be doubted. Facts are then customs re-described so as to mask their very character as customs. Facts are glosses for re-described customs now warranted as trustworthy and secure. Facts are authentic because they are speeches that exemplify customs worth preserving.

The critical character of science lies in its re-laying of the ground of custom by re-establishing a rational foundation in fact. Science the modernizing, moralizing enterprise conducts its questioning of custom under the auspices of a desire to resurrect on unassailable grounds the self-same customs. Consequently science will 'disturb accepted beliefs' by restoring and perfecting those beliefs as beliefs worthy of being trusted.

The science of sociology will describe and explain social facts, but this programme is a gloss for the deep impulse of the science to construct typifications of society as rational typifications. The ideal promoted by sociology then becomes the man who acts with scientific knowledge of custom, and such an ideal is exemplified by the inquirer idealized in

Durkheim's programme. The man acting with scientific knowledge of custom is the ideal rational member, for he is one whose speaking rests upon the most secure – communal, authentic – base.

III

Sociology will be the new first science, but its firstness will not be based upon its claim to study whatness, for it will study the foundations of belief; since every special science rests upon an unexplored belief, sociology will take priority through its pre-occupation with belief itself. Belief is a metaphor for the unexamined authorization which grounds every act and so, sociology will take as its topic the problem of the grounds of belief. Sociology will reformulate the problem of the Good which animates speech as the belief which ought be believed. Since such a belief will be located in that which is most apparent as an experience to all, it may be identified with 'society' as the first common experience. Sociology will seek to describe this experience by exemplifying it as an object – matter – of rational belief on the grounds that only this experience can serve as an ethical ideal for speaking. To believe in society is not to be a believer because society is authentic (an object of knowledge and not belief). Sociology begins with the recognition that speaking is community building and claims to be first not because it is a science but because it exemplifies the ideal type of relationship which science itself is concerned to create as a standard of knowing. The firstness of sociology consists in its attempt to create itself as an imitation of what is first when firstness is understood as what is most apparent. Sociology will be the first science because it will be the only science that understands the communal ground of science itself as an icon of the democratic conversation; and sociology's firstness will reside in its programme for speaking in such a way as to exemplify the communality which all aesthetic speaking seeks to produce.

Sociology will study belief by constructing images of the only belief worth believing. Since the social relationship that is society underlies all belief, sociology will study society by constructing images of the society which ought ground speech. Sociological description will represent the rational society of co-speakers as an ideal by making its description 'things' to be believed; sociology studies belief by constituting it-self as an aesthetic display – an appearance of – the only grammar worth believing.

Sociology will seek to demonstrate the authority of aesthetics by showing the radically common character of the experience of the apparent in its organization of this experience as itself a common experience. Such organizations of experience re-appear to men as common experiences while serving to orient men to them as possible ideals of conduct. These organizations justify themselves by exemplifying what they organize (the common experience) as the only rational ideals for any speech to follow.

The aestheticization of firstness leads to this: that what is present to a man is present to his eyes and ears, to his body, a man's body coordinates a time and place and what is most immediate to him is the time and place where he is (where he exists). When totally aestheticized the environment present to a man as time is history, and as (the more comprehensive) time and place is society. The firstness of society resides in its (external) immediacy and apparency to the man that is a body. The firstness of society also consists in the fact that of all the immediate appearances which are present to a man, it is the one external presence which he shares with all men. Society is first because it is the most inclusive environment present to a body, i.e., it is the most common and immediate presence for man as a body. Being both common and immediate society satisfies conditions that other environments cannot. The experience of the first is the experience of what is most common and immediate, of what is most concrete.

To speak under the auspices of society is to speak in a way that preserves the concreteness of this experience because only such a speech will re-produce the very experience on which it is founded. To reproduce *this* common experience in speech is the goal of theorizing, of rational speaking – and such a re-production will idealize concrete speaking – speaking which respects the immediate and the common – as the rational order for speech to follow. The method of correct speaking is the method which coerces men to speak about the common and immediate as a thing that is external to them. In following such a method, men will construct speeches which will themselves be seen as immediate and present (as common) when they are oriented to as external things.

Just as Descartes' programme required a concentration of effort, a collectedness of mind which organized itself under the auspices of rational interest, so the possibility of a science requires such a collectedness which directs towards a common interest the severalness of minds. Descartes' method was intended to consolidate the attention of the mind, to draw it towards a common factor, and to avoid the dispersion of attention and effort. His programme required the act of will necessary for creating the collectedness of knowledge.

We must desire and will to fix our minds on this rather than that object. Our minds must be directed properly at the outset of our inquiry and this direction is dependent on our will to do so.[1]

---

[1] See L. J. Beck, *The Method of Descartes*, Oxford: Clarendon Press, 1952, p. 57.

If the power of reason is equally available to all, the perspectivial differences that arise must be due to the misuse of these when it is directed not by reason but by will. Will must then be brought into line with reason and it is this relationship – the grounds of the authority of method – that is at once essential to Descartes' programme and simultaneously unexplored. The method then involves fixing the mind voluntarily upon the more simple things and excluding as extraneous 'other matters.' To be loyal to the method is then to will a simple starting point and to renounce all other impulses towards hasty and precipient entry. Opinion, impression, and premature conclusion must be controlled as the mind searches for a simple beginning beyond which nothing intelligible can be spoken. What Durkheim located in his project was the fact that the drive for the simple beginning as a quest for the common is simultaneously an affirmation of the communal (of one standard of communality). Durkheim acted upon the recognition that an efficient project must affirm and exemplify the communal ideal which grounds the project itself.

The simple beginning is the point at which all men can agree; beyond this point, sense, body, opinion, and perspective shatter agreement. The point at which all men agree is the point at which men agree to begin. It is the point which men elect to be first. Custom and convention provide for the recognition of such a point not in the sense that it is immediately apparent to all but in that its apparency will become available to anyman if divisive forces of differentiation such as impulse, interest, character, perspective – are eradicated. The differences between men must be eliminated and they must be provided with some commonality which will organize their beginning together at the beginning. Such a common condition must be deeper than method, for it must be a condition so immediate and apparent that it can arouse the will to submit which makes the use of the method possible, and it must be a condition so common that its arousal will be concerted. In other words Descartes never raised the question of what rules the method, and tended to treat the method as self-generating and its rationality as self-evident. Durkheim in contrast, raises the question of that to which the method is responsible and locates such a responsibility in the communal ideal which furnishes the project both with its goal and with its common start. Men must be encouraged to renounce the differentiating forces of individualism in order to choose to begin together. Yet men can only make this choice by understanding it through the very individualized capacities for differentiation which they are encouraged to repudiate. Men must then come to believe in the desirability of renunciating their humanity when this very ability to believe is grounded in their humanity. While sociology can only save aesthetics by recognizing the extra-ordinary origin of theorizing, the grammatical solution of 'method' only serves to perpetuate the illusion because the acceptance of the method is extraordinary (the method is not apparent) and this creates the very problem which the method sees it-self as having to resolve.

Durkheim wants to instruct us into the following: that authority is a communal achievement of will which will be secured when men learn to start at the beginning at the same point. The easiest way to start at the beginning is to start with a topic to which all can orient, and the most distinctive topic is the problem of how men can start together. The distinctiveness of this topic is grounded on two reasons: first, philosophy asserts the authoritativeness of starting together but leaves the question unexamined; and, secondly, in speaking about their special classes of 'things' all disciplines begin together and use such a beginning as an unexamined resource. Sociology will then establish its authority on the basis of its claim to be the modern version of the Royal Art. Sociology will claim to replace dialectic only because thinking has been aestheticized by epistemology; sociology will seek to earn its way on the basis of its claim to fill in the crevices left empty through the ascendancy of the modern project. The very unreflexivity of the modern project makes a place for sociology because sociology will appropriate as its topic the restoration of reflexivity. Yet, the task is confounded by the fact that sociology can only proceed under the auspices of the project it corrects, i.e., it can only proceed as an exemplification of the very unreflexive mode which it seeks to perfect.

To begin together is to begin with togetherness in hand and then, by building upon such togetherness it is to achieve discoveries. Throughout, the original togetherness is secured because any achievement is only intelligible as an instance of such togetherness. That is, any achievement will be an instance of the togetherness in which it begins because any achievement is controlled by the order to which its outcome makes reference. Therefore, any achievement will meet the fundamental requirement of preserving its starting point in the common by reconstructing this starting point as an authentic object for all.

In contrast, from a dialectical perspective beginning together is only an occasion for speech. Such a beginning is not a point to be certified, secured, and protected as the first element of a record, because the very possibility of beginning together hints at that which has been covered-over by the convention of deciding to begin together. Beginning together is merely an occasion to initiate inquiry into that which differentiates men as a step in the creation of speech about the real togetherness that can be addressed through dialectic. The modern starting point hides the differences between men which must be brought to speech as intermediate topics *en route* to the achievement of authentic togetherness.

Authentic togetherness occurs when man can speak in a way that conforms to his nature – for he is then together with his nature – and this achievement requires that the superficial ability to speak together as the prototype of beginning together be dissolved as part of the movement of inquiry. Thus, the dialectical enterprise is actually devoted to showing that the very idea of beginning together which the modern projects celebrates as the simple and authoritative starting point is the most spurious kind of 'being together' because it suppresses as divisive just those conditions which join man together in his essential relationship to his nature.

In its decision, sociology takes as its conception of the social the conventional agreement of men to begin together. Dialectic treats such an agreement as an instance of how man hides his nature from himself behind the authority of convention. What dialectic takes as a provisional occasion for speaking that is soon to be surpassed and dissolved, sociology will take as its topic.

Durkheim establishes as his task the problem of instructing the many to begin as a One, just as Descartes similarly instructed his thinker to consolidate his perceptions in order to begin with the idea. Both are interested in creating a collective and they accomplish such a criterion by stipulating the common starting point. Since to begin together is to organize the attention of the many by directing it to its oneness, that which provides for this unity can only be the many's consciousness of itself, that it is a One. The togetherness of the beginning is provided for by their concerted attention to what is first, and that which is first (before all else) is their togetherness as a One. Thus, the self-consciousness – of the many as a One – is to speak in such a way as to make reference to Oneness by showing that the attention of the many is organized by their understanding of this Oneness. Durkheim's conception of self-consciousness – the treatment of the many things as a one thing – is the consciousness of the many as being a one simple thing. For the many to re-cognize that they are one is for the many to recognize that what is first – as immediate presence – is what is common to them all, i.e., society.

To agree to begin together is then to agree to begin with the simple; the character of the simple resides only in the fact that it is the point at which the many can agree to begin. Thus, the simple is that recognition of the oneness of the common, it is to re-cognize that having in common makes the many a One. This re-cognition is grounded in the desire for peace and order as expressed in the unanimity of agreement. Note that whereas the moderns begin with the harmony of common speech, Socrates' comment that a harmony follows rather than leads its elements is meant to suggest that the harmony is already an analytic achievement which remains to be explored, and that any attempt to secure it as a foundation suppresses the analytic character of the beginning. In contrast to the modern project the beginning is not itself apparent. This point will be found because its recognition is an expression of what is common to reasonable men; (to men who Will to reason about the beginning). Desire as the grounds of the impulse for the analytic is then the Will for the simple as that which is covered-over by speech. To locate the simple starting point is to identify the minimal communal speech which men can understand. Thus, the rationality of the method is grounded in the belief that if men start together, their speech will proceed under communal control, i.e., they will speak under the constraint of some notion of simple togetherness. The passion required to locate this simple beginning (this first which is apparent and immediate) then serves to deny its claim to simplicity. That the method itself is not first – is not a simple beginning – that it is not apparent and immediate, means that aesthetics has to liquidate itself by invoking the inexplicable 'passion' of genius which its very programme was concerned to normalize.

Sociology wants to study precisely this problem of how men start together and it wants to conduct the study not as an aggregate of isolated men but as itself an exemplification of such togetherness. To start together is to guarantee finishing in an intelligible way, for only through a common start will community be preserved throughout the speaking that follows. If the achievement is to be an intelligible affirmation of communality men must begin together so that any conclusion in speech which they achieve will be assessable in terms of whether or not it re-produces their communal start.

Sociology does not understand its beginning as a simplification that surpresses the divisiveness of what is other to speech and thus believes in its beginning *as* a beginning whereas dialectic recognizes any beginning as a result; the moderns use their beginning to *achieve* the peace of release from doubt through the *praxis* of re-cognizing the common, whereas dialectic shatters its beginning in order to address the Good which the beginning covers over.

Sociology will then start with the harmony of the simple as that re-cognition which makes reference to agreement on what is common, and this speech will become the topic of sociology. Such speech is oriented to its requirement of having to come to terms with the understanding of anyman. Thus, the goal of sociology is to create the speech of anyman as the simple and secure condition of beginning together, and all exploration will be conducted under the auspices of such a constraint. The emergence of sociology as a discipline requires that men relinquish dialectical impulse and Desire for another kind of speech, and that they come voluntarily to submit to the ideal of a common speech by seeing common speaking as Rational speech.

IV

Sociology is in a peculiar position. It is in a fight for its life with other disciplines (other topics) and all of these disciplines operate under the same constraint of having to find some commonality about which to speak (some part of whatness to 'cut off'). Instead of locating yet another commonality Durkheim proposes that sociology take up as its topic the very idea of commonality. Sociology appropriates as its own the methodological pre-supposition of every discipline; sociology takes as its topic the very notion of commonality which every other topic uses as a resource; sociology takes as its topic that which makes every other topic possible. However, in its taking up, sociology will re-formulate commonality as the ideal of communality. In this re-formulation Durkheim authorizes the common life – the authority of common usage and procedure and routine – as the rational standard of community.

In one move Durkheim handles two problems: he selects a topic for sociology, and in so doing he authoritatively declares the pre-eminence of sociology as the topic of topics. The authority of sociology will rest upon its particular selection of a topic, for where every discipline has something in common about which to speak, sociology will study as its own the very idea of commonality. In this sense, sociology appropriates for itself the topic of reflexivity; since the idea of commonality grounds and makes possible every conceivable practice, sociology will take as its own the topic of whatness itself which every other practice glosses and covers over; this 'whatness' is the common which the special sciences cut up. Sociology is then not just another practice, but the practice that takes as its own the problem of the grounds of any practice. Sociology will re-lay the grounds of all projects in the common life and will become the first science because it elects to take up the common itself and to promote it by re-formulating it as an ideal for speaking. The common as common experience is resituated in the metaphor of society.

We obtain a new warrant for sociology, because its authority is not based upon some notion of inclusiveness or generality, or the fact that it studies collectives rather than individuals, or social systems rather than personality systems. Sociology studies and exemplifies reflexivity, but it is the reflexivity of the practical interest: which means that sociology declares that it owns as its topic the concern that all other topics gloss; sociology inquires into the idea of commonality upon which all intelligible speech is grounded, and in such an inquest sociology re-formulates commonality as a rational orientation to communality. In this sense, the firstness of sociology is based upon the fact that it is the only practice that shows belief in commonality as grounds for communality; that sociology is the only practice which takes science seriously by attempting to exemplify science as the rational authoritative organization for everyday life.

The reflexive claim of sociology is seen in its treatment of the common experience that is society as first. The highest level of consciousness is attained when society (as the common experience) orients to it-self as what is immediate, present and common to it; society experiences it-self as its most authentic presence. Society's experience of it-self as the common experience re-presents sophisticated aesthetic reflexivity and society acts upon this re-cognition to speak in a way that preserves this experience as itself an icon of this re-cognition. Such icons become descriptions. Whereas Durkheim locates the firstness of society in a way that alters Descartes' notion of immediacy and presence, Durkheim's society orients to it-self in exactly the same way that Descartes' inquirer intuited the apparent. Whereas Durkheim departs – to a degree – from epistemology, Durkheim's society – the Rational society – is an epistemologist.

The topic of sociology will then be the idea of commonality and Durkheim's very search for a topic is an instance of the idea of commonality into which he inquires. What Durkheim's discipline will have in common is its inclination to study the common. The connection between commonality and reflexivity is apparent: if every practice formulates for itself a common topic, such an appropriation is only possible though the use of an unanalyzed notion of commonality as a resource. Sociology appropriates to itself this resource by converting it into a topic and an ideal. Sociology will be prepared to speak about what other practices take for granted but sociology will not speak neutrally about this taken-for-granted resource; sociology will seek in its speech to affirm and to exemplify the ideality of commonality itself. In this sense sociology is first vis-à-vis other sciences because sociology is the only science which is serious about its ground; the seriousness of sociology however, is not reflected in its thoughtful care for the achievement of its grounds as a Rational achievement, but in its political concern to affirm its grounds as an authoritative standard of rational community. Sociology will study the foundations upon which other practices unreflexively build by affirming these foundations consciously and purposively as communal ideals. What is common to the sciences in general is that they all rest upon an unanalyzed and tacit notion of science as the best possible world and this notion itself presupposes a rational communicative ideal. Consequently sociology will speak under the auspices of this re-cognition by speaking in such a way as to exemplify the communal power of science as an organizing device. Sociology will speak from the standpoint of the epistemological society, the society which knows it-self as the (society) common experience which it is. Sociology will personify this knowledge, this society which re-cognizes its commonness and apparency, its firstness.

V

Note how Durkheim's early concern with the exterior and constraining character of matter was his way of developing new speech about the common. Because the common has potential for being equated with the prevalent or the general, it can be formulated in terms of the topics of psychology and biology. In contrast, sociology will address the common only insofar as it is formulable as a standard, i.e., only insofar as it is re-formulable as an ideal for community: if the common is to be seen as a standard it must be formulated in such a way as to provide for its external and constraining character. The common must be translated into a rule. The common must be seen as that which rules and the common must be re-formulated as that which men respect and to which they seek to comply as ruler. Consequently, sociology's real contribution to the study of the standards which govern speech is to speak about such standards as rules. Sociology will provide the authoritative method for talking about the common as a rule and sociology will be known as the practice which speaks about the common as a rule. Sociology will accomplish this by speaking about the common as rights and duties. Sociology will show how common experience rules and why it ought rule by speaking in such a way as to exemplify its own speech as speech that is so ruled.

To speak about commonness as rule is to speak about it in the most sophisticated way. To speak about commonness as rule is to speak in the way of science. Sociology will speak about commonness' consciousness of itself, it will address the highest self-consciousness of commonness in its unity with itself. Sociology will address how the common experience which is society experiences itself as a common experience; how society is ruled by the need to experience it-self as a common experience. Sociology will require of this commonness that it make reference through the *praxis* of action to its understanding of it-self as common. Action and behaviour will be the key terms and the 'actor' will personify the rational member. Sociology will then legislate upon authentic commonality, i.e., sociology will argue for authentic commonality as an instance of community and will make decisions upon inauthentic commonality by forcing every notion to pass through its court and to meet the requirements of its method. Sociology will test every such notion in terms of its possible formulability as a rule, which is to say that sociology will decide upon the communality of every formulation of commonality. The adequate description will be the description that displays itself as the 'what' that it describes, the description of the common experience which is it-self a common experience.

Commonness' understanding of itself is shown in science and the rhetoric of science reflects commonness' highest understanding of itself. In this case science alone re-presents authentic communality and the task of sociology is to scienticize the world, i.e., to re-formulate ordinary activities so as to exemplify their possible self-conscious character as instances of scientific communality. In this sense sociology can accomplish this merely through its own speech, i.e., by showing its own speech as the exemplification of such an ideal. Sociology must weed out the inauthentic and inadequate; all other ideas of the common are unreflexive because they each create a One out of the many through the stipulation of a rule whose analytic status is left unexplored. That is, the stipulation as itself a rule is not addressed. The method for converting commonness into rule must pass one stringent test which all other practices and forms of thinking ignore: the method for deciding the presence of rule must itself be an instance of rule. This is to say that the speech must show the selfsame character of externality and coerciveness as that which it describes. A description is ruled by common experience only when the description it-self can rule as a common experience. The rhetorical character of describing is clear, for a description is adequate to the extent to which it constitutes itself as the kind of common experience that can rule; the acceptability of the description depends upon whether it can be organized as an authentic (apparent and immediate) presence.

To say that the method is itself a rule is to say that the method is a demonstration of commonness; moreover it is to say that the method exemplifies the communal aspiration in terms of which commonness is formulable. The method makes reference to the selfsame community which its use is designed to accomplish. The adequate use of the method will guarantee a fair decision with respect to what the method intends to accomplish. This is because the method was developed in order to make fair decisions highly probable, just as Descartes' method was developed to make truth certain without leaving language. The method then exemplifies communality when it can be seen as a development of democratic, re-presentative procedure. The only way for sociology to tell if its translation of commonality into rule is successful is in terms of whether such a translation itself conforms to rule; scientific sociology's advantage over all other discipline is that it demands of itself that it conform to itself in a way that is assessable. Sociology then has two distinctive features; while it shares its reflexive requirement with all

204

sciences (the demand that its course of action conform to its rule), it takes as its unique topic the problem of how courses of action conform to their rules. Whereas all sciences use rules and reflect upon these rules, sociology appropriates to itself the topic of rule. Sociology then appropriates for itself the topic of what rules method, i.e., of what rules speech, and sociology speaks itself as an exemplification of that rule. *The firstness of sociology lies in the fact that it recognizes its ruler to be the ideal of scientific communality.*

Durkheim wants to create a society (the society that is a sociological description) that will look exactly like the society sociology intends to study because only through such a creation will the society be re-experienced as an authentic experience. Given the co-respondence of speech to things, if sociology can exemplify *what* it studies in its very action of studying, the very existence of sociology will testify to the truthfulness of its speech. Sociology wants to show how men understand commonness and are constrained by it, and sociology itself will exemplify this understanding in its speaking.

The starting point is the method as a social fact for the observer – as a thing external and coercive to him – the method as an expression of the desire for a common order. This is the point at which men can agree to begin together; given the security of this point, the rest follows. The starting point is authoritative and the essential feature of its authority resides in the fact that it is submitted to, i.e., that men give it life by deciding to be ruled. Men subject themselves to the authority of this re-cognition, to the authority of the common order, by voluntarily and spontaneously deciding to be ruled. It is not that men *have* this authority in common, but that they *understand* their commonness to consist in their submission to rule. Such an understanding is grounded in the fact that they re-cognize that only through such submission will rational community be achievable.

This is why Durkheim's early notions of exteriority and constraint had to be superseded since these notions provide only the most concrete picture of authority. To formulate authority analytically is to begin to address the source of authority in passion, i.e., it is to begin to address how authority is authorized.

Durkheim re-interprets the constraining character of authority by addressing the grounds of authority in passion. Authority makes reference to the willed moral obligation to voluntarily adhere to a method as a duty. Method comes to be more clearly delineated as a willful commitment, and exteriority and constraint appear as achievements rather than as grounds of belief. Yet if passion inspires this authorization and if the method is designed to eliminate passion by producing speech which is passionless, this speech can only be re-experienced if it is oriented to with passion.

Sociology will count its own opinions and beliefs adequate to the extent to which they can be evolved as objects of belief. Sociology will qualify as knowledge rather than opinion when what it speaks can be *believed* to be apparent. Sociology will speak truly by speaking concretely. Sociology will speak truly when it can convert its speech into what is present to anyman. Sociological truth is grounded in an image of a social discourse in which men communicate by making their speech apparent and immediate to one another and the good speech is one that exemplifies such a standard as the only Rational grounds of community – by recording what is apparent in a way that is apparent. Sociology will call its beliefs knowledge on the grounds that such beliefs exemplify the highest self-consciousness of a rational member (one oriented to the necessity of law-abiding communication as the standard of community) and consequently, any speech made under the auspices of such a standard will be at one with reason. The criterion of sociological knowledge will be a criterion internal to sociology itself as its standard of clear speaking: clear speech will validate the standard which is constructed to make clear speech an adequate validation. Thus, the standard itself will be protected from any examination that would surpass it because any surpassing is to be treated as unintelligible speech.

In Descartes' system, the agreement of men to begin with what the self methodically registered through a common procedure actually obscured the question of how the procedure became a common resource; what was obscured was the social character of self and how it became possible for the self to generate through *praxis* a conception of it-self as Other. With consummate ingenuity Durkheim identified society as the new metaphor for the emergence of the self through *praxis* and for its grounding in the experience of the common.

VI

Durkheim notes that all ideas are socially embedded, by which he means that any intelligible idea as an historic achievement is an outcome of language; any intelligible idea pre-supposes a language in terms of which it comes to life. Since language is a concerted achievement of men acting under the auspices of rules and procedures, language is essentially a 'social' phenomenon. The intelligibility of language justifies the claim that society is first. All of the ideas invented by philosophers make reference to society, i.e., make reference to their sociality. Society is the foundation of all thought and action because any intelligible speech is a move within a language and language is an icon of the social. The idea of society then serves as a metaphor for the foundations of thought and action.

In this sense 'society' is the fundamental concrete pre-supposition of all thought and practice because language is a social achievement. Language is caused by society. Furthermore the fundamentality of this pre-supposition is itself not a matter of opinion or belief because such a pre-supposition cannot even be denied without affirming what it recommends. Thus 'society' is the fundamental topic because it is the fundamental material cause of language and its recognition as such is not open to doubt. This is the way in which society is the common experience.

Furthermore, ideas are themselves icons of society because ideas collect through speech, and collectives are metaphors of the social. Society grounds and founds because the collectedness of speech is a bringing to appearance of society. There is nothing 'beyond' society because to even make the attempt to see beyond is to do so through language (from the vantage point of society). Consequently, society becomes the modern metaphor for Being, as that which grounds all as the source of thought and action; society then encapsulates history, experience, body, and mind as the most fundamental ground, as that which is first. If all thought conceals an act of submission to belief in its rule, the very possibility of rule and of method makes reference to intelligibility and intelligibility is social. Society depicts the social character of intelligibility and replaces the Good of an earlier formulation. Durkheim equates a concrete condition or material cause with what is Desirable and Good; he takes the fact that men as bodies *happen* to exist together (happen to speak together) as the mandate for identifying how speech is spoken with a standard for how it ought be spoken to truly say. Society is Durkheim's grammar.

Since sociology and all science is an expression of society, sociology cannot directly confront society as a 'thing' because sociology is itself an instance of that which it describes. In producing it-self sociology will make reference to the society of which *it* is an icon. Thus the differences between practices lie in their understanding of themselves as an instance of society and in the consciousness that their every speech makes reference to the authoritativeness of society. However, if Durkheim does nothing more than argue for the aptness of society as a metaphor for grounds to replace the various other historic metaphors he must still come to demonstrate more than that the study of this problem is possible, but that any attempt to accomplish a study testifies to the primacy of society and therefore, that the best study is the one that proceeds under the auspices of its understanding of such primacy, i.e., that the best study is the one which exemplifies in its very act of studying the grip of speech in the control of society. Thus, rational thought (the most adequate thought) is thought which grasps itself as a result of society and such a grasp is shown through sociology's speech about society. Sociology must speak in such a way as to make reference to it-self as an instance of society; sociological reflexivity is demonstrated through speech that makes reference to its grasp of its conventionality, i.e., to the fact that its status as a conventional product is understood. Durkheim conceives of sociology as that conventional practice which differentiates itself from other practices and establishes its priority vis-à-vis other practices simply by virtue of its understanding of conventionality; sociology will provide for a display of such understanding in its very speech by speaking the most conventional speech, i.e., the speech that personifies the social (the speech that imitates the common experience by becoming a common experience).

Sociology is under the control of society as is everything else and sociology distinguishes itself from everything else by showing through its description of society that it understands this relationship. Sociology certifies this understanding – makes it public and intelligible – by constituting itself as the rhetorical arm of society. Sociology seeks to preserve and to cultivate the highest development of society thinking of itself by exemplifying through its speech the personification of this consciousness.

To describe society is to chart the concrete influence of the social, i.e., to determine how the social causes. Yet, society as an amorphous, indistinct 'source' – as the bedrock field of sources – cannot be inspected directly, for the observer himself in his very inspection is a product of such forces. The force of society must be 'seen' through its works. The problem is to show how one can see 'being in the grip of rule' (being in the grip of a convention) in all thought and conduct. To describe society is to see how it makes itself visible as 'being in the grip of convention.' In this way, to describe society is to elect to describe convention. While Hume pointed to the power of custom as the unanalyzed grounds of action, Durkheim chooses to describe custom and to appropriate this enterprise as the topic for sociology. Yet, custom can only be described conventionally, since the resources of describing are instances of convention. Sociology then takes its very action of describing as a metaphor for the action through which society constitutes itself. Since the action of describing makes essential reference to the creation of society, the very possibility of sociological description testifies to the truthfulness of *what* sociology describes. Sociology then exists on the basis of Rousseau's analytic equation of science and society: the science of sociology is a society and its emergence reproduces the emergence of society. Sociology is then distinct from all other sciences in its display of description as an icon of the action of society creating itself and in so doing, in its display of its understanding of itself as such an impersonation.

Sociology is in a peculiar position as the programme becomes articulated in Durkheim's writing. Sociology is the discipline which seeks to make reference to society as the source of all speech from the perspective of an effect of that to which reference is being made. In other words, sociology is in the grip of that which it is describing; consequently sociology can make its case not on the basis of differentiating itself from that which it describes, but only in terms of its efficacy in affirming the authority of that which it describes as authorizing its very description. Sociology must necessarily rhetoricize, for in its very speech it makes reference to the authority of that which it seeks to describe.

The central principle is established: if society as the ultimate source can only be known through its works (its effects, influences), and since inquiry itself is such an effect, society can be known through inquiry. That is, in the act of understanding itself inquiry understands society because inquiry is itself an effect of society and to understand the effect is to re-produce an understanding of the cause. Moreover inquiry as conducted under the auspices of a programme is Rational inquiry and thus exemplifies the highest development of society understanding itself. Therefore if inquiry can understand itself, it exemplifies knowledge of society in its highest form. The highest form of self-conscious knowledge of society of it-self is society's understanding of its very conventionality. Sociology guarantees itself that it understands society when it understands itself because sociology itself is the paradigmatic expression of society. Sociology is the paradigm of convention because it speaks about convention for the purpose of displaying its own conventionality; sociology speaks only and exclusively to demonstrate its law-abiding character.

Durkheim's task is then to show how all ideas and conduct represent the collective (rule, authority, belief). The collective as society is represented in conduct when it can be shown to cause the conduct. Sociology then takes as its study the task of understanding the causal power of society as convention and in this way, sociology transforms the classical impulse to contemplate grounds as Being into the descriptive study of grounds as societal convention.

Durkheim is still vulnerable to the essential problem: that his very idea of society is itself an idea rather than a concrete society and that grounds cannot be an idea because grounds transcend all ideas. Durkheim then trivializes and concretizes Being. Furthermore, since the observer himself is 'an effect of society' (or convention) and in his formulation serves to exemplify the causal power of convention, Durkheim's very study of the force of society is an instance of such a force. Somehow, Durkheim must demonstrate that this programme is exempt from such an influence although every such demonstration merely exemplifies this influence.

It is here that Durkheim's ingenuity appears by making sociology the discipline which exemplifies convention by studying it; that is, he makes the question of authentic reflexivity totally irrelevant by converting unreflexivity into a strength and virtue which he formulates as the sociological attitude. If sociology is itself a result of society (convention), then any speech which sociology makes will be a conventional speech. Sociology *has* to be conventional because it is caused by what it studies. Sociology can no more disregard its conventionality than it can disregard the fact that it speaks. Sociology then has to be distinguished from other arts not by its lesser or greater conventionality because all such arts are instances of society, but by the display of its understanding of the convention that causes it. Sociology has to distinguish itself from other sciences by its greater understanding of its conventional character. The criterion for true speaking in sociology will then be whether its conventional speech shows that it understands its conventionality; as compared to other conventional speeches, sociological reflexivity as *the* conventional speech shows that it understands its conventionality by orienting to that conventionality as an authoritative, rational ideal for communal re-organization. Sociology understands society because sociology understands the link between science and community and acts in its speaking to exemplify this link as an ideal through speech. Sociology is like realistic cinema which *chooses* to be realistic on the grounds that cinema is a realistic medium and is to be understood analytically (ought to be understood) as realistic (naturalistic).

Sociology then acquires its authority vis-à-vis other conventional practices on the basis of its claim to exemplify the convention of which it is an expression. Sociology is the self-conscious conventional practice and such self-consciousness constitutes sociology's claim to be different than common sense. Sociology is the practice which truly understands convention and in this sense is the critical practice; the critical character of sociology lies in the fact that it not merely accepts convention as a rule but that it understands the *necessity* of accepting convention and of promoting the ideal recommended by convention as a standard worth speaking for. Sociology is the only discipline which understands how the common experience authorizes speech and why it must, and sociology is first because it seeks to enact this imperative Rationality.

Because such understanding is achieved by virtue of method, the difference between analytic and concrete thinking is a difference which depends upon the invocation of method as a rule. The kind of rational thought which Durkheim's method is designed to achieve is thinking's grasp of its relationship to society, i.e., to convention. The ideal rational course of thinking is then exemplified in thought which understands its conventional character and which orients to it as ground and as aspiration. Consequently the tables have been completely turned on the classicists who sought to surpass convention by beginning with it as a point of departure for a theorizing which sought to hear resonances which convention covered-over. Now, with sociology we get the exaltation of convention as the standard for which speech speaks. The nature of thought in this programme is that which makes reference to its own typicality and which shows in its conventionality its societal character. Adequate thought then becomes thought which understands its responsibility to convention, or thought which exercises such responsibility by making reference through its speech to the necessity of convention as its source and as its rational standard. Reflexivity then becomes re-defined as the attempt to understand and to maximize the conventionality of one's speech under the assumption that such maximization contributes to the development of a communal impulse. To show reflexivity is then to demonstrate the conventionality of speaking through speech which makes reference to its own typicality. All genuine critique of sociology is irrelevant because sociology makes no claim to be thoughtful, seeking only to affirm conventional wisdom as a rule to which men ought to orient.

The conventional speech is the best speech because it enacts in its occurrence the typical understanding of the collective when that understanding is re-formulated as the rational understanding of membership, i.e., from the scientific point of view. To orient to the rule of conventionality is to transform thinking into a social relationship by producing speech that can be oriented to, i.e., as a topic. However, the conventional character of sociological speech is not sufficient, for such speech must conventionally say what is true about convention. To say what is true about convention (to speak truly about convention) is to speak conventionally, i.e., with the power and force *of* convention. That is, conventions are true when they cause or force agreement, and conventional speech speaks truly when it forces itself upon an Other, when it causes an Other to accept its influence and to fall under the grip of its rule. Now, any forcing is a sufficient exemplification of true speaking when it forces itself upon an other in such a way as to allow the other to participate in this forcing, i.e., *conventional speech reaches its highest powers through speaking when its forcing is democratic.*

VII

Like everything it studies, sociology is an instance of convention, it is yet another convention. Sociology must assert its superiority on the basis of its force as a convention. Though sociology asserts itself on the basis of its claim to reflexively grasp convention, it can only demonstrate such reflexivity conventionally. Sociology exists because it understands the relationship between society and speech; however, sociology is itself a speaking within society, a thought within convention. In its every attempt to think, sociology will carry within itself the society (convention) about which it thinks. Sociology will then have no way of thinking about its thought that is free from that about which it thinks: lacking an independent 'test' of itself, sociology will have to become the most powerful, i.e., convincing, art of them all (the persuasive art). Sociology can only demonstrate its truthfulness by creating its own conditions for true speaking and by making speech which is designed to meet the requirements of the very conditions which it lays down for itself. Sociology will call its speech 'true' when it can convince and such convincingness shall constitute its truth; convincingness will require that the conditions of true speaking have been seen by an other as independent of that which authorizes them. True speech as convincing speech will be that which preserves the immediacy and which demonstrates the authenticity of the common experience. Sociological method will then provide for speech that meets these conditions: reflexivity is re-defined, for an understanding of how one's thought is controlled by society is displayed through the very use of society as a resource for creating intelligible speech.

Self-conscious thought is thought which reflects upon itself; this 'itself' upon which thought reflects is thought – thought thinks of thought. But, thought cannot think of thought in any old way, i.e., it cannot in the Cartesian programme think of itself as a concrete operation. Thought must think of itself under the auspices of an ideal of rational (perfect) thought; thought then does not think of itself concretely, *but as an ideal*, and consequently, what thought thinks is the attainment of the ideal. Reflexive thought is not then introspective thought but thought that is utopian. Reflexive thought is thought which thinks under the auspices of this idealization and which seeks to think and practice what the idealization recommends. Sociology becomes thought which thinks of it-self as inspired by the common experience, speech which speaks *as if* it was a common experience.

How is such an idealization possible? Durkheim radically alters the notion of the ideal in terms of which thought thinks, or in terms of which speech speaks. Thought grasps itself essentially when it conceives of itself under the auspices of the ideal of a social relationship. The ideal of a social relationship is the ideal of a community of men who democratically and re-presentatively collect their speech as an instance of community building. Thought grasps itself essentially as an instance of the very language through which it thinks; as soon as thought starts thinking of itself it starts thinking of the social because language is essentially social. When thought thinks of itself, it thinks of language because the essence of thought is linguisticality. Thus Durkheim demotes the Cartesian notion of the nature of thought as a rational ideal by re-interpreting nature as that which is common to all thought. What is common to thought is its linguisticality, i.e., its social source. Therefore thought grasps itself essentially, i.e., thought exemplifies rationality when it thinks under the control of a standard of commonality. Thought which orients to such control is thought which seeks to exemplify commonality as the standard for community. Reflexive thought is thought which grasps its character in this sense.

Thought which grasps its conventional character is thought which understands that it must be understood and that it has a responsibility to implement such an understanding. Thought which grasps its conventional character is thought which grasps the necessary requiredness of a social relationship. Thought which grasps its conventional character is thought which understands itself as necessarily requiring a democratic community. Thought which reflectively exercises its responsibility to this requirement of community is thought which cares for its intelligible character, i.e., thought which understands both community and responsibility. In showing that it understands its own conventional character, thought then shows that it knows what convention is. Rational thought in Durkheim's programme is thought which seeks to exemplify in its thinking and speaking the ideal of democratic community as the only ideal worth speaking for.

The difference between true and false speaking is then drawn differently, for the distinction is no longer one between nature and convention. Convention is all there is and yet, within convention speech can speak truly or falsely. True speech is speech that shows an understanding of itself as both an effective convention (founded upon common experience), and as a cause of other conventions (a common experience it-self). Speech speaks truly when it efficaciously understands itself as an exemplification of communal rationality and when it provides for the creation of community through its speaking. Reflexive speech is totally concrete; it is speech that understands how it must be concrete and which shows this understanding as the required condition of a democratic relationship. When speech complies with these requirements it can be said to understand itself and to speak truly no matter what it concretely speaks. Reflexive, speech is guided by an idealization of typicality and intelligibility and orients to such an idealization as a maxim of conduct that is external and coercive, i.e., as an object of belief. In contrast, false speech fails to make reference to such an understanding. False speech does not see itself as a methodical accomplishment of society and fails to prepare itself as an icon of that on which it is founded. Therefore, the difference between true and false speaking is a difference between following the rule of method and failing to adhere to this rule on the one hand, and between convincingly producing communities (predicting, controlling) and speaking without efficacy and power, i.e., speaking in such a way as to fail to realize concrete community. True speech is the action that is a self-conscious orienting to the order of community, and false speech is personified somewhat in a Weberian notion of behaviour; this is how sociology comes to both study action and to exemplify it.

As in Socrates, the starting point of sociology is its decision to agree to begin with convention. Yet, there is a difference: where Socrates used convention as a place to initiate inquiry into that which convention itself covered over, Durkheim uses convention as the source of intelligible inquiry. Where Socrates violates convention by creating the *aporia* in order to understand how the security of convention conceals the possibility of true speaking, Durkheim secures convention as the force and cause of all speaking. Both Socrates and Durkheim utilize society as resources: in the first case it is a resource for the creation of playful discussion which shall eventuate in serious inquiry – inquiry which will eventually shatter the conventional bond which made the beginning possible; in the case of sociology, society will be used seriously as a resource to do the work of inquiry and consequently, it will come to limit and to frame the possibilities of inquiry. In making society its topic, sociology not only appropriates to itself the ordinary, conventional, and mundane, but it asserts itself necessarily as the practice which must exemplify ordinaryness, conventionality, and mundaneity in its thought. In other words, sociology destroys the impulse to theorize inherited from the classicists by conceiving of that impulse as (strictly speaking) extraneous to the practice of science; sociology then celebrates the practical attitude as an exemplification of the scientific attitude towards speech, and in such a celebration authorizes practical rationality as a standard for which speaking ought speak.

In preserving the authority of the practical interest, sociology then takes language as its topic and calls language the 'social.' That is, sociology listens to language only insofar as language *says* that it is a shared experience. Men must then be induced to start with a common language and to exorcise any desire for the uncommon, the rare, and the excellent. Men start together by learning to hear in language only the common, and so, men begin as users of a language which is already divested of its resonance, depth, and history. Men begin as a One which adopts a common stance towards speech, i.e., a One which looks at speech as speaking what is common.

Men who achieve such an understanding will certify it in their own speech. That is, sociological speech will show its grasp of the common in its very ability to develop a common language. Sociology will demonstrate that it understands the conventions which produce it not only by re-producing itself as yet another convention, but as the first convention, i.e., the convention which understands the nature of convention itself. The test which sociology shall arrange for itself will reside in its ability to create assent to what it speaks because of the apparency of what it speaks.

Sociology has radical consequences. The sociological view of society whether of Durkheim or Weber rests upon a notion of unity as simple and common, i.e., as sharing the common experience. This results from segregating unity from difference as two 'things' or ideas and from treating difference as analytically central and similarity as a concrete source or ground. In contrast, dialectic views unity and difference as themselves instances or appearances – of a unity in which the inquirer is grounded. Even when unity is treated analytically in sociology, it re-appears as 'culture,' i.e., as common opinions, beliefs, norms, and rules. However, this can never be an authentic unity because in bringing *it* to speech the sociologist always makes reference to the unity in which *he* is grounded and which necessarily is a unity that is higher, i.e., that provides for his differentiation and for the bringing to speech of this unity. The idea of unity as convention is actually a differentiation of the given. Because the speaker sees *this* difference as unity, he has to see what he speaks *about* as different from the grounds of speech. This results from the fact as in Durkheim that in formulating society as the unconditioned common unity or source of speaking, he exempts the very activity of formulating from exposure; such an exemption allows Durkheim to write as if the unity he describes is unconditioned and primary only because he has not exposed its achievement. To expose the achievement of this unity would be to make reference to a higher unity which allows for the bringing to speech of the unity of the common.

In establishing the unity of community and democracy sociology elevates the notion of communality to authoritative status by transforming it into the normative order which rules speaking. Further, sociology shows a radically concrete understanding of unity as the unconditioned source of speaking – as the power of commonality which unifies differences – and in such an understanding it exempts its own achievement of this understanding from exposure. Moreover, sociology affirms the irrelevance of such an exposure on the grounds that it serves to invite dialectic and to undermine the security of the common beginning. Thus, sociology exists through its status as an antidote to theorizing; through its exemplification of the practical concern as the only rational grounds of community.

The power of sociology then curiously resides in its ability to disregard serious thinking on the grounds that serious thinking disturbs democracy: sociology – like Machiavelli and Rousseau – disregards theorizing not apologetically, but as a necessary condition for the creation of civic virtue and productive community. Sociology then completes the modern argument and brings it to its radical conclusion: theorizing is destructive and the destructiveness of theorizing resides in the fact that it undermines the commonness of the shared experience as an authoritative standard, and that it promises to deflect men from productively establishing political communities. Sociology affirms itself as the art which recognizes the inescapably practical character of community building and which acts upon such a recognition to speak in a way which affirms the good of such practical speaking. The firstness of sociology resides in the fact that it is the first art to recognize the incompatibility between theorizing and community building and to act upon such a re-cognition by re-formulating the desire to theorize as anti-social. Such a re-cognition is grounded in the modern concretization of the idea of the communal relationship by seeing it as the common experience idealized in the authority of grammar, rather than as an icon of the relationship of man to Being.

Despite the contemporary critique of Durkheim directed concertedly by 'schools' of sociology such as symbolic interaction, phenomenology, naturalism, and the 'critical science,' we might now note that the critique obscures its character as an affirmation of the aesthetic structure of Durkheim's programme. As an affirmation of total aestheticism the critique accuses Durkheim of not authenticating the experience which is common – the experience of society – as an immediate and indubitable presence. The critique is grounded in the claim that Durkheim is not sufficiently aesthetic and thus, the critique only exposes its own participation in the collective aspiration to totally aestheticize speech which Durkheim initiated but failed to complete. The most radical critics of Durkheim fail to see their togetherness because the criticism of Durkheim as a concrete thinker (as the objectivistic positivist) is grounded in the regret that he is not radically concrete. Just as Sartre's critique of 'orthodox' Marxism reflects the desire to totally concretize that grammar, so for example, does (so-called) phenomenology's critique of Durkheim express the demand to totally aestheticize the common experience as that appearance which is incorrigible in its presence. Durkheim failed to see the promise of aesthetic speech which contemporary sociologists grasp; that sociology can become the radically aesthetic speech, that sociology can be made to speak more concretely than even Durkheim dreamed, that sociology has it within its power to make silent speech (speech that says nothing), that sociology *can* become cinema.

Speech which knows its conventionality is speech which thinks that it is second because it is owned by a speaker and speakers are different. Speech which understands itself in this way knows that it is essentially difference to be overcome. Rational speech attempts to complete perspectiviality because it understands incompleteness as the manyness of perspectiviality rather than as the unspeakable relation between speech and its grounds. Incompleteness is seen as the interminability of pluralism or as the indefinite expandability of speech, rather than as the essential difference between speech and what is other than speech. If to complete means 'to end,' rational aesthetic speech tries to end interminability ('end' is seen as 'finishing' without respect to excellence) – instead of showing the 'end' of speech to be its display of the interminable as a trace of what is (other than speech).

8
Unity and Difference

I

Sociology, says Weber, is the science 'which attempts the interpretive understanding of social action to arrive at a causal explanation of its course and effects.'[1] Sociology is then identified with science; 'sociology is a science which. . . .' In this formulation, Weber equates sociology with science. However Weber's notion of sociology as science is specific; it is a science which has various instrumental goals. Sociology is a science only under the condition that it is the kind of science which attempts whatever Weber formulates it as attempting. Sociology is not any science because any science does not attempt the interpretive understanding of social action. Sociology is a particular science because it engages in such an attempt. The science of society has a particular goal which differentiates it from other sciences. The idea of the analytic identity of science as residing in its 'goals' re-introduces the idea of the hierarchy of sciences.

To say that sociology is a science 'which attempts the interpretive understanding' is to identify science with the achievement of under-standing. Historically science's character as a mode of understanding has been recognized. Yet Weber's conception of sociology as a science which attempts to achieve understanding goes further, for the under-standing that the science attempts to achieve seems to serve as a means for something other than the understanding itself. The understanding that the science achieves is displayed in the goal of the understanding, i.e., in the production of causal explanations of the course and effects of social action. But 'causal explanation' cannot be a *goal* of the science – as if understanding was achieved *in order* to causally explain, for what is the Good of causal explanation? Causal explanation is Good only insofar as it discloses the achievement of understanding, and so it is causal explanation that serves – by bringing to appearance – under-standing and not vice versa. This is to say that science's capacity to

[1] M. Weber, *Theory of Social and Economic Organization*, Glencoe: Free Press, p. 88.

causally explain makes reference to its achievement of understanding. Causal speech is an icon of the understanding which the science seeks to achieve as its goal.

In its identification with a science of understanding, through the icon of causal explanation sociology transforms the idea of science; sociology is the kind of science whose success in achieving interpretive understanding only appears through its causal explanations. Causal speech discloses or brings to appearance the understanding which the science *has*. Sociology then concretizes the notion of understanding by situating its visible character in speech understood as causal explanation. This is to say that if it is causal speech which discloses the understanding that is achieved, how can true speaking appear as some-thing as concrete as causal speech? The primordial question pertains to the relationship between such speech and an analytic conception of 'understanding,' i.e., how causal speech is 'understood' as a Rational appearance of knowledge.

For Weber, interpretive understanding recommends the formulation of meaning. 'Sociology is the science that attempts to formulate the meaning of social action in order to arrive. . . .' Yet the 'formulation of meaning' as a paraphrase for interpretive understanding is what the idea of social action recommends. Therefore, social action which is the matter to which the science addresses itself, is an instance of the very interpretive understanding that the science seeks to achieve. Sociology is the science which attempts the interpretive understanding of interpretive understanding and which shows the success of its attempt in causal explanation. The matter which sociology seeks to understand – its object, social action – is then displayed in its very act of understanding because sociology is the science which *acts* in order to grasp action. Therefore sociology is the peculiar science which has its object in front of it all along; sociology is the science that displays that very matter about which it seeks to achieve understanding. Sociology is the science which becomes what it studies, for in studying interpretive understanding, sociology produces it-self as an instance of interpretive understanding.

The production of a causal explanation of the course and effect of social action as the goal leaves the Reason of sociology unexplored. Such rationality cannot end at this point, i.e., sociology cannot permit itself to be grounded solely in its desire to produce causal explanations because the very notion of causal explanation must itself be grounded in some higher, Rational purpose. Therefore to call sociology 'the science which attempts to achieve causal explanation' is to leave unexplored and unexamined the question of the rationality of causal explanation, the question of the purpose and Reason of causal explanation. Yet, for Weber, causal explanation displays the science's achievement of understanding and in this lies its Reason; the goal or reason of the science is to display understanding, and consequently, Weber's notion of the production of causal explanation serves as a display of such an achievement. Sociology is then the science which attempts to understand understanding and which treats the understanding of understanding as its highest purpose and ground – as displayed in causal explanation. It is *this* idea of understanding that grounds the doing of sociology with its moral purpose. The important question then, is how does sociology understand understanding? What does sociology do to the idea of understanding?

Understanding is a metaphor for the kind of social relation that is knowing. Understanding 'appears' through causal speech. Understanding is valuable only because it is a metaphor for the creation of unity. This science is generated when an observer tries to understand an other. To understand an other is to stand under him in a togetherness that is unitary. It is to create a togetherness between you and he by collecting both of you as a one under some law. Though the other is different, the observer decides on the basis of what he and the other have in common (the resources of what is given) in order to determine whether other is understood. The goal of the science is to bring self and other into concert on the grounds of their putative difference; given their difference, the problem of the science of sociology is to understand other, i.e., to understand some-thing different, by employing resources which unify both the one engaged in the understanding and the one whom he is trying to understand.

To understand is then to create unity, it is to establish the unity between self and other, or to restore a unity which the observer's initial formulation had shattered by beginning with a difference that is apparent other than Real. The science which achieves understanding is the science which assimilates other, (i.e., the difference) to itself, and which can show in such an assimilation the adequacy of its procedure. Sociology is then the science which builds community: the interpretive understanding of social action is the understanding of other and to understand other is to understand what is non-ego or what is different. Sociology is then the science which attempts to understand what is different from the author of the understanding, i.e., the science which seeks to bring into contact differences by establishing their related character. As such a science, sociology employs custom as a resource – as a concerted resource – to understand what other is. Therefore, sociology is the science which uses similarities to understand difference; it is the science which attempts to understand what the other is. It is the science which attempts to explore the relationship of the one to the one, of the parts to the many. Yet, note that the very notion of Other recommends that the science begins with similarity. This is to say that the very idea of an other pre-supposes the related character of the differences that are being created. The science which attempts to understand the other is the science which creates the other – as different – in order to re-assert the related character. Sociology creates the other as difference by equating the apparent with the Real and then unifies by showing the related character of what is apparently different. Sociology re-establishes a relationship among appearances. Sociology is the science which starts communally, and then shatters communal bonds in order to restore community on a firmer and more authentic foundation. We can then see what sociology does to the idea of understanding: it transforms it into a metaphor for the creation of a simple unity between different things.

II

> In 'action' is included all human behaviour when and insofar as the acting individual attaches a subjective meaning to it.[1]

Through the use of the term 'attach' Weber makes it appear as if we are dealing with two discrete kinds of 'things' – behaviour and subjective meaning – which the idea of 'attach' cements together. Thus, attach already pre-supposes the break between behaviour and subjective meaning which Weber is attempting to delineate. Obviously, the problem can become tortuous, for if Weber is read as instructing an observer, then the observer must do some attaching of his own; the behaviour which he witnesses (of an individual attaching . . .) must have meaning 'attached' to it. Yet, all of this pre-supposes the conception of 'one who can be treated as attaching subjective meaning to his behaviour' and this is the problem which we must address.

Weber introduces a distinction between behaviour and subjective meaning by producing the *possibility* of attachment, or by generating the idea that behaviour and subjective meaning are independent kinds of forms. Imagine what it would be like for an individual not to be seen as so attaching. If we translate 'subjective meaning' as 'to understand' then he is saying: action will be recognized as human behaviour which shows that it is understood by the agent performing it. But since all conduct can be provided with such a reading, it becomes difficult to imagine one who is not understanding what he is doing. It is that what the agent does or does not understand is the understanding which the observer has; thus, to re-cognize action is to treat one as showing that he understands what he is doing in a certain way. What an actor might be assumed to understand is that he is ruled by the observer, i.e., that he and the observer are joined together in their understanding. So, the difference between subjective meaning and behaviour is this kind of

[1] *Ibid.*, p. 88.

difference: that one who is seen as acting, i.e., as assigning subjective meaning (as understanding), is one whose behaviour displays his attempt to unify difference, one who shows his hearing or orienting to the rhetorical possibilities of his own speaking. Since the rhetorical possibilities of speaking recommend the difference between ego and Other, action can be seen in behaviour that displays the agent's orienting to the requiredness of overcoming disparity and difference through his conduct. In this sense an actor is exemplified in the observer: if the observer is an ideal scientist, (i.e., one who orients to the need to overcome the rhetorical propensity of speech by restoring unity), then the actor is one who displays this selfsame understanding. The actor exemplifies through his conduct that he is ruled by the same concern that rules the observer. The actor is seen as understanding that he and the observer are joined together in a community of understanding, i.e., that he displays the understanding which the observer formulates and recommends as an ideal understanding.

To see action is to understand conduct as making reference in its accomplishment to the agent's understanding of the conduct; in this way the conduct performatively displays the actor's knowledge, it is an icon of the understanding. To see action is then a way of recognizing conduct as a display of communal or scientific reflexivity.

The observer then begins with what *he* can assume the other to understand. The other becomes an actor when his conduct can be treated as a display of the observer's understanding of what he (the other) understands. Since what he understands is equivalent to what he knows, action is conduct that is done as a method of showing what the actor knows. To see an actor is to formulate one who is reflexively orienting to his conduct as a display of knowledge, whereas to see behaviour is to formulate the interests of other as oriented to self-interest rather than communal interests. Yet, both kinds of other cannot be recognized unless *they* are understood and to understand them is to participate in their intelligibility; so the actor must be the type of other (for the observer) who displays a particular kind of understanding. Thus, it is not reflexivity *per se* that distinguishes the one who acts, but a certain kind of reflexivity; the reflexivity of communal rather than self-interest. The actor is reflexive only in the sense that he is public spirited, that is, that he displays his public spirit which in it-self enunciates his thought-ful orientation to the problem of the conditions required for the creation of communicative order as the ideal relationship that is knowledge.

Action is social insofar as, by virtue of the subjective meaning attached to it by the acting individual (or individuals), it takes account of the behaviour of others and is thereby oriented in its course.[1]

---

[1] *Ibid.*, p. 88.

Here we have it. It is not merely that the concept makes reference to the agent's knowledge, but that it displays *what* he knows – that he is together with others, that he begins together with others. Action is recognized when an agent's conduct makes reference to his being together with others. The actor then, as compared to the one who behaves, is one who shows in his conduct that he is oriented to the speech of other and is seeking to overcome their differences (he is public spirited, a public speaker, one whose speech is controlled by the public). In the very same way, Weber is oriented to the speech of other – whether actor or one who behaves – as a display of difference, and under the auspices of a desire to restore their unity. Therefore, the actor is recognized as a facsimile or impersonation of Weber himself, and Weber recognizes action when he can conceive of conduct as displaying the ideal rationality which his very formulation recommends as adequate and to which he subscribes as a rule of inquiry.

Behaviour then, is not merely self-centred aestheticism or genius, but it can be seen by a modern like Weber in dialectic itself. As a modern metaphor behaviour can catch not only the self-centred aestheticism of empiricism (which Weber thought of as different from his 'rationalism,' his grammar), but also, the faithfulness of dialectic which shows the lack of public spirit. Where 'charisma' will symbolize aesthetic speaking, 'tradition' will symbolize dialectic (in such a way as to include both Plato and Aristotle and to equate them with the pre-historic).

If all conduct can be seen as making reference to the actor's knowledge, not all conduct makes reference to the actor's orienting to the scientist's relevance. This is to say that not all understanding displays itself as an understanding of the rhetorical propensity of human conduct and as the desire to overcome this rhetorical possibility in order to achieve community. Because neither classicism nor empiricism displays such a spirit, neither the classical nor the modern theorist is an actor. In this case though, action does make such reference, i.e., action and only action displays the understanding of the scientist interested in preserving community. What the actor understands then is his commonness; in other words his understanding displays his grasp of his commonness with others. To formulate an actor is to construct an other who is ruled by his commonness, i.e., as one whose conduct displays itself as grounded in the rule of his commonness. In this sense, the agent's understanding of such commonness is seen as the reason for his conduct. However, what the agent has in common is precisely the difference between himself and other, and so he is oriented to the requiredness of overcoming these differences. To overcome these differences symbolized as rhetoric and danger – through speech – is to understand these differences and the requiredness of silencing them which is what the actor displays. In this sense the actor displays precisely the understanding and desire of the observer; both observer and actor are oriented to the rhetorical danger of difference – of the difference between self and other – and they display in their conduct their grasp of the requiredness of overcoming these differences through their speaking. This actor is the inquirer totally aestheticized: he accepts and orients to the need for unity as that which is immediate, present, and good (its goodness residing in the fact that the need for such a unity is convincing, i.e., it is apparent as the good method for overcoming difference).

The point to grasp is not merely that the actor is one who can be assumed to show understanding of his commonness with other, but that he is one whose understanding of this commonness *is* an understanding of difference. In other words, both actor and scientist – or actor as exemplification of scientist and scientist as idealization of actor – understand their commonness to consist of difference, and both display their understanding of commonness in their desire to overcome difference through speech which creates and restores unity.

From the Socratic perspective, when man's conduct does not display his understanding of having something in common, he is showing that he does not understand the relationship between his speech and Reason (as demonstrated by the various interlocutors of Socrates). However, for Socrates, the commonness to be understood was the unity of the belonging-together of language and Being. The speaker had to show that he understood that the medium for his unity with his audience was more than the capacities to speak together, but was a deeper relationship which this very common speech covered-over. A knower was one who understood how his speaking encounter concealed a deep relationship to Reason, a relationship whose commonality consisted only in the fact that it was a human possibility. Consequently, a knower was one who acted on the basis of such an understanding. Such an 'actor' demonstrated his understanding through his creation of the *aporia* and through his search for essential speech.

In contrast, with sociology we obtain another version of understanding one's commonness. The very impulse which makes dialectic possible is treated as an instance of privatization. To demonstrate reflexivity is to display through speech respect for the conventional character of unity, and is to affirm through speech this respect as a display of solidarity. One displays his respect for communal solidarity by demonstrating a grasp of the conventions which rule speech, and by respecting such conventions as both a starting point and limit of speaking. Where dialectic treats commonness as a relationship only hinted at by a concerted capacity to speak together, or as a problem which concerted speaking raises, sociology treats this problem as settled by the fact that we do speak together.

Sociology decides to use what we have in common as the basis for solidarity, as that nature to which the 'action' of inquiry is responsive, as that nature which it will imitate. Despite our differences – the difference between ego and other – what is common is that we participate in the same experience. What we have in common is not that we could think, but that we are exposed to the same concrete environment. Whereas Durkheim re-formulates this environment as the nature that is society, Weber re-formulates it in terms of the ethical ideal of communicative rationality. In Durkheim what we share is that we could speak as participants in this common experience, whereas in Weber, we could speak as loyalists to this ideal. To speak 'as if' provides the grammatical element in both programmes.

That which is common is the fact that men understand their commonness, and this fact is secured and protected through speech. To show that one protects this fact is to demonstrate the reflexivity of an actor. An actor is one who makes reference to this commonness by showing that he understands the limit which commonness imposes upon Desire. An actor shows that he knows the limits and that his conduct is guided by such knowledge; he is *ruled* by this knowledge. An actor is then a responsible agent, i.e., a One who is mindful of his obligation to be ruled by his commonness rather than by Desire. The actor is one who reflexively decides for unreflexivity; he is the paradigmatic exemplar of practicality. Therefore, the speech that makes reference to the speaker's understanding of his commonness is the speech that takes much for granted; the reflexive actor is the common sense member impersonating and impersonated by the ideal rational scientist. The scientist then becomes the exemplar for the actor and comes to exemplify the actor through the scientific rationality.

The question is this: how does sociology show itself as acting under the rule of its understanding of its commonness? Since all of the sciences seem to operate under the auspices of such an understanding, what is distinctive of the science of sociology? This query raises two particular questions: on the one hand, if science is the method for inducing men to behave with knowledge of their conventionality in order to achieve community, then sociology is no different from any science in the fact that it is grounded in this responsibility to a collective. That is, science is the method *par excellence* for asserting the authoritativeness of the common and for demonstrating the communal character which must underlie the common. Sociology must then differ from the other arts by refusing to let this ideal lie and by actively seeking to promote it as an object of inquiry. Sociology finds in the other an imperfect facsimile of the conventional understanding which sociology as a science itself exemplifies; thus, the other must be transformed into an impersonation of the very understanding – science – which creates it, and hence, into an instance of scientific rationality. Since scientific (conventional) understanding provides the limits of rationality, sociology must use every inquiry as an occasion to re-affirm such an authoritative stand by creating the actor. The actor is one who is designed to impersonate the ideal of concrete (communal) rationality, and in his conduct is constructed to display the omnirelevance of this rationality on any and every occasion.

Since conventional rationality is the understanding that reflexively grasps responsibility to a standard of convincing speech because such a standard exemplifies the relationship that is knowledge, sociology constructs puppets to enact and personify this understanding. Sociology preserves this understanding by demonstrating its omnirelevance, and it accomplishes such a demonstration by re-creating ordinary life as an impersonation of this understanding as an ideal social relationship (as a possible society). Thus, an actor is one who is constructed to exemplify what the sociologist knows and every actor is an exemplification of the rationality of sociology. Consequently, an other must exhibit the potentiality of such a grammatical understanding (of mathematicity) in order to be formulable as an actor (which is exactly what the notion of 'good data' recommends). The other is not external or independent to the sociologist, nor is he a one who is to be engaged; rather, he is a feature of sociologizing itself in that he is only recognized through the sociological understanding, and he is only made intelligible as an exemplar of the selfsame understanding, i.e., whether as one who departs from or conforms to such a standard.

The actor is then not only one who impersonates, but he is the achievement of an impersonation. It is through his construction of an actor that the sociologist impersonates the rational ideal of scientific belief as an authoritative grammar for reconciling difference (as the image of the kind of relationship which is aesthetic conviction). Whereas sociology ultimately poses the question of whether its impersonations are real, such questions can only be answered in terms of the standards used to construct impersonations (such as causal adequacy and adequacy at the level of meaning). However, the only responsible question that can be asked is whether the standard of rationality is itself worth impersonating, because any test or demonstration of the adequacy of the impersonation can only occur under the auspices of the standard; the other cannot be treated as a 'test' for sociology because every such test is done sociologically. (Which means that he is only a concrete alter and does not personify real otherness.)

All conduct is treated as an inarticulate attempt to impersonate society (to belong together in a unity with society as an instance of its conventional wisdom); consequently, all conduct is re-constructed as such an impersonation. Theory takes upon itself the task of producing speech which is designed to intimate conventional rationality and which is only different from that about which it speaks by its understanding of such a relationship. The theory-practice distinction is then political in the deepest sense because theory becomes speech which enlarges the scope of conventional understanding by introducing it as a standard on any and every occasion. Theorizing is the act of keeping alive the standard of scientific rationality, i.e., of community through speech. Sociology then distinguishes itself from other practices by its desire to make the world rational through its very speech, where such rationality is understood as the scientific self-consciousness of the ideal member; sociology seeks to accomplish this by creating a total community through its speech and by asserting and affirming the community as authoritative through its use of standards furnished by the speech. Through sociology, rationality becomes redefined as scientific self-consciousness – which is just a gloss for the politicization of the practical interest – rather than as Reason.

The political character of sociology is seen in its assertion of the authoritative character of communal self-consciousness (of the actor) against which it treats all other forms of consciousness as instances of privatization or distortion. Sociology is the populistic discipline, because in creating and sustaining the authority of the concrete speaking community it celebrates the rationality of the city as the only thing worth speaking for. Weber presents a new role for the science of sociology; sociology will proceed with the rationalization of the world and it will accomplish such a task by converting the other into an actor. Consequently, sociology will re-make the world in its image and will produce itself as the discipline which re-presents the highest development of communal thought. The highest development of communal thought – the ideal 'state' of sociology – is reflected in the image of a collective acting concertedly under the auspices of scientific rules (i.e., a democracy). Thus, sociology will close its mind to the fact that any relationship between the other and the actor cannot test sociology because it already pre-supposes its existence, and it will pretend to discover what it has had in hand all along, using this pretence as a way of diverting questioning from the Goodness or Rationality of that which it has in hand.

Under Weber's influence, sociology becomes a metaphor for thought which is at one with the political character of speaking and which thinks under the auspices of such an understanding. This is because convincing speech is a politicization of the idea of a relationship. Sociology becomes a metaphor for the rational-legal development of thought and sociological rationality becomes typified in the reflexivity of the rational-legal agent – the typical, conventional scientific actor. Alter is neither respected, preserved, nor educated to face the

Good, but is treated as a possible exemplification of the scientific rationality. To accomplish this transformation sociology must epitomize rationality in its very own method, i.e., in its speaking. The task of inducing respect for the law – which both Descartes and Durkheim confronted – must be completed by arguing for the political advantage of such respect. The authority of the law is based upon its technical superiority and upon the fact that only through such submission will a rational-democratic society be created. Where both Descartes and Durkheim argued that the rule of method will create a rational society because it answers to some self-evident process of adequate thinking, it was Weber's task to complete this argument by presenting his picture of the self-certifying and grounding society which permits no escape within speech and which justifies itself through its good works. In other words, Weber completed the process begun by earlier thinkers by arguing that the efficacy of the scientific community could only be justified by the peaceableness and efficiency it created and by its production of good works. Weber's particular advance upon Durkheim was to convert the ideas of productivity and good works into notions of 'causal adequacy' and prediction. Weber demonstrated the political possibilities of prediction as a way of masking the thoughtlessness of science and of delaying the critique which science inevitably invites.

III

Sociology is then distinguished from all other sciences by this fact: sociology alone is the science which promotes the ideal of science as the only rational, efficient, and productive ground of community. Sociology is then the first science because it is the political science, i.e., it is the science which promotes the ideal of science it-self as a method for organizing the ordinary communal affairs of men. Sociology is first and acquires its power in this sense; that as such an active pro-pagandizing science it is the science which asserts the communal power and good of science itself as grounds of communal living. Sociology then must ground its claim by arguing for the superiority of science as a method of achieving peace, efficiency, and good works and this is the task which sociology sets out for itself.

There are three pure types of legitimate authority. The validity of their claims to legitimacy may be based on: 1) rational grounds – resting on a belief in the 'legality' of patterns of normative rule and the right of those elevated to authority under such rules to issue commands (legal authority); 2) traditional grounds – resting on an established belief in the sanctity of immemorial traditions and the legitimacy of the status of those exercising authority under them (traditional authority); or finally, 3) charismatic grounds – resting on devotion to the specific and exceptional sanctity, heroism or exemplary character of an individual person, and of the normative patterns or order revealed or ordained by him (charismatic authority).[1]

In one case, we submit to the 'legality' (for which we should read 'adequacy') of a methodic discipline, i.e., the discipline of our method which acquires its adequacy through legal grounds. In the traditional case, we submit to another sort of discipline for which the adequacy is similarly stipulated. Nevertheless, there is a difference between the two cases, for in one, the adequacy of the method has been decided through a willful act of belief which could have been otherwise, while in the other the question of adequacy was never a topic for the believer.

Also, in each of these cases, the speech which is produced acquires a different status: 'the right of those elevated to authority under such rules to issue commands' refers to the *reality* of the speech, i.e., that the speech which is elevated to 'authority' under the auspices of such a method (the speech which acquires 'legitimate' ontological authority) is the speech which *issues commands*. That is, the speech that is produced through such procedures as a bona fide and 'real' topic of inquiry comes to command its producer (the theorist). The speech that is produced comes to acquire authority and to command the theorist simply by virtue of its production; that is, the authoritativeness of the speech is based upon the fact that it is produced through these rational procedures. The speech is authoritative because it is loyal to method and demonstrates its loyalty through its rational accomplishment. The speech acquires its 'real' status because it is ruled by method. The speech that is ruled by method is authoritative because method guarantees that the speech imitates nature and so, speech that follows method follows nature. Method as a plan for producing convincing speech is organized to re-present the real (the unquestioned need) for order that is the rational community.

In this sense, we might appreciate that this view of grounding the authority of speech only and exclusively in terms of its conformity to method is a variation of an ancient project since the authority of the method is not itself addressed as a topic. That is, the question of what rules the method is concealed. What we obtain instead is an anticipation of the notion of scientific definition; simply by virtue of its production, a speech acquires command over the theorist (with the qualification that the method is 'legal,' i.e., judged to be adequate). The Rationality of the authoritative notion of legality however remains unspoken. Paradoxically, the method is ruled by an ideal of communality – of

[1] *Ibid.*, p. 328.

democracy or of democratic community – commitment to which is itself an instance of the very traditional authority and belief against which this rational-legal formulation is opposed. This is to say that the method which is grounded in the democratic ideal of openness thrives on secrecy because it divests all concern with its rationality.

The notion of 'sanctity' introduces a different emphasis from 'legality,' for whereas the latter at least hints that the method is grounded in a decision for belief that participates in a rational agreement to begin together, the 'sanctity of immemorial traditions' suggests that such a decision is not accomplished under the auspices of a rational understanding of its character, but is closer to common sense unreflexive knowledge. This is to say that traditional authority does not *require* a decision with respect to adequacy because the decision was not a topic of thought. Consequently, the difference between the two procedures for Weber is that one is the achievement of a decision-with-respect-to-adequacy while the other is the outcome of a process within which such a decision was not a necessary feature. While the speeches produced by both methods exercise their authority by virtue of their accomplishment, they are accomplished in different ways. Thus, the agency that provides speech with its status as 'real,' i.e., analytic speech, is in both cases the method used, and yet, whereas one method requires of speech that it make reference to itself as an instance of method (that it show understanding of the method), the other requires no showing of such public spirit.[1] Tradition is a metaphor for speech which does not subject what it says to the standard of convincingness stipulated as the authoritative communal rationality. Yet, Weber can only establish a distinction by exempting his own speaking from scrutiny: the very grounding of his distinction between the rational-legal and the traditional exemplifies the traditionality of belief which he denigrates; it is only possible for Weber to make such a distinction on the basis of his misconstrual of the idea of belief (by concretizing it and by treating it as a paradigm for unreflexive knowing). This is to say that his very notion of rational-legal belief rests upon, is grounded in, and displays in its very accomplishment the authority of a traditional commitment which was never a topic for rational-legal procedure in itself. The grammatical distinction which Weber makes affirm his traditionality and he masks this only because he banalizes the ideas of tradition, faith, and belief by concretizing them as ignorance and as ego-centricity. Is there a better example in

[1] This is the negative sense of traditional method which we get from Heraclitus: 'One need not act and talk just like the parents' children,' p. 109 in Cleve, where tradition is equated with opinion, with listening, but not really *hearing*, etc. We also find this notion of tradition in Meno, cf. F. Cleve, *The Giants of Pre-Sophistic Philosophy*, The Hague: Martinus Nijhoff, 1965.

the history of thought of what sociology has done to thinking than Weber's treatment of tradition? To exempt it by saying that it is a 'sociological treatment' only affirms what is being said.

In contrast to these two methods, charismatic authority specifies the theorist's relationship to the contingent, fortuitous world of appearances which he is required to manage through his method. In this case, the theorist produces speech grounded in his perceptions of the unstable flux of the appearing world; consequently, the authority of a speech which is produced through these methods of perceiving is the authority of an object of perception rather than of knowledge.[1]

The connection between a sense datum philosophy of appearances and charismatic authority is instructive because such authority commands in terms of the way in which it manifests itself in appearance. This also makes intelligible Socrates' attempt to induce Protagoras to terminate his set speeches in *The Protagoras* and enter into dialogue: Protagoras' false equation of perception and knowledge was exemplified in the method of charismatic authority which he sought to employ in the dialogue; charismatic authority inevitably creates the anarchy of Protagoras' maxim, 'every man is the measure.' In this respect, charismatic authority appears as a metaphor for self-centred thinking and we may note why charismatic authority is essentially unstable and why charismatic authority must in Weber's language be 'routinized.'

Charismatic authority is unstable in the way that the collection of sense data and opinions is unstable: the essentially contingent character of the world of the senses can be all things to all men, i.e., the contingency of time, place, observer, use etc., guarantee the essential instability of any one perceiver's speech insofar as that speech makes a descriptive claim to knowing. Because charismatic authority exalts a standard of free speaking as authoritative it must dissolve into the anarchy of perspectiviality unless it is organized by force (by the rational-legal state). This leads to the conclusion that knowing is more than perceiving or recording and that it requires a pre-selected organization of understanding for its normalization. The grounds of knowledge are not achievements of perception but are more like organized understandings which make any perception possible. The routinization of charisma is thus another way of formulating the inevitable stabilization of percepts through knowledge, the collecting of the essential together-

---

[1] 'Knowledge then seems to be nothing but the perception of the connection of and agreement and repugnancy of any of our ideas. In this alone it Exists. Where this perception is, there is knowledge, and where it is not, there, though we may fancy, guess or believe, yet, we always come short of knowledge.' J. Locke, *An Essay Concerning Human Understanding*, ed., A. C. Fraser, New York, 1959, 2 volumes, II, 167–168.

ness of things and the bringing of them to light and permanence.[1] Whereas charismatic authority makes reference to the authority of self, both traditional and rational-legal authority point to communal ideals that are more competitive. The real question is whether tradition (faith) or rational-legal authority (science) will organize speech. The question of what is the best state only masks the aesthetic desire to save speech from nihilism by restoring and re-affirming a Reason for which speech ought to speak.

Weber conceives of the rational-legal method as superior to the traditional: traditional authority is uncritical and naive; it is either the paradigm of unreflexive, ordinary thinking, or at its best, of egocentric genius. What grounds does Weber use to provide for the superiority of rational-legal authority as a solution, for such grounds are certainly not self-evident in the quote? That is, how does Weber formulate such authority so as to provide for its superiority?

In the rational type it is a matter of principle that the members of the administrative staff should be completely separated from ownership of the means of production or administration. Officials, employees, and workers attached to the administrative staff do not themselves own the non-human means of production and administration. The seare rather provided for their use in kind or in money, and the official is obligated to render an accounting of their use. There exists, furthermore, in principle complete separation of the property belonging to the organization, which is controlled within the sphere of office, and the personal property of the official, which is available for his own private uses.[2]

This is a fine quote on what the rational-legal method of theorizing intends to accomplish, although he still does not provide for the Reason of such an accomplishment. Read 'ownership of the means of production and administration' as a method for speaking about the legitimate scope of the theorist's 'interests' in his activity of theorizing, i.e., he must operate under the auspices of the rule of official disinterest vis-à-vis the world which his theorizing intends to describe. The theorist does not 'own' his theory in the sense that he is not free to behave as he wishes (without respect to official standards). The theorist is not a free speaker, that is how he differs from ordinary men. So, the quote reads as a method for inducing 'scientific' responsibility in the theorist, for forcing him to be responsible and responsive to certain features of his practice which he cannot alter and manipulate at will. The way to accomplish this is to create a version of what theory is and then to stipulate certain rules, compliance to which must be enforced so as to

---

[1] In fact, Heidegger's description of man, the gatherer of Logos, in *Introduction to Metaphysics* is essentially a formulation of the routinization of charisma in this sense.

[2] Weber, p. 331.

232

insure the production of this type of theory. The best theory is that which will control man (the free speaker) by preventing free speech from undermining community. Rational-legal theory is superior because it is construed as a solution to the problem of free speech which it itself creates as the problem of theorizing (in the metaphor of rhetoric). Thus, the rational-legal method is an attempt to enforce in the theorist, loyalty to method and to its rules rather than to self.[1] The task is to provide for the rational limit of Self as exhausted through its commitment to method by arguing for the requiredness of the rational-legal as the only method for overcoming difference and rhetoric through the creation of community.

Separating staff from ownership is a way of converting theorizing from that which is 'private' and under the control of the personal interests of the theorist into that which is public and under the control of the collective. The first principle then states: theory should be a public product (i.e., it should become a topic) so that it can be evaluated without respect to the personal interests of the theorist. To achieve a public product, the theorist must agree to begin (with others) with the method where such an agreement wills as anti-social (anti-communal) that which would undermine this agreement by differentiating man from others. This then ties into the point that the theorist is required to 'render an accounting' of his use of the 'means of production and administration' in the sense that he is required to make public his methodic production of the theory (i.e., his methods for using whatever ideas and 'data' he uses). The theorist is required to use his speech to make reference to the typicality of the speech under the assumption that such typicality affirms his communality with others.

The rational method is then the method for enforcing the public character of theorizing. To say that theorizing must be public is to stipulate the official irrelevance of the congeries of interests, involvements, and attitudes that are particular to the theorist and which promise to separate him from those with whom he is required to begin. The attempt to institutionalize the public character of theorizing is a systematic effort to control for the effect of extraneous factors upon the course of inquiry, where the major class of such factors of interest to Weber is that which can be treated as a dangerous and lively source of his possible differences from others. To create the passionless science is to legislate as anti-social the passions. In this sense, the passion which is theorizing (essentially) cannot be the subject of theorizing itself because theory only addresses that which can be rendered passionless as

---

[1] For our purposes, what is most interesting is the condition(s) or form of life under which loyalty to method becomes loyalty to self, for this is what such an emphasis requires as a condition of its success; *this* was the theme of *The Protestant Ethic and the Spirit of Capitalism*.

a topic of conversation. The attempt to 'rationalize' theory by making it public can be seen analytically as an effort to create a collective, because a public theory is a *topic* of concerted treatment, i.e., for assessment and review. Weber re-states the Durkheimian instruction to treat ideas as things, by recommending they be treated as topics. The method accomplishes this by inducing the theorist to respect and to comply with rational-legal maxims because the essential feature of such a law is its guarantee to convert ideas into *topics* (i.e., into objective knowledge), and thus, the superiority of rational-legal methods is grounded in the expectation that they will transform ideas into topics (or, what is outside of the domain of the collective into what is inside).

The superiority of rational-legal methods is marked: its efficiency and fairness leads to its tendency to maximize the re-presentativeness of its speeches as answering-to most standardly the free-speaking possibilities of its contributors by organizing these contributions in terms of a standard of whether or not they can uniformly convince the many in the same way that one convinces him-self of what is present to him. It makes decisions assessable and reviewable and controls excesses of motivation, and imagination (of desire). Further, rational-legal method creates topics by terminating discussion and rhetoric through its enforcement of a common beginning, a plan for work, and a common (communal) ideal. It makes possible authoritative and legal terminations of discussion on the radically new grounds that such termination is a legitimate obligation incurred by those who accept the mandate recommended by the scientific ideal of commonality.

The description of the separation of personal from public property follows in the same vein, with the qualification that the 'property belonging to the organization, which is controlled within the sphere of office,' is the corpus of knowledge relevant to theorizing, while the 'personal property of the official' are those extraneous features which are regarded as officially irrelevant. In other words, this is a comment on the possibilities of *bias* and on how rational-legal methods work to eliminate the capricious and interested mind of the scientist as an analytic feature of his inquiry. 'Office' is then a metaphor for the class of intellectual resources of relevance to inquiry, i.e., it is an attempt to guarantee that the theorist's orientation to his inquiry proceeds under the rule of law and that it not operate to pervert the inquiry. Such interests are controlled by being made visible, reportable, and public through the inquirer's careful delineation of his activity, i.e., through the medium of self-report. Essentially, rational procedures consist in their transformation of impulse into product; in making theorizing communal, they seek to guarantee objective assessments of knowledge without respect to those interests which undermine the possibility of community by introducing the 'effects' of one man's differences from others.

Thus, Weber's principal concern is to demonstrate that theory grows out of a relationship (which both Descartes and Durkheim glossed) by formulating the essential features of such a relationship. This is the communal relationship of man to his fellows which is undermined by the divisive, private, self-interested and unreflexive. It is the method which if followed, strengthens the inquirer's resolve to overcome rhetoric, because the method promotes his compliance to the ideal of scientific commonality as a legitimate object of belief on the grounds that compliance to such an ideal provides the only efficient means for guaranteeing *both* peaceableness and achievements and for establishing such a guarantee in a manner that intrinsically silences disputatiousness.

For illustration, let us briefly turn to Weber's discussion of bureaucracy.

> Each office has a clearly defined sphere of competence in the legal sense. The office is filled by a free contractual relationship. Thus, in principle, there is free selection.
> Candidates are selected on the basis of technical qualifications.
> The office is treated as the sole, or at least the primary, occupation of the incumbent.
> It constitutes a career.
> The official works entirely separated from ownership of the means of administration and without appropriation of his position.
> He is subject to strict and systematic discipline and control in the conduct of the office.
> The role of technical qualifications in bureaucratic organizations is continually increasing.[1]

This collection of features requires for its understanding a further clarification of the notion of 'office.' What is the *office* of the theorist? We might conceive of office as the locus of rights and obligations of the theorist-as-theorist; it is that to which the theorist – in his capacity as theorist – is responsive and responsible. That is, the idea of 'office' suggests the authority to which theory is responsive, its Good or Reason. The office of theory depicts the relationship of theory to its nature and consequently, 'office' is an icon of the nature to which theory ought to belong.

When Weber speaks of the 'office' of theory he is addressing the age-old problem of the nature of theory; to what ought the idea of theory be responsible. Of course this question pre-supposes a commitment to an idea of the nature of theory as the authoritative and Rational commitment. Weber's notion of 'office' will reflect the election of the scientific project.

[1] Excerpted from Weber, pp. 333–335.

While some might say that the theorist is responsible to Logos, to Will, to a party, or to humanity, Weber is saying that the theorist's primary responsibility as-a-theorist is to his *problem*. This is a way of formulating the Being of theorizing, that which makes theorizing theorizing and not something else. In one's capacity as a theorist, he is responsible only and exclusively to the *problem* (office) which calls him. Weber then re-formulates the nature of theory – the Reason of theory – in such a way as to transform it into a responsibility to an external problem. To formulate the nature of theory as problem-solving is to assume the secure and well-founded character of this nature since such security is pre-supposed in any conception of a problem. This re-formulation then re-orients theory away from itself (its nature) by making it dependent upon some 'problem' external to this nature. Theory acquires its analytic status through its contingent relation to external problems, while the very recognition of such problems pre-supposes the availability of such a nature. Theory which serves a 'problem' is speaking that subjects itself to topics that *happen* to the present and timely. It is speech that is controlled by what *appears* as present to a time and a place (to a body). Since what is present to a body is the fact that it is mine, 'problem-oriented' theory seeks to overcome the perspectiviality of concrete speaking.

The 'problem' is a metaphor for the danger recognizable in difference, and the normalizing task of theory is to exemplify the overcoming of rhetoric in its speech. We then get the classic paradigm of sociological theory in its formulation of the 'problem' for when 'problem' is understood analytically as the re-cognition of the destructive, divisive implications of rhetoric, the 'success' of theorizing is tested by its capacity to overcome difference, to silence rhetoric, and to communalize discussion. To define theorizing as 'problem-solving' is to affirm the political and conventionalized community-building impulse of sociology.

Weber's discussion of bureaucracy succeeds in showing the goal of rational-legal authority, and consequently, the grounds of his claim to its superiority. Rational-legal authority is superior because it provides for the solution of problems; one forces his thought to conform to method because such conformity will be realized as the solution of a problem. True speech is then equated with a solution to a problem, where every such 'solution' is concretized through metaphors of communalization that succeeded in creating silence (analytically) by producing standard and univocal hearing rules; yet, every such hearing is only possible because it sacrifices the very idea of hearing for a mundane standard of listening. Problem-solving then appears through metaphors like 'causal explanation' and 'prediction' where every such 'solution' only 'succeeds' by virtue of the same standard that produced the problem in the first place.

In this way, the 'clearly defined sphere of competence in the legal sense' refers to the clear identification of a problem; his conception of the office as the 'primary occupation' of the incumbent is a way of instructing the theorist to disregard everything extraneous to the problem (everything extraneous to the need to make that which is present to me present to all); the fact that the office constitutes a career means that the problem is formulated as the successive stages in its clarification, as it progressively moves towards a solution (as convincing speech). This is the same very concrete conception of the location and formulation of problems that Merton described in his paper on 'problem finding in sociology':[1] first, the problem is formulated, then it is 'specified' in terms of certain dimensions through a process of 'progressive clarification,' and then (if we add those many repetitions of the one paper written by Lazarsfeld on the 'movement from concepts to indicators') we obtain a complete profile of the 'stages' through which the career of the problem proceeds.

There are other implications. For example, the notion that the office is filled by a 'free contractual relationship' is just another way of talking about so-called value neutrality. That is, the theorist is free to select his 'problem' in terms of the limits of his interests. However, that this is not completely true is suggested by the remark that 'candidates are selected on the basis of their technical qualifications' which really means that not any *problem* is selected (even if the inquirer has an interest in it), but only those which are amenable to description and specification in terms of the rational programme. What is not formulable cannot be a topic and only invites silence (yet if what is formulable is formulated so concretely that what is said is nothing, then even programmatic speech is silent). Finally, Weber's remark that the role of such technical qualifications are increasing can be seen as a suggestion that problem selection which is increasingly governed by the authority of a rational-legal programme promises to assimilate these (and any) problems to its legal requirements and in the process, to radically distort (fail to 'hear') speech by making what it speaks so apparent as to be not worth speaking. This is why Weber decried the rationalization to which he was him-self contributing. He had tried to save speech from apostasy and genius by idealizing a relationship that could only make speech speechless.

Thus, if sociology follows the method as its rule it will demonstrate its authority (i.e., efficiency) because it will solve problems, it will produce community. Since a problem is nothing more than a version of the speaker and hearer as independent, to solve problems is to convert Other into an actor (into a re-presentation of the theorist). In this way, sociology will solve problems when it creates rational actors,

[1] See Merton in Broom, *et al.*, *Sociology Today*.

and every such creation constitutes a 'solution' inasmuch as it inserts a rational sociologist into the world under the cover of a puppet which impersonates him. To solve problems is then to conceal the sociological impulse to rationalize the world (to rationalize other) under the cover of speech which parades as description.

Talk about 'solving problems' then permits the sociologist to speak as if he has an independent criterion for deciding the adequacy of sociology because it sounds as if the problem is external to sociologizing itself rather than a product of its creation. Sociology uses this criterion as grounds of its authority and as a test of its claims and it can only do so by treating the problem (the other) as external to its language. Yet, every such 'solution' instead of testing sociology pre-supposes it, and thus every solution keeps alive the very 'problem' it intends to solve.

In solving its problems, sociology makes reference to its principal problem: sociology solves problems by transforming other into actor, and each transformation uses a conception of actor as both resource and standard. The problem which sociology raises for itself concerns the standard of rationality which it employs, for this standard is the unspoken ground of every occasion of inquiry (this 'problem' is pre-supposed in every solution).

> Bureaucratic administration means fundamentally the exercise of control on the basis of knowledge. This is the feature of it which makes it specifically rational. This consists on the one hand in technical knowledge which, by itself, is sufficient to ensure it a position of extraordinary power. But in addition to this, bureaucratic organizations, or the holders of power who make use of them, have the tendency to increase their power still further by the knowledge growing out of experience in the service. For they acquire through the conduct of office a special knowledge of facts and have available a store of documentary material peculiar to themselves. While not peculiar to bureaucratic organizations, the concept of 'official secrets' is certainly typical of them. It stands in relation to technical knowledge in somewhat the same position as commercial secrets due to technological training. It is product of the striving for power.[1]

The general features of bureaucracy which Weber lists: its transformation of world into uniform events and situations through the organization of uniform tasks, serves to locate as a primary organizational problem, the trouble of responding to unique events. Again, the rationality of the organization requires insulation from the external pressures to which it is vulnerable, just as the rationality of the method of theorizing requires protection from the vagaries of mood, interest, polity, and Desire to which the theorist is vulnerable. Furthermore,

[1] Weber, p. 339.

just as the specialization of bureaucracy can work to undermine the generality of goals, the conception of Other as external to speech can produce an atomistic and concrete approach to that world which theorizing seeks to transform. Bureaucracy is an icon of the mathematical project in terms of its emphasis upon a calculable standard for generating a uniformity of units and a comparability of speech. The superiority of bureaucracy co-responds to the ethical claims of grammaticality as putative solutions to the descriptive 'problem' of aesthetics.

It is instructive to note that the primary instability to which rational-legal theorizing is vulnerable re-produces the typical vulnerability of bureaucracy, the problem of organizing the unique and contingent features of the world in terms of recurrent and uniform classes of situations and events (i.e., variables). This is to say, that since the rational-legal method of theorizing makes a world in its image, it raises as the only question worth asking whether that which the imitation copies is worth speaking for. Rational-legal method *is* a procedure for transforming the particular and unique into the general, standard and recurrent (just as bureaucracy is a method for conquering personal caprice). The chief threat to rational-legal method is not that this-or-that event will prove unformulable – for the method requires any event it processes to be formulable, and, thus *makes* any event so formulable – but that such transformations of events (such speech) will eliminate authentic Reason from its world. In fact, this is not even a question, for the rationalization of theory makes Reason impossible by concealing the achieved character of the transformation, i.e., the 'result' is treated as some-thing external to the experience of wresting it from concealment. The notion of 'official secrets' speaks to this point by serving as a metaphor for the rational-legal reluctance to expose its authoritative commitment to analysis behind its resourceful and tacit use of the commitment to do productive speaking (just as Aristotle did).

In the same way that the specialization of offices into differentiated spheres of competence can work to undermine general organizational goals, the transformation of particular ideas into 'concepts' substitutes the mere mathematical concept of the idea for its Being. Another way of putting this is that the generality of rational-legal method is an achievement which serves to mathematize Desire. This is a high price to pay for methodicalness, for it amounts to saying that the method *essentially* perverts that which it intends to display. In the same way that increasing bureaucratization re-presents the progressive methodical subordination of the personal, rational-legal methods of theorizing promise the subordination of Desire to the requirements of method by affirming the Rationality of a watered-down standard of commonality; a standard which is itself based upon an unquestioned equation between commonality, peaceableness, and the Good where the achieved character of such an equation is protected from scrutiny.

In order to engage successfully in the conflict with the divisive and changing flux of false and inessential appearances Weber forces his practical actor (the other) to accept the 'office' (the problem) of theorizing. Thus Weber creates order (community) by transforming other into an actor who is responsible to *his* (Weber's) theoretic interest in the problem which they are both forced to share. Such environments are called ideal types. Weber's discovery was that he could coerce the irrational into the rational by constructing a fanciful society in which the irrational was induced to submit to the methodic discipline of the rational. This contribution amounted to the assertion that although ordinary men in their mundane environments tend to relate to knowledge in terms of the traditional and charismatic relationships described earlier, he would portray them *as if* they oriented to knowledge in the same way as he, i.e., under the auspices of a rational-legal methodological discipline. In proceeding, Weber created as his version of knowledge the standard of practical rationality.

Thus, each of Weber's societies was constructed through actors who employed rational-legal methods of knowledgeably relating to and organizing their environments. Regardless of the kind of substantive content that was entered into the society as their 'problem,' the grounds were the same: in order to have a society in common, one required actors making their speech (their particularities) public as a topic of concerted treatment through objective methods.

Weber's programme is designed to be used by the theorist as his rule for acting upon Self as other. The method is a procedure for re-creating Self as an actor; the rational theorist is one who acts under the auspices of this understanding to produce himself as an actor. Recall the notion of 'actor' as one who acts under the auspices of his understanding of his commonness. Weber's inquirer is then one who seeks to make himself rational in this sense: he seeks to comply to the communal standard of rationality in order to overcome the difference between self and subject (his 'data') by re-establishing their unity in a communally assessable way (in a way that satisfies the standard of convincingness that is the rational community). The fact that rational-legal theorizing transforms other into an actor while using the selfsame conception of an actor which it intends to create means that rational-legal theory never moves outside of itself. This recommends that the rational-legal theorist begins with the requirement of rationality secure and in-hand as a binding object of belief.

From the perspective of rational-legal theory, charisma and tradition (custom, usage, behaviour) are forces which divide the inquirer (or separate him) from his obligation to rationality. In Weber, each and all of these notions are metaphors for various types of inarticulated and undeveloped rationalities; they specify in their several stages the imperfect integration between Self and Reason. They personify actors who are not yet communal, or communities which are not yet rational. These various disarticulations are 'other' for Weber and 'other' only becomes 'actor' under the conditions of rationality. Rationality then stands as the absolute of rational-legal theory, the perfect unity between Self and Reason which the grammar of 'actor' encapsulates. Note though, that it is a rational-legal version of rationality, a rationality which treats its understanding of itself as a secure sub-position and not as a matter of possible discussion.

Rational-legal theory can only criticize itself as an imperfect realization or articulation of its ideal of rationality. Such a critique cannot bring the ideal into question, for the ideal is used as the grounds and source of all questioning. Thus, rational-legal theory can only criticize itself by addressing and formulating itself as a failure of rationality and by assigning responsibility for this failure to its weakness of will (i.e., to its reluctance to submit to the rule of method).

From a dialectical perspective, the rationality in which rational-legal theory terminates is not the unproblematic absolute but the beginning of inquiry. The rationality of Weberian theory is the starting point of conversation and inquiry, the primitive joining together of men through speech which subsequently dissolves through the force of theorizing. Dialectically, the rational-legal absolute is first addressed through the erotic attachment between fellows (charisma) in which they concertedly re-collect through *anamnesis* (tradition) their essential relationship to Reason. Dialectic reverses rational-legal historicity because it submits to critique the absolute which the rational-legal project protects from scrutiny. Unlike rational-legal theory, dialectic does not gauge its 'success' in terms of solving problems, but counts itself fortunate when it can raise problems by making reference to their transparency as appearances of the crisis (not the problem) of language.

The relation between self and other only becomes intelligible on the basis of an inarticulate version of what is other to this relationship and this genuine otherness (which we have situated in the rational-legal commitment) is never faced because Weber's grammar stipulates it competes itself (that its rationality is self-evident). By identifying what is with the rational-legal commitment Weber *shows* the grounds of this commitment to lie in what it is not (in what is other to it). Norms, like concrete perspectiviality, is an achievement of otherness (of what is other than speech) and to topicalize them as 'grounds' is to deceive oneself that there is nothing other than speech (that speech is first, that it can complete itself).

9
Rule and Language

I

Modern theorizing, particularly as it is reflected in sociology, is animated by an ideal of democratic communality as a typification of Rational organization. Such an ideal is seen as the only Rational method for organizing differences; that the organization of differences proceeds through the use of relevances which these different contributors share; consequently, the notions of commonality and sharing become decisive, socially relevant features of the environments of members insofar as they orient to these as the only relevances respect for which will produce order and peace, i.e., truth.

Community as the moral transformation of the common becomes personified in the notions of essence and central character where each such notion expresses the commonness of what is different. Community appears as the method for creating unity out of difference.

The method of communalization certifies itself as adequate insofar as it displays genuine communalization in its very accomplishment: that is, insofar as its ordering activity is exposed to, and rebuttable by, the very differences which it organizes (insofar as its occurrence is created as an instance of convincing that which it had dismembered). To meet such a requirement, the method of communalization must segregate such differences from itself – as Real differences – on the grounds that only the unity of Real differences can be assessed and reviewed. If these differences are unreal – are artifacts or appearances of the method itself – then the re-unification is guaranteed and the method of communalization merely explicates as a result its very own beginning. The method would then become a way of treating its explicated beginning as an independent result or 'product.'

The method of communalization then begins with a mathematical relationship between whole and part, with the idea of unity and difference as independent 'things' that are produced through inquiry and which are discovered as a concrete relationship, rather than re-collected as appearances of a relationship which they cover-over.

Difference and unity stand as origin and result of the process of communalization: difference frames the limits of the relevance to be employed, and unity furnishes the criteria for every successful employment. The very possibility of difference is left unexplored, for the examination of such a possibility would make transparent the unity in which these differences are grounded: to ask for how the differences *are* different would lead to the recall of their real status on the grounds that they appear as icons of the unity which pre-figures and foreshadows them.

Thus, if it is necessary for the method to begin with difference, such a beginning only conceals the unity in which it is grounded. On the other hand, to treat the difference as difference is to take the contrast, e.g., between the observer and what he observes, as moments or re-presentations of the unity from which it has been wrested. To take the difference-as-difference is to take the very activity of creating difference as a display of the unity which permits such differentiation; it is to take difference as achieved. In contrast, to begin with difference as Real is to employ the notion of unity as a tacit resource by concretizing this resource through its transformation into an independent result.

Not only is the achieved character of the beginning and of the commitment which underlies it protected from exposure, but this very insulation transforms the commitment into something other than it is, into a concrete result or product: the commitment becomes 'public' through its works and these works re-present the commitment in the form of a concrete standard of togetherness, i.e., in the form of concrete social relationships. All concepts, tests, predictions, and re-productions are metaphors for such relationships.

We owe the formulation of the mathematical paradigm to Aristotle. Aristotle recommended in contrast to Plato, beginning with difference and disregarding unity on the grounds that only in this way could rhetoric and difference itself be overcome in the inquestive community; it was necessary to start with difference in order to create the unity of a social relationship. When Aristotle accused Plato's accounts of failing he intended only this: that Plato's pre-occupation with unity could never lead to the production of a stable social relationship – the relation which Aristotle calls knowledge, or truth. Plato's failure to 'solve the problem' only means that Plato's speaking could not silence rhetoric (as indeed Aristotle's own disputatiousness bears witness).

In speaking about the Aristotelian root of the development of mathematics Klein says,

> Necessary though it be to pre-suppose numbers of 'pure' units in order to understand the prior knowledge of numbers which is revealed in our daily calculating accounting, yet we must not, on that account, conceive

of their being as independent and separate or 'absolute'. The mode of being of the pure numbers can simply not be sufficiently determined from the point of view of the attempt to 'account' for the possibility of counting and calculating. Rather the dependence and bondage is indicative of the being of number. The whole difficulty is here precisely to bring this character of all possible numbers, and also of pure and mathematical number into consonance with the purely noetic nature of the latter.[1]

Note here how it is only Aristotle's very concrete reading of Plato's notion of unity which allows him to make such an accusation. In other words the Platonic version of unity – of the groundedness of the unity which makes activity possible – is transformed by Aristotle into the idea of unity as *a* unity (a pure, absolute, and separable kind of thing): on the basis of *this* reading Aristotle can then accuse Plato of not seeing the ways in which the differences which appear as icons of the unity serve as essential ingredients. But this move is only possible because Aristotle has read Plato's notion of unity, i.e., of the form, as specifying or describing a concrete kind of absolute. To continue

> How will we be able, we must ask, to extract all the single parts, the single 'constituents' of a thing which we get hold of in the logos one after the other. . . . Clearly only in this way: that in each case we *disregard* certain attributes of the thing in question ignoring the nexus of being which links them all to one another. This 'disregarding of . . .' is able to produce a new mode of seeing which permits something to come to life. . . . In particular, the possibility of subjecting the numerical aspects (or the dimensions) of *aisthetia* to an apodeictic discipline is based on this 'disregarding' of every particular content. This, as Aristotle says, assures us 'that there may be definitions and proofs (i.e., a science) of sensible magnitude, though not insofar as these are objects of sense, but insofar as they are just such.[2]

Aristotle then recommended that as the mathematical aspects become intelligible in their purity and segregated from all of the particularities of content, they may be isolated within the whole and may be without detriment lifted off or segregated from the whole. Aristotle proposed that this not only promises no danger but that it is a constructive, positive, and regional feature of inquiry.

> If someone, positing things as separated from that which (otherwise) goes with them, examines them for that about them by which they are such (namely 'separable'), there will be no more falsification because of

---

[1] Jacob Klein, *Greek Mathematical Thought and the Origin of Algebra*, Cambridge, Mass.: The M.I.T. Press, 1968, p. 102.

[2] *Ibid.*, pp. 102–103.

this than when someone draws something on the ground (for the purpose of demonstrating geometric theorems) and says that it has the length of a foot when it has not.[1]

In other words, this mode of studying not only does not falsify, but is itself a particular method for attaining clarification, because it aids each thing to be viewed in its best way and thus 'one posits that which is not separated (i.e., which has no separate existence) as separate, just as the arithmetician and the geometer do.' As Klein says, this is the way in which the mathematical formations first become objects of science for Aristotle in that what has to be accepted – their whatness – is accepted as given.

> Moreover, science simply has to 'accept' the 'being' of the various original formations, namely, of the 'one. . . .' Because. . . . Science studies those objects which in respect to their being are not 'detached' as if they were detached or separated. . . .[2]

Therefore, Aristotle proposed the positive requirement (as we indicated in chapter 2) of disregarding the wholeness of difference, of disregarding the groundedness of a unity which the differences displayed or to which they made reference, because of the requiredness of unifying inquiry. In other words, it was only on the basis of such a disregard that science could get on with its business by first subjecting an object to consideration and concern, and then by doing collective work on the object in an orderly way which would permit members of the collective engaged in the work to make assessable and concerted decisions. It only becomes possible for science to silence rhetoric – for theorizing to overcome difference – if difference is started with as a real origin, i.e., on the grounds that the unity of being in which the differences participate and which these selfsame differences display become silenced as matters to be disregarded.

Therefore, the mathematical recommendation to begin with difference as Real is itself grounded in the image of an adequate social relationship typified as the rational ideal of democratic communality. The rationality of the ideal rests upon its capacity to silence rhetoric. The essential liaison between mathematics and democracy is expressed in the recommendation to disregard grounds (which is what the mathematical conception of the whole-part, one-many, unity-difference relationship suggests) in order to create a particular kind of social relationship (a relationship which is personified in the very same mathematical conception of the whole-part, one-many, unity-difference relationship). Mathematical theory then rests upon this conception of a social relationship as *both* its resource and ideal: in this dependence, the character of

[1] *Ibid.*, p. 103.
[2] *Ibid.*, p. 104.

relationship as relationship remains unexplored. Its rationality is presumed to be self-certifying and self-justifying insofar as it re-produces itself in inquestive communities which stand to it as 'result,' 'confirmation,' and 'product.' To say that the mathematical conception of theorizing is grounded in a mathematical conception of a relationship means something like this: the connection between the similarity and dissimilarity of putatively but comparable unlike things grounds the notion of theorizing and of being-together. Consequently, the model of the relationship between subject and predicate frames the possible conceptions of relationships between one man and another man, or between similarity and difference. This is to say that the idea of a relationship is itself inherited mathematically and comes to stand for the similarity or relatedness through similarity of unlike but comparable things. Consequently, both ideas of similarity and of difference are treated as unexplored starting points which resolve themselves through and by themselves. The alternative idea of relationship – of the con-nection between similarity and difference taken themselves as a unity or as part of the unity – and of something beyond is then left unex-plored. The notion of community is treated as a question which asks for the similarities between different things and the question becomes – what is the essence or central feature (commonness) of these different things? rather than – what grounds and provides for (what is the source) the intelligibility of these different things as comparable rather than as something else? In other words the mathematical version of relationship takes the very idea of the relationship for granted by asking for its essence or centrality or characteristic instead of asking for how the relationship itself essences, becomes characterizable, becomes relevant as some-thing rather than no-thing? The mathe-matical notion of a relationship organized as it is around ideas of similarity and commonness situates what is common in rules of usage or laws: the parallel to this question can be seen in the way in which the mathematical version of theorizing grasps language. This notion of language directs attention to the common features or properties of language use rather than to the possibility of language itself; attention is directed to the essence of language rather than to how language essences. The question which begins by asking what is the centre, heart, or analytic essentiality of language creates an answer by res-ponding to the commonness which underlies and concerts the various possible different appearances of language; on the other hand, the alternative question asks for the possibility of language by seeing its very occurrence and the multiple differentiated forms in which it *appears* as expressing or making reference to something that rules it and is beyond it. The rule of language in mathematics then becomes the feature which organizes the expressive articulation and accomplishment of language, which unites its various occurrences; instead of marking a concern with that which rules language, and with that to which language is responsible and responsive. As mathematics examines the shifting relationships between oneness and twoness already secured and unexplored, the way in which twoness is multiplied into manyness and in which oneness is expanded, dialectic in contrast starts with Oneness and seeks to make its origin transparent, always holding fast to the question – how does Oneness come to be? What is Oneness compared to Nothing? The dialectical concern directly faces the question of the difference between something and nothing, whereas mathematics begins with something and seeks to multiply its appearance in well-defined and clearly articulated ways. Dialectic then recognizes an essential contradiction in the mathematical version of theorizing – the contradiction that is expressed in various ways through the whole-part, unity-difference, commonality-community, relationship; dialectic recognizes the essential contradiction to inhere in the very mathematical ideal of a relationship as the rational ordering and coming-together through the similarity of unlike things. The conflict or contradiction which dialectic recognizes is one between the unity in which things participate and the manyness which speaking creates; the contradictory nature of this relationship is expressed in the fact that unity must be ignored to create a speaking unity and dialectic finds this contradictory on the grounds that the speaking unity is only a servant of the unity from which it is wrested.

II

Note how Marx's conception of the contradiction of capitalistic society provides a nice reading of the contradiction of which we have been speaking in the mathematical. Capitalist production is essentially social in character and yet the means of production are privately owned, i.e., production is for profit and not for use. The contradiction then is not an extrinsic accident but belongs essentially to the socially organized character of the society. In the same way theorizing, i.e., critical speaking, is essentially social insofar as it is a way of making reference to an authoritative commitment which provides for it, licences it, and grounds it as intelligible. On the other hand the sociality of speaking is denied through the stipulation of an authoritative rule which requires an official 'disregarding' of that very unity. The contradiction is then expressed in this sense: that the procedure of mathematical theorizing requires as a positive feature of its programme the disregarding of that which makes the programme possible, distinctive, and which brings it to life. The contradiction of speaking can be expressed through various metaphors: as the conflict between the social character of speech and the authoritative creation and self-justifying commitment to private language, or between the subject as speaker and what is spoken about, or between speaking as saying and as referring. For each of these metaphors the idea of contradiction emerges thusly: that in authorizing itself to rule itself language in such an endeavour denies that to which *it* is subject, and in such a denial deprives itself of saying by succumbing to the easy temptation to merely refer and speak. The Marxist notion that man must become conscious of himself as simultaneously the subject *and* object of the historic process means nothing less than that man must become aware of his being subject, i.e., of his language's subjectitude to logos. The Marxist notions of history and totality are ways of pointing to Being and to the embeddedness, dependence, and gratitude which speaking ought to display (ought to say).

Thus, mathematical theorizing just like capitalism conceives of itself as independent and free and formulates itself as self-grounding and self-justifying by authorizing its very speaking as the limits and boundaries of intelligibility. In such an act speech forgets its history or the unity which makes it possible. Since this unity is the ruling commitment to which speaking is subjected, speech forgets it-self by submitting itself to external constraints. The individualism which Marx often speaks of is then the forgetfulness of the false speaking which forgets that which rules it, and which surrenders to the path which it lays down for itself. To understand oneself then, is to understand more than what one concretely is, but is to understand and to orient to the unity through which one's very speaking comes to life; this understanding of self is destroyed by the drive of the mathematical project to unify its speakers at a common starting point through their concerted disregard of the very commitment which gives them life. If all speakers are so formulable and characterizable, in Marx's theory the proletariat come to typify the self-consciousness of speakers labouring under this constraint, of speakers who crystallize an awareness of the way in which their very speaking alienates them from their commitment. In his theory, the proletariat through this typification become possibility and youth – the Marxist metaphor for Platonic love and for youth as student and as possibility. The proletariat then re-present the possibility of youth for re-assessing the source of their alienation and in such a re-assessment for transforming themselves into authentic speakers. No concrete 'facts' or 'predictions' are implied, for the proletariat is an icon of love, youth and possibility.

The notions of history and totality stand as Marx's metaphors for the forgetfulness that occurs when speaking detaches itself – is indifferent to – that which rules it, to the commitment in which it is grounded. When speech speaks as if it was self-sufficient and when it authorizes itself as ruler of what it speaks by virtue of the fact that it gives it-self life, it leaves unsaid that which gives it its grant. If, in Heidegger's language true thinking thanks, then speech is the medium which displays this gratitude.

Marx's idea of contradiction then points to the irreconcilable character of this forgetfulness: a contradiction that is essential to the kind of speech that forgets how it comes to speak, or to the kind of speech which chooses to remain silent and indifferent to its Reason for speaking. Speech that invokes the immunity of genius shows such a contradiction; so does speech that pretends to speak about only what appears, forgetting that its very own appearance is an appearance of something beyond it-self.

The idea of contradiction points with striking clarity to the essential conflict between the social and the private, between grounds and self, between origin and method. In treating one's beginning as a Real beginning, what is denied is its concerted and achieved character. In treating one's beginning as an enforced, common beginning, speaking subjects itself to the authority of this position which it lays down for itself as its authoritative beginning. In deciding to rule it-self speech abandons that which rules it. Speech contradicts itself – its very character as a saying rather than a mere speaking – by abandoning all concern with that which permits it to say. Speech contradicts itself – its analytic character – by authorizing it-self to rule.

Such speech is not conscious of itself – of speaking – as both the subject and object of the historical process (which is another way of referring to sophistry). Speech does not see its very speaking as possibility and achievement, as end and result. Speech does not see itself as an object of the historical process because speech does not address how its very speaking expresses its subjectitude to that which owns it. Speech cannot see itself as an object because speech cannot treat itself as being ruled by anything beyond it-self. Such speaking fails because it does not understand how Being speaks through it and gives it life. Such speaking does not grasp the very possibility of speaking itself because it treats possibility as given, certifying itself as authoritative on the basis of this denial. Such speech does not understand what speaking *is* and thus fails even as it begins to talk.

Unhistorical, bourgeois man is a metaphor for the speaker who starts with a result and who takes such a start as a secure beginning regardless of whether the security is euphemized in notions of provisionality, axiomatics, or hypotheses; the achievement of securing the beginning is never re-activated and is never re-experienced as an involvement of the speaking itself. It is an experience that is allowed to slip into forgetfulness as present-speaking cumulates its remarkable quantity of distinctions.

The contradiction is expressed in the fact that speaking in its forward march generates fetters for itself; such speech in its very speaking perverts the idea of speech. Such speech does not seek to say what is (to speak truly), and in such a denial turns its back upon the kind of saying that speech is; such speech turns its back on what speech is, on the isness of speech; such speech turns away from any consideration of how speech is and how it comes to be some-thing rather than nothing. Speech then violates itself, it does violence on it-self by treating its speaking as referring rather than as saying.

Even when mathematical speaking takes the historical turn it can only do so mathematically: the totality or 'history' which gives speaking life is itself re-presented in the various mathematical metaphors of 'culture,' 'society,' or 'weltanschaaung,' the image of a concrete relationship that causes and forces speaking. In this reflexive turn, the analytic character of Being – of that which causes and permits all things to be and to endure and persist – is transformed into the conventional social relationship that is spoken of by moderns as 'society' or as 'culture.'

Mathematical (bourgeois) speaking cannot grasp how its every attempt to speak about itself must fail because the very idea of speaking *about* only re-presents its authority. Mathematical speaking cannot understand the idea of speech as a saying because the relationship of saying cannot be spoken about; it is a relationship to which the mathematical cannot itself relate without abandoning the very conception of relationship which makes relating intelligible mathematically.

III

Marx says that production is a social fact, that production pre-supposes a form of life. In the same way, Wittgenstein said that naming pre-supposes language. The making of products – the gathering of things through speech – is a re-collecting. If producing is speaking and consuming is hearing, the belonging-together of production and consumption recommends the relational character of speaking, i.e., that speaking follows in the path of hearing and answers to or corresponds to hearing. That is, true speaking follows in the path of hearing, it seeks to *relate* to what is heard. Speaking then, does not just explode into the world without having its way prepared by hearing; speaking is a heeding and a listening that produces only under the call of what is heard.

Therefore, when Marx says that production is social he recommends that production is not self-evident but historical, which is another way of making reference to the social character of speaking. Speaking as it accomplishes itself, speaks under the auspices of how it hears itself. Speech is ruled by it-self only under the condition that we understand such a rule as its being governed by its hearing of it-self. Speech speaks under the auspices of its hearing of it-self; yet what speech hears is not speech speaking but what speech *says*. Speech says what is more than speech, speech says what is Real and Rational. In this sense, speech as speaking of itself is ruled by how speech hears itself as making reference to Reason, how it hears itself as saying what is through itself and this is what speech tries to grasp in its speaking.

The relationship which rules speech is the relationship that is speech's speaking: speech tries to speak in such a way as to follow in the path of what it hears. Yet what speech hears is something other than speech, it is the Reason which rules all authentic speaking and all authentic hearing. Therefore the relationship which speaking is subjected to is the relationship between what is other than speech *and* what says through speech – Being – and the hearing of Being that prepares the way for authentic speaking to heed. We can see this through a metaphoric reading of one of Marx's more famous quotations.

> In the social production which men carry on they enter into definite relations that are indispensable and independent of their will; these relations of production correspond to a definite stage of development of their material powers of production. The totality of these relations of production constitute the economic structure of society, the real foundation on which legal and political superstructures arise and to which definite forms of social consciousness correspond.[1]

Because of Marx's notion of social production which we are using here as a metaphor for speaking, the section of the quote can read as follows: when men speak, i.e., produce, they enter into relationships that are indispensable, i.e., necessary and independent of their will, i.e., over which they have no choice. What is the character of such a relationship generated by the very act of speaking? Speaking is a hearing, it follows in the wake of hearing; in other words, if speaking and hearing belong together, then the very accomplishment of speaking makes reference to the possible, Rational belonging-together of speaking and hearing. The accomplishment of speaking makes reference to the relationship that ought rule speaking, the relationship between speaking and hearing. Speaking and hearing relate in that speaking answers-to hearing; however the relation between speaking and hearing which rules and guides speaking is not a relationship between the separable, distinct activities of mouthing and listening, but is a relationship which is itself

[1] Karl Marx, 'Preface to A Contribution to the Critique of Political Economy', in *Selected Works*, Vol. I, Moscow: Foreign Language Publishing House, 1962, pp. 362–363.

a coming to appearance of something beyond speaking and hearing. This is to say that the very act of speaking makes reference to Reason which rules both speaking and hearing: authentic speaking speaks as an answering-to hearing, but what authentic speaking hears is beyond both speaking and hearing as the Reason that rules. Therefore, when Marx says that in speaking a relationship is generated which is independent of the will of speakers and indispensable to their speaking, he is making reference to the fact that speaking is controlled by its Rational relationship to hearing and in this relationship, that both speaking and hearing are (ought be) ruled by Reason. Because language is a disclosure of Being, every occasion of speech itself discloses the essential togetherness (relationship) of language to Being. Critical speaking tries to *show* in its speech that it hears this togetherness (not by categorizing it – as an 'it' or in speaking *about* it, but) by speaking in a listening way. Speech which speaks in a listening way is speech that speaks thinkingly. Rational speech is not convincing speech nor speech which *gives* good (Intelligent) reasons, but is speech which shows that it is controlled by the Desire to show that it hears, by the Desire to speak thinkingly. *This* is Rational because the togetherness of language and Being is the Good and the togetherness of speaking and hearing shows that speech is controlled by its Desire to affirm the Good.

Recall the Aristotelian model of speaking as a relationship between words and things. Words answer to things because of the basic Aristotelian ontology which stipulates the ways in which mental experiences appear as signs of things, sounds as signs of mental experiences, letters as signs of sounds, and words as signs of letters. The relationship of words to things is the primordial relationship that the very act of speaking affirms. Words relate to things; the very act of speaking flings man into relationships which are indispensable and independent of his will – relationships to things.

But if speaking creates such relationships, the relationship of words to things is not expressed in any old relationship. This is to say that the act of speaking makes reference to the possible belonging-together of speaking and hearing with Reason, and *this* relationship is that to which the act of speaking makes reference. In contrast to this is the relationship between words and things which is affirmed as a kind of referring, pointing to, signalling, and communicating. The Rational relationship between words and things that *ought* rule speaking is the relationship between words and things prepared by an authentic hearing of what words say, i.e., of what the connection between words and things show (in Heidegger's sense). An alternative relationship between words and things is demonstrated in the ways in which words name things in terms of standard conventions of meaning and naming. In other words, we get in the quote the notion that speaking generates two possible kinds of relationships, two different senses of relating as answering-to; in one sense, the very idea of speaking is the idea of how speaking says, shows, or makes reference to the Rational commitment which rules it; in the other sense, the very idea of speaking makes reference to speaking as a referring which is done under the auspices of common standards of naming, identifying, labelling, and referring. In the best sense, discourse that is Rational is speaking which shows that it hears; it is speaking which addresses its hearing as a belonging-together with Reason and which seeks to affirm that togetherness in its very act of speaking. This is to say that only one sense of answering, of dutiful speaking – the relation of speaking to Reason – makes reference to Rational speech, whereas the other sense of relationship makes reference to the common speech of referring under the auspices of the conventions of commonality (of the desire to unify difference and to communalize around the common).

> These relations of production correspond to a definite stage of develop-
> ment of their material powers of production.

The 'relations of production' make reference to the relationships which speaking generates, i.e., to the relationships which speech generates with it-self – with hearing – and through this conjunction of speaking and hearing with Reason. However these relations of production also make reference to the relationship between one speaker and another.

This is to say that speaking speaks under the auspices of a genuine (Rational) relationship, and of a notion of relationship that is concrete. Speaking which speaks under the auspices of a genuine relationship is speaking which speaks in such a way as to make reference to it-self as a belonging-together with what it hears, i.e., as a belonging-together with Reason. This is the strong sense of relationship; speaking which makes reference to the degenerate sense of relationship is a speaking which takes this essential relationship of it-self to Reason for granted and which proceeds to speak intelligibly under the auspices of con-ventions of adequate, communal hearing and speaking. Thus, Marx is beginning to describe what happens to the ideal of Rational speaking under certain circumstances. Marx is developing a metaphor designed to exemplify the forgetfulness of Being. The relations generated by the act of speaking – the rational, absolute for which speaking aspires to speak – is corrupted when speaking speaks. The occurrence of speaking as an answering-to the 'material powers of production' of speech itself means in one sense that speaking is ruled by the matter which underlies speech; the matter that underlies speech is the speaker, i.e., the one who speaks, and therefore, speaking which ought be oriented to its Rational belonging-together with it-self actually comes to be ruled by the matter which underlies the production of speaking. Since this matter is the speaker, speaking then answers to the speaker in the sense that the speaker authorizes speaking and establishes himself as the author-ity of speech. We then get a replay of the Marxian notion of contradiction: the very act of speaking generates the contradiction between Rational speaking and the alienation to which speech falls heir. The possibility for speech to speak thinkingly is denied when speech forgets that there is some-thing beyond self; speech answers to the self.

Self as one possible personification of the material powers of production is that to which speech answers. Speech ought answer to Reason – but instead, it answers to the self. The only possible source of common-speaking, of speech which unifies different selves – different speakers – are standard and conventional rules for hearing and speaking (is a notion of convincing speech modelled after speech which convinces one-self). Starting with self can only create an external solution. Speaking which ought orient to Being by speaking faithfully is controlled by conventions of common-speaking. We then obtain in the Marxist analysis two contrasting metaphors for social relationships which correspond to many of the distinctions we have been making. On the one hand the relationship of speech to it-self as a genuine belonging-together of speaking and hearing with Reason; on the other hand, the relationship of speaking to hearing (as different things) through the mediation of common symbols and rules.

> The totality of these relations of production constitute the economic structure of society . . . the real foundation on which legal and political superstructures arise and to which definite forms of the social consciousness correspond.

The notion of relationship has been concretized and what we have is a society of separate speakers concerting with one another on the basis of external requirements which idealize a concrete standard of speaking. The organization of speech by rules of common speaking can be read in Marx's terminology as the economic structure or real foundation. Economic organization then has nothing to do with 'economy' but makes reference to the practically organized accomplishment of mundane speaking under the auspices of common-speaking rules. The realness of the real foundation or economic structure makes reference to the firstness of rules of common-speaking: by firstness is intended that speaking accepts rules of common-speaking as the secure and unassailable starting point of subsequent speech. Speaking speaks under the control of influences to communicate – to clearly convince as a moral requirement – and to overcome rhetoric and difference; such speaking takes its very possibility for granted and begins with the authority of the 'material powers of production.'

Given the security and 'reality' of self as a point of origin, the material powers of production can be heard with the accent on 'powers' rather than 'matter' as the power and capacity of speaking to multiply itself through its making of products, of things. Speaking makes things not by addressing its own possibility – the possibility of speech itself – but by securing this possibility as a given – as a starting point – for subsequent speaking. Speaking can only make things when it silences any concern with the grounds of speaking by stipulating and enforcing a common beginning. Speaking which answers-to or co-responds to the material power of a self is speaking which accepts the security of it-self and which submits it-self to the requirements to make things, i.e., to create distinctions that are intelligible to a community. The making of things through speech recommends the business of moving ahead with the work. To move ahead with the work means to silence the interminable discussion that every concern with the grounds of speaking invites. Getting on with the work means the silencing of disputatiousness, the silencing of the rhetorical possibilities inherent in speaking; it requires commanding the assent of Other – of enlisting him into the cause – in a way that is both intelligible and rational for him (in a way that is convincing). To accomplish this, 'works' or results are produced, which means the making of two things out of one. Instead of addressing the creation of something out of nothing, such speaking treats its things as intelligible re-productions of the authority which grounds it, as separable and independent 'things' external to the authority. Speaking justifies itself in terms of products which can only be assumed to be independent of the authority which makes them possible: such speaking requires of itself that it produce products under the constraint that such products are generative and independent consequences of the method of speaking. For speech to answer-to the material powers of production is for speaking to preserve the fiction of the independence of it-self from history or totality on the grounds that only such a preservation will solidify the authority of the self. In this way, the 'progressive' drive to cumulate expressed in the idea of productivity is essentially linked to the self-centred character of concrete speech.

Thus, the notion of the 'material powers of production' makes reference to two intersecting possibilities. On the one hand, the authority of self as source of intelligibility is re-produced through products which confirm that authority by introducing it into new domains under the mask of independent 'tests.' This image disregards the belonging-together of self and things in a unity which prefigures and grounds: this unity must be disregarded because *it* cannot be produced as a product and such disregard merely affirms the authority of self. This unity is (on critical occasions) personified in surrogate objects which only concretize the notion of grounds by subjecting it as matter which the authoritative speaker can speak about. Such products are mere 'superstructures' which show their grip in the hands of self-centred speaking. Being no longer owns speech but is owned by speech as objects (products) which it talks about – much as superstructures are owned by the base. The two metaphors for these possibilities as self and difference (data) articulate in the idea of commodity.

> The mode of production of material life determines the general character of the social, political, and spiritual processes of life.

Think of other uses of 'to determine' besides the causal-influence usage: to determine means to settle or decide (a dispute, question, etc.) by an authoritative or conclusive decision, to fix possibilities, to conclude or ascertain, to fix the position of, to give direction or tendency to, to impel, to limit a notion, to lead or bring to a decision. The mode of production of material life determines in all these senses not because it causes but because it frames possibilities for thinking and speaking, i.e., thinking and speaking accept the constraint of the material mode of production by surrendering to its control. Speaking allows the mode of production of material life to control its possibilities; it is the mode of production of material life to which speech answers and by which it decides to be ruled. The mode of production of material life is the method of speaking, the method whereby matter (self) as difference is transformed into a unity (productive speech) because the method idealizes a programme of convincing speaking to be ruled by the method of speaking. Here, Marx can be heard as describing the gradual ascendence of one type of relationship generated by the speaking act. The relationship concerns the way in which the method of speaking (the ideal of convincing speech which is required by a self-centred notion of speaking) comes to control speech itself. Such speech loses sight of its own possibility – of what speech it-self is – in deciding to submit to the control of the method of speaking (it submits to a standard of rationality based upon the most concrete image of speech).

The entire quote suggests various possibilities which are generated by the act of speaking. On the one hand the accomplishment of speech as an intelligible activity makes reference to the grounds or Rational ideal which speech ought serve, the relationship of it-self and language with which it is essentially concerned; on the other hand the accomplishment of speech falls increasingly under control of the 'material powers of speaking,' and speech is concretely seen as the tangible product of the individual speaking practices of concrete individual men and the fact that speaking so conceived is seen as being ruled by and answering-to the methods used by a collection of men to speech that concretely convinces.

IV

Just as capitalist society converts social relationships into exchange relations between producers and consumers of commodities, so concrete speaking is exemplified in the externalized speaking practices between members who must decide and warrant the convincing character of speeches. Just as capitalist society transforms the notion of value, so concrete speaking transforms the idea of the weight of speech by silencing resonance and discussion under the authority of usage. Just as capitalism expands and grounds itself on the basis of its quantity of products, so concrete speaking reaches into every corner of life with its news, its researches, and studies. Where the value of a social relationship resides in the exchange values of commodities, so the value of concrete speaking resides in its capacity to silence opposition, to command assent, to impose one hearing rule upon the assembly. Both capitalism and concrete speaking silence interaction by transforming speech into an external and oppressive concrete 'object.'

The product comes to dominate man because it is through the product – through his speaking and gathering of things – that man makes reference to his manliness. In order for man's speaking to make such reference it must acquire value. Value is the Marxian notion of how speaking makes reference to the commitment of the speaker, how speaking in its occurrence does more than utter but *says*. Value is like Heidegger's notion that speaking is a saying and that speaking enters into its only authentic relationship with it-self when it conceives of itself as a saying, as a togetherness with what it hears.

In capitalist society, the pre-conditions for the product's acquisition of value is not only that it is due to labour but that it has a use value for others, i.e., that it can be used by others. Products acquire their value as commodities when they have a use value for others. If it is only through his product – through his speech – that man can make reference to his commitment not all speaking becomes a valuable resource in the community. Commodity might be Marx's term for resourceful speaking – for speaking that is directed by the practical interest – for speaking that seeks to take matters into hand and to get down to business, that seeks to make many things. In order to be resourceful, speech has to have a social use value which means that it must acquire its value vis-à-vis Other's hearing of it.

When Marx says that 'the value of a commodity represents human labour in the abstract, the expenditure of human labour in general'[1] he means that the value of a product – of speaking – when seen under the auspices of the practical interest (which is what 'commodity' makes

[1] *Ibid.*, p. 363.

reference to) is assigned by ignoring the way in which speaking makes reference to its relationship to it-self – to its commitment – as a required Rational display, and is instead seen as an expression of some abstract and general notion of speech. Such a notion of speech is reflected in the conception of speech as usage, an idea of how speaking is accomplished. To assign value in this way is to treat speech concretely rather than analytically in terms of the general conditions of speaking practice rather than as an icon of the authority which permits speech to speak. It is to treat speech as reflected in rules of usage rather than as a way of making reference to the commitment which grounds the production of such practices that become formulable as rules.

In saying that a man's product is viewed generally or concretely it is said that speaking is uprooted from history and context and is externalized in a standard formula. Speaking is seen as other than it is. Essentially what speech *is* is a display, a making reference to an achievement; the product as speech encapsulates the collecting and gathering which entered into its achievement. Now however, the product is secured and it is seen in every way other than for what it is: it is seen externally in terms of what it proposes, asserts, or predicates; the product is seen in terms of the *what* which it recommends rather than the *how* of its possibility; it is seen as a new thing rather than an old thing, a resource rather than a display.

When Marx says that commodities are expressed in relative values, he can be heard as saying that only for this kind of practical speaking what speech *says* cannot be expressed in terms of it-self but can only be expressed relative to the 'material powers of production.' In other words, the value of speech can only be assessed vis-à-vis the method for the production of speech. In contrast, to express the value of speech in terms of it-self means that the value of a notion only comes to light when we ask 'how it can come to be?' or 'how it could come to be something rather than no-thing?' To express the value of speech in terms of itself is what all analytic thinking and speaking attempt; to address or to make reference to its own grounds and to evoke a sense of its accomplishment as an achievement. In this sense, valuable speech heeds and listens to it-self – its speaking – as the answering-to a rational history; valuable speech is speech that is oriented to itself as a hearing. Valuable speech is speech that is in tune with what it hears, and that in its speaking makes reference to its belonging-together with what it hears as a disclosure of the togetherness of language and Being.

However, the logic of practical speaking – of the commodity – requires as an essential condition of its accomplishment that the value of speech be seen in terms of another product. My speaking acquires its value vis-à-vis your hearing; you and I are assumed as two discrete individuals, one speaking and one listening, one speaking *to* an other.

Speaking and hearing have become segregated and situated in two different, separable actors. The idea of commodity begins with the self-centred image of free speaking as a relationship. The value of my speaking depends upon your hearing and for you to hear my speaking is for us to share – to have in common – some rule which, by flattening out the particular evocative resonances of our speaking, manages to join us together. The question of speech's Real value as a way of making reference to its relationship to Reason is silenced and the security of speaking is posited as a common position from which we will begin to speak and listen. Speaking is then subjected to some general notion of the method for its production because it is only such a notion that unifies the speaking that is produced by separable, different speakers.

Speech's surrender to 'the material powers of production' means that speaking surrenders to its concern to make things, to be busy, to take things into hand. Speech surrenders to its concern to secure things where this concernful attitude towards things is reflected in the subjectitude of speech to itself, i.e., to its interests. Speech makes haste to get down to business and to take things in hand. Given the character of 'thing' as that which is taken in hand and is well secured, and given that thing acquires its thingful character only through the action of concernful taking in hand, speech which is controlled by the material powers of production is speech which is controlled by the attitude of concernful taking in hand and securing. Speech creates things, i.e., makes new things, through its very action of concernful taking into hand. Such speech could never question its beginning for then it would relinquish its grip over things and would have to find grounds for formulating thinghood itself as a possibility. Such speech transforms things into facts through a concernful taking into hand and thus requires its own speaking to follow the path with which this concern to take in hand lays down for itself. Speech which is ruled by the 'material powers of production' is speech that is ruled by the attitude of concernful taking into hand, speech which answers-to the conception of it-self as the authoritative source of speaking, speech which conceives of itself as the creator of new products. Such speech treats its very speaking as the creation of a commodity.

The value of a commodity is measured in terms of the methods which enter its production. Speaking has value only insofar as it is methodically produced. Just as each individual commodity is to be considered as an average sample of its class – as a typification – so each intelligible practice acquires its value in terms of how it typifies the artful, planful, intelligible display of method. Members who act to make their activities observable and reportable are members who orient to their speaking as commodities. Yet, it is the inquirer who must be kept in mind: the inquirer who orients to maximizing the observability and reportability of *his* speaking to the exclusion of its value as a kind of labouring power is orienting to his own speaking – to inquiry – under the auspices of a commodity orientation. He is one who treats speaking as the production of commodities and who, by equating truthfulness with convincing, identifies knowledge with power (with speech that has exchange value). Labour as labour power, as the action of re-producing and re-creating commitment through speech does not become typified in the speaking practices of men in the society which Marx invents. In this society labour is seen in the conditions under which it is done or in the methods under which it is accomplished as a socially intelligible display of labour. In this society – the society which exemplifies concrete speaking – labour power as commitment becomes a commodity and a concrete kind of product that re-presses the very power (grounds) which makes it possible.

The image of the material powers of production is an image of a collection of individual speakers each producing his own product. This is the aesthetic society of free speakers each orienting to what is present to one as a possession. Under such conditions, speech becomes valuable only when it is seen as a transformation of many possessions into what is commonly possessed. Valuable speech then becomes speech which can be expressed in terms of general conditions for the production of speech, and the notion of commodity personifies the locus of such values. For example, commodity acquires value only through exchanges, and the valid exchange values of a given commodity express something equal because for two commodities (two speeches) to have an equivalent exchange value, there must exist in equal quantities something common to both, i.e., the two speeches must be equal to a third which in itself is neither one nor the other. Exchange value pre-supposes some standard which is external to the two commodities as two speeches. To provide for the concerted character of the speeches of different speakers some external standard must be available which can unify these differences. This standard must be totally comprehensive because the differences which it intends to organize are the most concrete differences among speeches. Such a standard must be concrete enough to organize the most concrete differences among men (it must express the lowest common denominator). Since the external standard must be derived from common features shared by the different producers of speech, the usual locus of such authority is expressed in terms of methods of speaking and rules for the production of speech. Speaking then acquires its value in terms of how it conforms to requirements of method, rule, or to some external standard which is extracted from and built upon the common characteristics shared by superficially different speakers. In contrast to this, is the underlying theme of the Marxian argument that valuable speech ought be speech which displays its commitment, i.e., speech which makes reference to the labour power used in re-creating things?

Marx's notion that men relate through labour makes reference to the fact that men relate through their commitments, that men through their speaking say or show their manliness. Marx's description of the way in which speaking suppresses a concern with commitment by transforming the idea of labour into the product in which it issues, i.e., into a commodity which expresses the general commonality of a collection of different speakers, typifies the alienation to which speech falls heir. Marx's metaphor helps us to see the instabilities of a rational-legal ideal of speaking which drives to unify differences under rules of method developed from an image of commonality. Marx helps us see this by showing how the Rational character of speaking is forgotten under the condition of such speaking interests.

The notions of exchange and commodity typify the idea of speaking as mere reference. Speaking which enters into relationships to things by referring to things is speaking which is done under the auspices of general conventions and rules for referring: such rules include the corpus of conditions required for referring to things intelligibly: the conventions of re-cognizing, naming, conceptualizing, and asserting only have unifying potential because different speakers are not that different, i.e., they are similar enough to be themselves beings who disclose Being.

The notion of speaking as mere referring asserts the primacy of method and rule as the source of the unity of intelligible speaking. Speech which answers-to the 'material powers of production' is speech which answers to the unifying power of method by submitting to its rule; such rational-legal speaking accepts the rule of method because it subscribes to the ideal relationship which is pre-supposed by such a rule. The rational-legal ideal of a relationship is personified in Marx's conception of the exchange value of a commodity as typifying the value of common-speaking.

Though speaking generates different possibilities for conceiving of the relationship between words and things, the rational-legal model of this relationship as mere referring – as concerted referring – diminishes the possibility of grasping the kind of relationship which true speaking is – the saying of speaking as an answering-to Being. To fail to understand this relationship is to fail to grasp the analytic character of speaking as a way of showing the togetherness of thinking and Being. To avoid this relationship is to ignore all that speaking, thinking, and Being is; it is to abdicate responsibility because it withdraws Rationality from speech. In this sense, the modernization of thought exemplified in the rise of sociology does nothing more or less than re-present the way in which thinking has become alienated from Being through the emergence of a mathematical conception of the idea of relationship. Stripped of its causal, concrete imagery, capitalism is an apt metaphor for such an alienating condition.

V

Marx's analysis of labour necessarily suggests that all human activities insofar as they are instances of labouring are addressable with his metaphor. This recommends that theorizing itself can be conceived as an instance of labour, as labour power which issues in products. Marx says that men relate through their products, but their products are produced through labour; so men relate through their labour. But what does labour mean? Labour creates products? Labour creates new values? Labour is a metaphor for the re-thinking that is theorizing and so, to say that men relate through their labour is to say that they relate through their re-thinking. But, men who relate through their re-thinking are men who relate through their commitments to speech and thought. Therefore, Marx's notion recommends deeply that the idea of relationship is exemplified in the notion of men relating through their commitments. The primordial relationship is exposed in the co-relation between speaking and authority *as* the idea of commitment and is shown in the speaking which displays its Desire to be a hearing.

Think of the way in which an idea of labour enters into the conception of theorizing. In the *Theaetetus* Socrates spoke of the labour of theorizing as *anamnesis*, of getting Other to stop his premature march and to turn back, to re-member, to re-collect that upon which his speaking rests. Socrates referred to himself as a midwife attempting to bring an offspring to life. The labour of theorizing is that kind of turning back and bringing to life, that turn towards origins. The making of something that is captured in the sense of labour is a re-making, a taking of something already here for the purpose of re-constructing or re-membering the origin from which it is now detached. The terms that are used by Socrates and his various interlocuters are resting places to dwell and to re-consider; the facility with which we consider the terms and employ them in our routines only appear to Socrates as a sign of resonances which the terms cover-up. Socrates was not out to invent a better dictionary but better men, and he used the routine employ of terms as a method for arousing in men their desire to address their commitments; he sought to encourage men to face their commitments rather than to mask them under easy and positive chatter.

The terms are not springboards for action for their very occurrence testifies to their status as terminal points in actions long since cumulated. The terms are occasions to act or to re-enact a suppressed history; they are occasions for acting only if action is seen as thinking and not as keeping busy. The conversation arouses the action that is thinking and not the action that is making and moving, producing and doing. For dialectic, thinking is more like a re-producing than a producing because the thinker seeks to re-enact in thought the history of a notion already produced and secured. Thinking is action only in the sense that the thinker is one who re-enacts or imitates – who answers-to – Being. Thinking is acting only in the sense that thinking is an answering to the logos and in such an answering is a re-enacting or re-producing. Dialectically, thinking is the paradigmatic and supreme relationship of speech to things in the sense that it is a speaking which answers to a hearing.

Dialectically, the actor is one who seeks to hear the enunciation of the logos in things, one who seeks to re-enact in speech the enunciation of Reason. In contrast, the rational-legal actor is one without time to hear, one concerned to rush into things – into their midst – and take them up as objects of practical concern. The actor typified through rational-legal ideals is the convincing speaker (the rhetorician in the worst sense); his concern is to protect the well-secured things which his concern has itself produced as an object of concern. Whereas the dialectical actor speaks in a truly listening way, by treating his own speaking as a saying to which he ought orient as a hearer, the rational-legal actor speaks without listening to what his speech *says*, but only in such a way as to produce speech which complies with an external rule for correct speaking. The rational-legal actor regards hearing as self-evident, as something which is secure and at hand.

The kind of labouring in which Marx is interested is a re-creating; through his labour man makes reference to his commitment by 'calling it to mind,' by re-constituting it, and by evoking it. To say that men relate through their labour is then to say that men relate through their commitments, that they relate as men by making reference through their speech to their commitments. This is what speaking means in the strongest sense; not to chatter, to make sounds, to use words intelligibly, but to *say*. Through speaking men *say* and what they say is that they are men. The situation of theorizing is itself a speaking situation. Men speak in order to maximize the salience of commitments which provide for the intelligible character of speaking. It is only through such making reference that men speak with value, i.e., rationally; men who orient to their speaking as commodity accept the security of commitment as a posit – a common position – and protect this position from being explored while simultaneously employing it as a resource to do speaking which merely strengthens the unassailability of the position (while pretending to confirm its weight through the independence of descriptive tests). This is why the rational-legal interest is essentially conservative: it seeks to conserve the authority created by its own rule, the authority of its common-speaking starting point.

Alienated theorizing is speaking which does not care why it speaks and which treats such disregard as a necessary, required, and constructive feature of its speaking. Alienated theorizing is speaking that chooses to disregard its Reason on the grounds that such disregard is a required condition for the creation of the concrete community reflected in the ideal of a society of co-speakers who are present to their speech in the same way that any one of them is present to his body. Alienated speaking is speaking which is out of touch with it-self and with that which gives it life. Alienated speaking/theorizing is the speaking which treats what it speaks *about* – what it refers to – as that which gives it life, and consequently such speaking can never grasp what it essentially is. Alienated speaking regards its life giving power to lie in the objects which it produces for itself as objects of concern for speaking and as the methods and rules which it follows to make such objects intelligible to an other. In this sense alienated speaking looks in the wrong direction by looking away from what it is to everything other than it-self. Rational-legal theorizing exemplifies as its ideal the alienated state of speaking, speaking which submits to the control of method and which affirms such submission as a necessary condition for the achievement of knowledge as the icon of a rational association.

Mode of production makes reference to the method of speaking which lays down as the rule (law) for speech to follow the selfsame method of speaking now generalized as the normative order compliance to which will produce speech with value (meaningful speech). The conflict between the mode and relations of production then comes to this: that the transformation of method of speaking into rule undermines the essential relationship of speaking to Being, to its commitment, by undermining the possibility of thoughtful speaking.

The mode of speaking – the method – becomes the order which constrains the highest development of speaking itself. When mode of speaking is re-formulated as rule, empirical conditions of speaking become oppressive fetters upon speaking itself and upon the Desire of speech to say what is.

The mode of production makes reference to the general character of adequate speaking when seen from the perspective of the commonalities underlying diversities or differences in speaking. These commonalities become re-organized as the order of communality to which speaking ought orient to achieve its Rational character. In the process rationality is personified in speech that complies with mode-as-method (as enforceable project or plan) because only such compliance is seen to guarantee communal rather than idiosyncratic speech, i.e., valuable speech. Consequently, rational speech is treated as speech that seeks to display its self-consciousness by demonstrating its subordination to a standard for accomplishing anonymous speech. Self-conscious speech is that which shows its desire for anonymity and the anonymity amounts to its decision to be silent about its grounds.

The kind of speaking that displays such a desire – the desire for anonymity – is a speaking that attempts to show that it is not responsible for what it speaks; it is a speech that decides to show its nihilism; such speech is speech that is driven to re-nounce its responsibility. Yet, it does not abandon this responsibility in the classical way by making reference to how it is ruled by Being – the power which *says* through *its* speaking – but by conceiving of itself as the mute member of a two-party relationship between things and words. The conflict Marx speaks of is expressed in the fact that every such disclaimer of responsibility merely re-affirms responsibility itself, and that the responsibility re-affirmed through the desire for anonymous speech is the deliberate decision of speech to be indifferent to its reason for speaking. Like Plato, Marx then points to the essential nihilism of rational-legal speaking and to the essential and necessary forgetfulness of any speaking which speaks under such auspices.

Index

Harre, R., 42n
Hegel, 133
  and aestheticization of grammar,
    160
Heidegger, M., 1n, 9n, 14n, 30n, 34,
    34n, 39n, 42n, 43n, 67n, 82n
Heidegger and the Tradition, 6n
'High Sounding',
  and Aristotle, 10
  and Socrates, 7–9
History,
  and Marx, 248, 250
  elimination by Durkheim, 187–8
  Platonic discussion on, 5
History and Greek Philosophy, 65,
    65n
Hobbes, 139
  political philosophy of, 173
Hume, on power of custom, 208

Independence, man's consciousness
  of, 155
Individualism, possessive, 131–2
Intuition,
  as primordial action, 145–6, 147
  as undoubting conception, 145

Judgement, sound and correct,
  142–3

Kant, I,
  on aesthetics, 133, 160
Kapp, E., 111n
Kierkegaard, 93, 127
Kirk, G. S., 36n
Klein, J., 8n, 9n, 65n, 243–4
Knowledge,
  and Aristotle, 4
    scale, of, 97
  and rhetorical theorizing, 166
  belief as, 21–2
  classical notion of, 144
  collectedness of, according to
    Descartes, 196–7
  formulation of, 163
  perfect-grounded, 145
  Plato on, 141
  sociology as, 206

Socratic, 8
theory of, 74–5

Labour, Marx analysis of, 262–4
Language,
  absence of, 174
  and mathematical version of
    theorizing, 246–7
  and naming, 250
  as mirror of structure, 161
  as social phenomenon, 206
  as topic of sociology, 214–15
  as topic of sophist, 84, 85
  conception of, 48
  ordinary, 170
  scientific, 97
Law, inducing respect for, 228 *see
  also* Legality
Lazarsfeld, 237
Legality, authoritative notion of,
    229–30
Logic,
  of Aristotle and Plato, 111–13
Logos, 58, 84
  Aristotelian idea of, 19, 20–2, 36–7
  of theorizing, 101
  Socratic standard of, 7

Machiavelli, political philosophy of,
    173, 216
McIntyre, 39n–40n
McKeon, 30n–32n, 37n
Marx, K., 247, 248, 250–7, 258
  on labour, 262–4
  on speech, language and rule,
    260–1
Marx, W., 6n, 39n
Mathematical conception of theoriz-
    ing, 246–8
Mathematics,
  Aristotelian development of, 243–5
  Platonic science of, 56
Merton, R. K., 237
Metaphysics, as first science, 59,
    60–2, 98–9
  and questioning principles, 105
  self-consciousness of, 119–21
Metaphysics, 1n, 4, 39, 39n, 59